Jean Anouilh

Published by Hill and Wang

JEAN ANOUILH Volume I
    Antigone
    Eurydice (Legend of Lovers)
    The Ermine
    The Rehearsal
    Romeo and Jeannette

JEAN ANOUILH Volume II
    Restless Heart
    Time Remembered
    Ardèle
    Mademoiselle Colombe
    The Lark

JEAN ANOUILH Volume III
    Thieves' Carnival
    Medea
    Cécile, or The School for Fathers
    Traveler Without Luggage
    The Orchestra
    Episode in the Life of an Author
    Catch As Catch Can

THE CAVERN

Jean Anouilh

(FIVE PLAYS)

VOLUME I

A MERMAID DRAMABOOK

 HILL AND WANG – NEW YORK

Copyright © 1958 by Hill and Wang, Inc.
Standard Book Number (paperback edition): 8090–0710–x
Standard Book Number (clothbound edition): 8090–2700–3
Library of Congress Catalog Card Number: 58–6064

FIRST DRAMABOOK PRINTING MARCH 1958
SECOND PRINTING OCTOBER 1958
THIRD PRINTING FEBRUARY 1960
FOURTH PRINTING OCTOBER 1960
FIFTH PRINTING JANUARY 1962
SIXTH PRINTING AUGUST 1962
SEVENTH PRINTING APRIL 1963
EIGHTH PRINTING JANUARY 1964
NINTH PRINTING OCTOBER 1964
TENTH PRINTING MAY 1965
ELEVENTH PRINTING JANUARY 1966
TWELFTH PRINTING MAY 1966
THIRTEENTH PRINTING DECEMBER 1966
FOURTEENTH PRINTING MARCH 1967
FIFTEENTH PRINTING OCTOBER 1967
SIXTEENTH PRINTING MARCH 1968
SEVENTEENTH PRINTING SEPTEMBER 1968
EIGHTEENTH PRINTING APRIL 1969

The plays in this volume were first produced in Paris in the following years: *The Ermine*, 1932; *Eurydice*, 1941; *Antigone*, 1944; *Romeo and Jeannette*, 1946; and *The Rehearsal*, 1951.

Manufactured in the United States of America
by The Colonial Press Inc., Clinton, Mass.

CONTENTS

	PAGE
Antigone	1
Eurydice (Legend of Lovers)	55
The Ermine	121
The Rehearsal	195
Romeo and Jeannette	261

Jean Anouilh

ANTIGONE

A *Tragedy*

Translated by

LEWIS GALANTIÈRE

Antigone by Jean Anouilh, adapted and translated by Lewis Galantière. Copyright 1946 by Random House, Inc. Reprinted by permission of Random House, Inc.

All applications for permission to perform this play professionally must be made to Dr. Jan van Loewen Ltd., 81-83 Shaftesbury Avenue, London, W.1. Applications for amateur performance should be made to Messrs. Samuel French Inc., New York. No performance may take place unless a licence has first been obtained.

CHARACTERS

Chorus
Antigone
Nurse
Ismene
Haemon
Creon
First Guard (*Jonas*)
Second Guard (*a Corporal*)
Third Guard
Messenger
Page
Eurydice

ANTIGONE

ANTIGONE, *her hands clasped round her knees, sits on the top step. The* THREE GUARDS *sit on the steps, in a small group, playing cards. The* CHORUS *stands on the top step.* EURYDICE *sits on the top step, just left of center, knitting. The* NURSE *sits on the second step, left of* EURYDICE. ISMENE *stands in front of arch, left, facing* HAEMON, *who stands left of her.* CREON *sits in the chair at right end of the table, his arm over the shoulder of his* PAGE, *who sits on the stool beside his chair. The* MESSENGER *is leaning against the downstage portal of the right arch.*

The curtain rises slowly; then the CHORUS *turns and moves downstage.*

CHORUS. Well, here we are.

These people are about to act out for you the story of Antigone.

That thin little creature sitting by herself, staring straight ahead, seeing nothing, is Antigone. She is thinking. She is thinking that the instant I finish telling you who's who and what's what in this play, she will burst forth as the tense, sallow, willful girl whose family would never take her seriously and who is about to rise up alone against Creon, her uncle, the King.

Another thing that she is thinking is this: she is going to die. Antigone is young. She would much rather live than die. But there is no help for it. When your name is Antigone, there is only one part you can play; and she will have to play hers through to the end.

From the moment the curtain went up, she began to feel that inhuman forces were whirling her out of this world, snatching her away from her sister Ismene, whom you see smiling and chatting with that young man; from all of us who sit or stand here, looking at her, not in the least upset ourselves—for we are not doomed to die tonight.

CHORUS turns and indicates HAEMON.

The young man talking to Ismene—to the gay and beautiful Ismene—is Haemon. He is the King's son,

Creon's son. Antigone and he are engaged to be married.
You wouldn't have thought she was his type. He likes
dancing, sports, competition; he likes women, too. Now
look at Ismene again. She is certainly more beautiful than
Antigone. She is the girl you'd think he'd go for.
Well . . . There was a ball one night. Ismene wore a new
evening frock. She was radiant. Haemon danced every
dance with her. And yet, that same night, before the
dance was over, suddenly he went in search of Antigone,
found her sitting alone—like that, with her arms clasped
round her knees—and asked her to marry him. We still
don't know how it happened. It didn't seem to surprise
Antigone in the least. She looked up at him out of those
solemn eyes of hers, smiled sort of sadly and said "yes."
That was all. The band struck up another dance. Ismene,
surrounded by a group of young men, laughed out loud.
And . . . well, here is Haemon expecting to marry Antigone. He won't, of course. He didn't know, when he asked
her, that the earth wasn't meant to hold a husband of
Antigone, and that this princely distinction was to earn
him no more than the right to die sooner than he might
otherwise have done.

CHORUS *turns toward* CREON.

That gray-haired, powerfully built man sitting lost in
thought, with his little page at his side, is Creon, the King.
His face is lined. He is tired. He practices the difficult art
of a leader of men. When he was younger, when Oedipus
was King and Creon was no more than the King's brother-
in-law, he was different. He loved music, bought rare
manuscripts, was a kind of art patron. He would while
away whole afternoons in the antique shops of this city
of Thebes. But Oedipus died. Oedipus' sons died. Creon
had to roll up his sleeves and take over the kingdom. Now
and then, when he goes to bed weary with the day's
work, he wonders whether this business of being a leader
of men is worth the trouble. But when he wakes up, the
problems are there to be solved; and like a conscientious
workman, he does his job.

Creon has a wife, a Queen. Her name is Eurydice.
There she sits, the old lady with the knitting, next to the

Nurse who brought up the two girls. She will go on knitting all through the play, till the times comes for her to go to her room and die. She is a good woman, a worthy, loving soul. But she is no help to her husband. Creon has to face the music alone. Alone with his Page, who is too young to be of any help.

The others? Well, let's see.

He points toward the MESSENGER.

That pale young man leaning against the wall is the Messenger. Later on he will come running in to announce that Haemon is dead. He has a premonition of catastrophe. That's what he is brooding over. That's why he won't mingle with the others.

As for those three red-faced card players—they are the guards. One smells of garlic, another of beer; but they're not a bad lot. They have wives they are afraid of, kids who are afraid of them; they're bothered by the little day-to-day worries that beset us all. At the same time—they are policemen: eternally innocent, no matter what crimes are committed; eternally indifferent, for nothing that happens can matter to them. They are quite prepared to arrest anybody at all, including Creon himself, should the order be given by a new leader.

That's the lot. Now for the play.

Oedipus, who was the father of the two girls, Antigone and Ismene, had also two sons, Eteocles and Polynices. After Oedipus died, it was agreed that the two sons should share his throne, each to reign over Thebes in alternate years.

Gradually, the lights on the stage have been dimmed.

But when Eteocles, the elder son, had reigned a full year, and time had come for him to step down, he refused to yield up the throne to his younger brother. There was civil war. Polynices brought up allies—six foreign princes; and in the course of the war he and his foreigners were defeated, each in front of one of the seven gates of the city. The two brothers fought, and they killed one another in single combat just outside the city walls. Now Creon is King.

CHORUS is leaning, at this point, against the left proscenium arch. By now the stage is dark, with only the cyclorama bathed in dark blue. A single spot lights up the face of CHORUS.

Creon has issued a solemn edict that Eteocles, with whom he had sided, is to be buried with pomp and honours, and that Polynices is to be left to rot. The vultures and the dogs are to bloat themselves on his carcass. Nobody is to go into mourning for him. No gravestone is to be set up in his memory. And above all, any person who attempts to give him religious burial will himself be put to death.

While CHORUS has been speaking the characters have gone out one by one. CHORUS disappears through the left arch.

It is dawn, gray and ashen, in a house asleep. ANTIGONE steals in from out-of-doors, through the arch, right. She is carrying her sandals in her hand. She pauses, looking off through the arch, taut, listening, then turns and moves across downstage. As she reaches the table, she sees the NURSE approaching through the arch, left. She runs quickly toward the exit. As she reaches the steps, the NURSE enters through arch and stands still when she sees ANTIGONE.

Nurse. Where have you been?

Antigone. Nowhere. It was beautiful. The whole world was gray when I went out. And now—you wouldn't recognize it. It's like a post card: all pink, and green, and yellow. You'll have to get up earlier, Nurse, if you want to see a world without color.

Nurse. It was still pitch black when I got up. I went to your room, for I thought you might have flung off your blanket in the night. You weren't there.

Antigone [*comes down the steps*]. The garden was lovely. It was still asleep. Have you ever thought how lovely a garden is when it is not yet thinking of men?

Nurse. You hadn't slept in your bed. I couldn't find you. I went to the back door. You'd left it open.

Antigone. The fields were wet. They were waiting for something to happen. The whole world was breathless, waiting. I can't tell you what a roaring noise I seemed to make alone on the road. It bothered me that whatever was waiting wasn't waiting for me. I took off my sandals and slipped into a field. [*She moves down to the stool and sits.*]

Nurse [*kneels at* ANTIGONE'S *feet to chafe them and put on the sandals*]. You'll do well to wash your feet before you go back to bed, Miss.

Antigone. I'm not going back to bed.

Nurse. Don't be a fool! You get some sleep! And me, getting up to see if she hasn't flung off her blanket; and I find her bed cold and nobody in it!

Antigone. Do you think that if a person got up every morning like this, it would be just as thrilling every morning to be the first girl out-of-doors?

NURSE *puts* ANTIGONE'S *left foot down, lifts her other foot and chafes it.*

Nurse. Morning my grandmother! It was night. It still is. And now, my girl, you'll stop trying to squirm out of this and tell me what you were up to. Where've you been?

Antigone. That's true. It was still night. There wasn't a soul out of doors but me, who thought that it was morning. Don't you think it's marvelous—to be the first person who is aware that it is morning?

Nurse. Oh, my little flibbertigibbet! Just can't imagine what I'm talking about, can she? Go on with you! I know that game. Where have you been, wicked girl?

Antigone [*soberly*]. No. Not wicked.

Nurse. You went out to meet someone, didn't you? Deny it if you can.

Antigone. Yes. I went out to meet someone.

Nurse. A lover?

Antigone. Yes, Nurse. Yes, the poor dear. I have a lover.

Nurse [*stands up; bursting out*]. Ah, that's very nice now, isn't it? Such goings-on! You, the daughter of a king, running out to meet lovers. And we work our fingers to the bone for you, we slave to bring you up like young ladies!

[*She sits on chair, right of table.*] You're all alike, all of
you. Even you—who never used to stop to primp in front
of a looking glass, or smear your mouth with rouge, or
dindle and dandle to make the boys ogle you, and you
ogle back. How many times I'd say to myself, "Now that
one, now: I wish she was a little more of a coquette—
always wearing the same dress, her hair tumbling round
her face. One thing's sure," I'd say to myself, "none of
the boys will look at her while Ismene's about, all curled
and cute and tidy and trim. I'll have this one on my hands
for the rest of my life." And now, you see? Just like your
sister, after all. Only worse: a hypocrite. Who is the lad?
Some little scamp, eh? Somebody you can't bring home
and show to your family, and say, "Well, this is him, and
I mean to marry him and no other." That's how it is, is
it? Answer me!

Antigone [*smiling faintly*]. That's how it is. Yes, Nurse.

Nurse. Yes, says she! God save us! I took her when she
wasn't that high. I promised her poor mother I'd make a
lady of her. And look at her! But don't you go thinking
this is the end of this, my young 'un. I'm only your nurse
and you can play deaf and dumb with me; I don't count.
But your Uncle Creon will hear of this! That, I promise
you.

Antigone [*a little weary*]. Yes. Creon will hear of this.

Nurse. And we'll hear what he has to say when he finds
out that you go wandering alone o' nights. Not to mention Haemon. For the girl's engaged! Going to be married!
Going to be married, and she hops out of bed at four in
the morning to meet somebody else in a field. Do you
know what I ought to do to you? Take you over my knee
the way I used to do when you were little.

Antigone. Please, Nurse, I want to be alone.

Nurse. And if you so much as speak of it, she says she
wants to be alone!

Antigone. Nanny, you shouldn't scold, dear. This isn't
a day when you should be losing your temper.

Nurse. Not scold, indeed! Along with the rest of it, I'm
to like it. Didn't I promise your mother? What would she
say if she was here? "Old Stupid!" That's what she'd call
me. "Old Stupid. Not to know how to keep my little girl
pure! Spend your life making them behave, watching over
them like a mother hen, running after them with mufflers

and sweaters to keep them warm, and eggnogs to make them strong; and then at four o'clock in the morning, you who always complained you never could sleep a wink, snoring in your bed and letting them slip out into the bushes." That's what she'd say, your mother. And I'd stand there, dying of shame if I wasn't dead already. And all I could do would be not to dare look her in the face; and "That's true," I'd say. "That's all true what you say, Your Majesty."

Antigone. Nanny, dear. Dear Nanny. Don't cry. You'll be able to look Mamma in the face when it's your time to see her. And she'll say, "Good morning, Nanny. Thank you for my little Antigone. You did look after her so well." She knows why I went out this morning.

Nurse. Not to meet a lover?

Antigone. No. Not to meet a lover.

Nurse. Well, you've a queer way of teasing me, I must say! Not to know when she's teasing me! [*Rises to stand behind* ANTIGONE.] I must be getting awfully old, that's what it is. But if you loved me, you'd tell me the truth. You'd tell me why your bed was empty when I went along to tuck you in. Wouldn't you?

Antigone. Please, Nanny, don't cry any more. [ANTIGONE *turns partly toward* NURSE, *puts an arm up to* NURSE's *shoulder. With her other hand,* ANTIGONE *caresses* NURSE's *face.*] There now, my sweet red apple. Do you remember how I used to rub your cheeks to make them shine? My dear, wrinkled red apple! I didn't do anything tonight that was worth sending tears down the little gullies of your dear face. I am pure, and I swear that I have no other lover that Haemon. If you like, I'll swear that I shall never have any other lover than Haemon. Save your tears, Nanny, save them, Nanny dear; you may still need them. When you cry like that, I become a little girl again; and I mustn't be a little girl today. [ANTIGONE *rises and moves upstage.*]

ISMENE *enters through arch, left. She pauses in front of arch.*

Ismene. Antigone! What are you doing up at this hour? I've just been to your room.

Nurse. The two of you, now! You're both going mad, to

be up before the kitchen fire has been started. Do you like running about without a mouthful of breakfast? Do you think it's decent for the daughters of a king? [*She turns to* ISMENE.] And look at you, with nothing on, and the sun not up! I'll have you both on my hands with colds before I know it.

Antigone. Nanny dear, go away now. It's not chilly, really. Summer's here. Go and make us some coffee. Please, Nanny, I'd love some coffee. It would do me so much good.

Nurse. My poor baby! Her head's swimming, what with nothing on her stomach, and me standing here like an idiot when I could be getting her something hot to drink. [*Exit* NURSE.]

A *pause.*

Ismene. Aren't you well?

Antigone. Of course I am. Just a little tired. I got up too early. [ANTIGONE *sits on a chair, suddenly tired.*]

Ismene. I couldn't sleep, either.

Antigone. Ismene, you ought not to go without your beauty sleep.

Ismene. Don't make fun of me.

Antigone. I'm not, Ismene, truly. This particular morning, seeing how beautiful you are makes everything easier for me. Wasn't I a miserable little beast when we were small? I used to fling mud at you, and put worms down your neck. I remember tying you to a tree and cutting off your hair. Your beautiful hair! How easy it must be never to be unreasonable with all that smooth silken hair so beautifully set round your head.

Ismene [*abruptly*]. Why do you insist upon talking about other things?

Antigone [*gently*]. I am not talking about other things.

Ismene. Antigone, I've thought about it a lot.

Antigone. Have you?

Ismene. I thought about it all night long. Antigone, you're mad.

Antigone. Am I?

Ismene. We cannot do it.

Antigone. Why not?

Ismene. Creon will have us put to death.

Antigone. Of course he will. That's what he's here for.

He will do what he has to do, and we will do what we have to do. He is bound to put us to death. We are bound to go out and bury our brother. That's the way it is. What do you think we can do to change it?

Ismene [*releases* ANTIGONE's *hand; draws back a step*]. I don't want to die.

Antigone. I'd prefer not to die, myself.

Ismene. Listen to me, Antigone. I thought about it all night. I'm older than you are. I always think things over, and you don't. You are impulsive. You get a notion in your head and you jump up and do the thing straight off. And if it's silly, well, so much the worse for you. Whereas, I think things out.

Antigone. Sometimes it is better not to think too much.

Ismene. I don't agree with you! [ANTIGONE *looks at* ISMENE, *then turns and moves to chair behind table.* ISMENE *leans on end of table top, toward* ANTIGONE.] Oh, I know it's horrible. And I pity Polynices just as much as you do. But all the same, I sort of see what Uncle Creon means.

Antigone. I don't want to "sort of see" anything.

Ismene. Uncle Creon is the king. He has to set an example!

Antigone. But I am not the king; and I don't have to set people examples. Little Antigone gets a notion in her head—the nasty brat, the willful, wicked girl; and they put her in a corner all day, or they lock her up in the cellar. And she deserves it. She shouldn't have disobeyed!

Ismene. There you go, frowning, glowering, wanting your own stubborn way in everything. Listen to me. I'm right oftener than you are.

Antigone. I don't want to be right!

Ismene. At least you can try to understand.

Antigone. Understand! The first word I ever heard out of any of you was that word "understand." Why didn't I "understand" that I must not play with water—cold, black, beautiful flowing water—because I'd spill it on the palace tiles. Or with earth, because earth dirties a little girl's frock. Why didn't I "understand" that nice children don't eat out of every dish at once; or give everything in their pockets to beggars; or run in the wind so fast that they fall down; or ask for a drink when they're perspiring; or want to go swimming when it's either too early or too late, merely because they happen to feel like swimming. Understand! I don't want to understand. There'll be time enough to understand when I'm old. . . . If I ever *am* old. But not now.

Ismene. He is stronger than we are, Antigone. He is the king. And the whole city is with him. Thousands and thousands of them, swarming through all the streets of Thebes.

Antigone. I am not listening to you.

Ismene. His mob will come running, howling as it runs. A thousand arms will seize our arms. A thousand breaths will breathe into our faces. Like one single pair of eyes, a thousand eyes will stare at us. We'll be driven in a tumbrel through their hatred, through the smell of them and their cruel, roaring laughter. We'll be dragged to the scaffold for torture, surrounded by guards with their idiot faces all bloated, their animal hands clean-washed for the sacrifice, their beefy eyes squinting as they stare at us. And we'll know that no shrieking and no begging will make them understand that we want to live, for they are like slaves who do exactly as they've been told, without caring about right or wrong. And we shall suffer, we shall feel pain rising in us until it becomes so unbearable that we *know* it must stop. But it won't stop; it will go on rising and rising, like a screaming voice. Oh, I can't, I can't, Antigone!

A pause.

Antigone. How well have you thought it all out.

Ismene. I thought of it all night long. Didn't you?

Antigone. Oh, yes.

Ismene. I'm an awful coward, Antigone.

Antigone. So am I. But what has that to do with it?

Ismene. But, Antigone! Don't you want to go on living?

Antigone. Go on living! Who was it that was always the first out of bed because she loved the touch of the cold morning air on her bare skin? Who was always the last to bed because nothing less than infinite weariness could wean her from the lingering night? Who wept when she was little because there were too many grasses in the meadow, too many creatures in the field, for her to know and touch them all?

Ismene [*clasps* ANTIGONE'S *hands, in a sudden rush of tenderness*]. Darling little sister!

Antigone [*repulsing her*]. No! For heaven's sake! Don't paw me! And don't let us start sniveling! You say you've thought it all out. The howling mob—the torture—the fear of death. . . . They've made up your mind for you. Is that it?

Ismene. Yes.

Antigone. All right. They're as good excuses as any.

Ismene. Antigone, be sensible. It's all very well for men to believe in ideas and die for them. But you are a girl!

Antigone. Don't I know I'm a girl? Haven't I spent my life cursing the fact that I was a girl?

Ismene [*with spirit*]. Antigone! You have everything in the world to make you happy. All you have to do is reach out for it. You are going to be married; you are young; you are beautiful——

Antigone. I am not beautiful.

Ismene. Yes, you are! Not the way other girls are. But it's always you that the little boys turn to look back at when they pass us in the street. And when you go by, the little girls stop talking. They stare and stare at you, until we've turned a corner.

Antigone [*a faint smile*]. "Little boys—little girls."

Ismene [*challengingly*]. And what about Haemon?

A pause.

Antigone. I shall see Haemon this morning. I'll take care of Haemon. You always said I was mad; and it didn't matter how little I was or what I wanted to do. Go back to bed now, Ismene. The sun is coming up, and, as you see, there is nothing I can do today. Our brother Polynices is as well guarded as if he had won the war and were sitting on his throne. Go along. You are pale with weariness.

Ismene. What are you going to do?

Nurse [*calls from off-stage*]. Come along, my dove. Come to breakfast.

Antigone. I don't feel like going to bed. However, if you like, I'll promise not to leave the house till you wake up. Nurse is getting me breakfast. Go and get some sleep.

The sun is just up. Look at you: you can't keep your eyes open. Go.

Ismene. And you will listen to reason, won't you? You'll let me talk to you about this again? Promise?

Antigone. I promise. I'll let you talk. I'll let all of you talk. Go to bed, now. [ISMENE *goes to arch; exit.*] Poor Ismene!

Nurse [*enters through arch, speaking as she enters*]. Come along, my dove. I've made you some coffee and toast and jam. [*She turns towards arch as if to go out.*]

Antigone. I'm not really hungry, Nurse.

NURSE *stops, looks at* ANTIGONE, *then moves behind her.*

Nurse [*very tenderly*]. Where is your pain?

Antigone. Nowhere, Nanny dear. But you must keep me warm and safe, the way you used to do when I was little. Nanny! Stronger than all fever, stronger than any nightmare, stronger than the shadow of the cupboard that used to snarl at me and turn into a dragon on the bedroom wall. Stronger than the thousand insects gnawing and nibbling in the silence of the night. Stronger than the night itself, with the weird hooting of the night birds that frightened me even when I couldn't hear them. Nanny, stronger than death. Give me your hand, Nanny, as if I were ill in bed, and you sitting beside me.

Nurse. My sparrow, my lamb! What is it that's eating your heart out?

Antigone. Oh, it's just that I'm a little young still for what I have to go through. But nobody but you must know that.

Nurse [*places her other arm around* ANTIGONE'S *shoulder*]. A little young for what, my kitten?

Antigone. Nothing in particular, Nanny. Just—all this. Oh, it's so good that you are here. I can hold your callused hand, your hand that is so prompt to ward off evil. You are very powerful, Nanny.

Nurse. What is it you want me to do for you, my baby?

Antigone. There isn't anything to do, except put your hand like this against my cheek [*She places the* NURSE'S *hand against her cheek. A pause, then, as* ANTIGONE *leans back, her eyes shut.*] There! I'm not afraid any more. Not afraid of the wicked ogre, nor of the sandman, nor of the dwarf who steals little children. [*A pause.* ANTIGONE *resumes on another note.*] Nanny . . .

Nurse. Yes?

Antigone. My dog, Puff . . .

Nurse [*straightens up, draws her hand away*]. Well?

Antigone. Promise me that you will never scold her again.

Nurse. Dogs that dirty up a house with their filthy paws deserve to be scolded.

Antigone. I know. Just the same, promise me.

Nurse. You mean you want me to let her make a mess all over the place and not say a thing?

Antigone. Yes, Nanny.

Nurse. You're asking a lot. The next time she wets my living-room carpet, I'll——

Antigone. Please, Nanny, I beg of you!

Nurse. It isn't fair to take me on my weak side, just because you look a little peaked today. . . . Well, have it your own way. We'll mop up and keep our mouth shut. You're making a fool of me, though.

Antigone. And promise me that you will talk to her. That you will talk to her often.

Nurse [*turns and looks at* ANTIGONE]. Me, talk to a dog!

Antigone. Yes. But mind you: you are not to talk to her the way people usually talk to dogs. You're to talk to her the way I talk to her.

Nurse. I don't see why both of us have to make fools of ourselves. So long as you're here, one ought to be enough.

Antigone. But if there was a reason why I couldn't go on talking to her——

Nurse [*interrupting*]. Couldn't go on talking to her! And why couldn't you go on talking to her? What kind of poppycock——?

Antigone. And if she got too unhappy, if she moaned and moaned, waiting for me with her nose under the door as she does when I'm out all day, then the best thing, Nanny, might be to have her mercifully put to sleep.

Nurse. Now what *has* got into you this morning? [HAEMON *enters through arch*]. Running around in the darkness, won't sleep, won't eat—[ANTIGONE *sees* HAEMON.]—and now it's her dog she wants killed. I never.

Antigone [*interrupting*]. Nanny! Haemon is here. Go inside, please. And don't forget that you've promised me.

[NURSE *goes to arch; exit.* ANTIGONE *rises.*] Haemon, Haemon! Forgive me for quarreling with you last night. [*She crosses quickly to* HAEMON *and they embrace.*] Forgive me for everything. It was all my fault. I beg you to forgive me.

Haemon. You know that I've forgiven you. You had hardly slammed the door, your perfume still hung in the room, when I had already forgiven you. [*He holds her in his arms and smiles at her. Then draws slightly back.*] You stole that perfume. From whom?

Antigone. Ismene.

Haemon. And the rouge? and the face powder? and the frock? Whom did you steal them from?

Antigone. Ismene.

Haemon. And in whose honor did you get yourself up so elegantly?

Antigone. I'll tell you everything. [*She draws him closer.*] Oh, darling, what a fool I was! To waste a whole evening! A whole, beautiful evening!

Haemon. We'll have other evenings, my sweet.

Antigone. Perhaps we won't.

Haemon. And other quarrels, too. A happy love is full of quarrels, you know.

Antigone. A happy love, yes. Haemon, listen to me.

Haemon. Yes?

Antigone. Don't laugh at me this morning. Be serious.

Haemon. I am serious.

Antigone. And hold me tight. Tighter than you have ever held me. I want all your strength to flow into me.

Haemon. There! With all my strength.

A pause.

Antigone [*breathless*]. That's good. [*They stand for a moment, silent and motionless.*] Haemon! I wanted to tell you. You know—the little boy we were going to have when we were married?

Haemon. Yes?

Antigone. I'd have protected him against everything in the world.

Haemon. Yes, dearest.

Antigone. Oh, you don't know how I should have held him in my arms and given him my strength. He wouldn't

have been afraid of anything, I swear he wouldn't. Not of
the falling night, nor of the terrible noonday sun, nor of
all the shadows, or all the walls in the world. Our little
boy, Haemon! His mother wouldn't have been very imposing: her hair wouldn't always have been brushed; but
she would have been strong where he was concerned, so
much stronger than all those real mothers with their real
bosoms and their aprons around their middle. You believe
that, don't you, Haemon?

Haemon [*soothingly*]. Yes, yes, my darling.

Antigone. And you believe me when I say that you
would have had a real wife?

Haemon. Darling, you are my real wife.

Antigone [*pressing against him and crying out*].
Haemon, you loved me! You did love me that night,
didn't you? You're sure of it!

Haemon [*rocking her gently*]. What night, my sweet?

Antigone. And you are very sure, aren't you, that that
night, at the dance, when you came to the corner where I
was sitting, there was no mistake? It was me you were
looking for? It wasn't another girl? And you're sure that
never, not in your most secret heart of hearts, have you
said to yourself that it was Ismene you ought to have
asked to marry you?

Haemon [*reproachfully*]. Antigone, you are idiotic. You
might give me credit for knowing my own mind. It's you
I love, and no one else.

Antigone. But you love me as a woman—as a woman
wants to be loved, don't you? Your arms around me aren't
lying, are they? Your hands, so warm against my back—
they're not lying? This warmth that's in me; this confidence, this sense that I am safe, secure, that flows
through me as I stand here with my cheek in the hollow of
your shoulder: they are not lies, are they?

Haemon. Antigone, darling, I love you exactly as you
love me. With all of myself.

They kiss.

Antigone. I'm sallow, and I'm scrawny. Ismene is pink
and golden. She's like a fruit.

Haemon. Look here, Antigone——

Antigone. Ah, dearest, I am ashamed of myself. But this

morning, this special morning, I must know. Tell me the truth! I beg you to tell me the truth! When you think about me, when it strikes you suddenly that I am going to belong to you—do you have the feeling that—that a great empty space is being hollowed out inside you, that there is something inside you that is just—dying?

Haemon. Yes, I do, I do.

A pause.

Antigone. That's the way I feel. And another thing. I wanted you to know that I should have been very proud to be your wife—the woman whose shoulder you would put your hand on as you sat down to table, absent-mindedly, as upon a thing that belonged to you. [*After a moment, draws away from him. Her tone changes.*] There! Now I have two things more to tell you. And when I have told them to you, you must go away instantly, without asking any questions. However strange they may seem to you. However much they may hurt you. Swear that you will!

Haemon [*beginning to be troubled*]. What are these things that you are going to tell me?

Antigone. Swear, first, that you will go away without one word. Without so much as looking at me. [*She looks at him, wretchedness in her face.*] You hear me, Haemon. Swear it, please. This is the last mad wish that you will ever have to grant me.

A pause.

Haemon. I swear it, since you insist. But I must tell you that I don't like this at all.

Antigone. Please, Haemon. It's very serious. You must listen to me and do as I ask. First, about last night, when I came to your house. You asked me a moment ago why I wore Ismene's dress and rouge. It was because I was stupid. I wasn't very sure that you loved me as a woman; and I did it—because I wanted you to want me. I was trying to be more like other girls.

Haemon. Was *that* the reason? My poor—

Antigone. Yes. And you laughed at me. And we

quarreled; and my awful temper got the better of me and I flung out of the house. . . . The real reason was that I wanted you to take me; I wanted to be your wife before——

Haemon. Oh, my darling——

Antigone [*shuts him off*]. You swore you wouldn't ask any questions. You swore, Haemon. [*Turns her face away and goes on in a hard voice.*] As a matter of fact, I'll tell you why. I wanted to be your wife last night because I love you that way very—very strongly. And also because—— Oh, my darling, my darling, forgive me; I'm going to cause you quite a lot of pain. [*She draws away from him.*] I wanted it also because I shall never, never be able to marry you, never! [HAEMON *is stupefied and mute; then he moves a step towards her.*] Haemon! You took a solemn oath! You swore! Leave me quickly! Tomorrow the whole thing will be clear to you. Even before tomorrow: this afternoon. If you please, Haemon, go now. It is the only thing left that you can do for me if you still love me. [A *pause as* HAEMON *stares at her. Then he turns and goes out through the arch.* ANTIGONE *stands motionless, then moves to a chair at end of table and lets herself gently down on it. In a mild voice, as of calm after storm.*] Well, it's over for Haemon, Antigone.

ISMENE *enters through arch, pauses for a moment in front of it when she sees* ANTIGONE, *then crosses behind table.*

Ismene. I can't sleep. I'm terrified. I'm so afraid that, even though it is daylight, you'll still try to bury Polynices. Antigone, little sister, we all want to make you happy— Haemon, and Nurse, and I, and Puff whom you love. We love you, we are alive, we need you. And you remember what Polynices was like. He was our brother, of course. But he's dead; and he never loved you. He was a bad brother. He was like an enemy in the house. He never thought of you. Why should you think of him? What if his soul does have to wander through endless time without rest or peace? Don't try something that is beyond your strength. You are always defying the world, but you're only a girl, after all. Stay at home tonight. Don't try to do it, I beg you. It's Creon's doing, not ours.

Antigone. You are too late, Ismene. When you first saw me this morning, I had just come in from burying him. [*Exit* ANTIGONE *through arch.*]

The lighting, which by this time has reached a point of early morning sun, is quickly dimmed out, leaving the stage bathed in a light blue color. ISMENE *runs out after* ANTIGONE. *On* ISMENE'S *exit the lights are brought up suddenly to suggest a later period of the day.* CREON *and* PAGE *enter through curtain upstage.* CREON *stands on the top step; his* PAGE *stands at his right side.*

Creon. A private of the guards, you say? One of those standing watch over the body? Show him in.

The PAGE *crosses to arch; exit.* CREON *moves down to end of table.* PAGE *re-enters, preceded by the* FIRST GUARD, *livid with fear.* PAGE *remains on upstage side of arch.* GUARD *salutes.*

Guard. Private Jonas, Second Battalion.

Creon. What are you doing here?

Guard. It's like this, sir. Soon as it happened, we said: "Got to tell the chief about this before anybody else spills it. He'll want to know right away." So we tossed a coin to see which one would come up and tell you about it. You see, sir, we thought only one man had better come, because, after all, you don't want to leave the body without a guard. Right? I mean, there's three of us on duty, guarding the body.

Creon. What's wrong about the body?

Guard. Sir, I've been seventeen years in the service. Volunteer. Wounded three times. Two mentions. My record's clean. I know my business and I know my place. I carry out orders. Sir, ask any officer in the battalion; they'll tell you. "Leave it to Jonas. Give him an order: he'll carry it out." That's what they'll tell you, sir. Jonas, that's me—that's my name.

Creon. What's the matter with you, man? What are you shaking for?

Guard. By rights it's the corporal's job, sir. I've been recommended for a corporal, but they haven't put it through yet. June, it was supposed to go through.

Creon [*interrupts*]. Stop chattering and tell me why you are here. If anything has gone wrong, I'll break all three of you.

Guard. Nobody can say we didn't keep our eye on that body. We had the two-o'clock watch—the tough one. You know how it is, sir. It's nearly the end of the night. Your eyes are like lead. You've got a crick in the back of your neck. There's shadows, and the fog is beginning to roll in. A fine watch they give us! And me, seventeen years in the service. But we was doing our duty all right. On our feet, all of us. Anybody says we were sleeping is a liar. First place, it was too cold. Second place—— [CREON *makes a gesture of impatience.*] Yes, sir. Well, I turned around and looked at the body. We wasn't only ten feet away from it, but that's how I am. I was keeping my eye on it. [*Shouts.*] Listen, sir, I was the first man to see it! Me! They'll tell you. I was the one let out that yell!

Creon. What for? What was the matter?

Guard. Sir, the body! Somebody had been there and buried it. [CREON *comes down a step on the stair. The* GUARD *becomes more frightened.*] It wasn't much, you understand. With us three there, it couldn't have been. Just covered over with a little dirt, that's all. But enough to hide it from the buzzards.

Creon. By God, I'll——! [*He looks intently at the* GUARD.] You are sure that it couldn't have been a dog, scratching up the earth?

Guard. Not a chance, sir. That's kind of what we hoped it was. But the earth was scattered over the body just like the priests tell you you should do it. Whoever did that job knew what he was doing, all right.

Creon. Who could have dared? [*He turns and looks at the* GUARD.] Was there anything to indicate who might have done it?

Guard. Not a thing, sir. Maybe we heard a footstep— I can't swear to it. Of course we started right in to search, and the corporal found a shovel, a kid's shovel no bigger than that, all rusty and everything. Corporal's got the shovel for you. We thought maybe a kid did it.

Creon [*to himself*]. A kid! [*He looks away from the* GUARD.] I broke the back of the rebellion; but like a snake, it is coming together again. Polynices' friends, with their gold, blocked by my orders in the banks of Thebes.

The leaders of the mob, stinking of garlic and allied to envious princes. And the temple priests, always ready foɪ a bit of fishing in troubled waters. A kid! I can imagine what he is like, their kid: a baby-faced killer, creeping in the night with a toy shovel under his jacket. [*He looks at his* PAGE.] Though why shouldn't they have corrupted a real child? Very touching! Very useful to the party, an innocent child. A martyr. A real white-faced baby of fourteen who will spit with contempt at the guards who kill him. A free gift to their cause: the precious, innocent blood of a child on my hands. [*He turns to the* GUARD.] They must have accomplices in the Guard itself. Look here, you. Who knows about this?

Guard. Only us three, sir. We flipped a coin, and I came right over.

Creon. Right. Listen, now. You will continue on duty. When the relief squad comes up, you will tell them to return to barracks. You will uncover the body. If another attempt is made to bury it, I shall expect you to make an arrest and bring the person straight to me. And you will keep your mouths shut. Not one word of this to a human soul. You are all guilty of neglect of duty, and you will be punished; but if the rumor spreads through Thebes that the body received burial, you will be shot—all three of you.

Guard [*excitedly*]. Sir, we never told nobody, I swear we didn't! Anyhow, I've been up here. Suppose my pals spilled it to the relief; I couldn't have been with them and here too. That wouldn't be my fault if they talked. Sir, I've got two kids. You're my witness, sir, it couldn't have been me. I was here with you. I've got a witness! If anybody talked, it couldn't have been me! I was——

Creon [*interrupting*]. Clear out! If the story doesn't get around, you won't be shot. [*The* GUARD *salutes, turns, and exits at the double.* CREON *turns and paces upstage, then comes down to end of the table.*] A child! [*He looks at* PAGE.] Come along, my lad. Since we can't hope to keep this to ourselves, we shall have to be the first to give out the news. And after that, we shall have to clean up the mess. [PAGE *crosses to side of* CREON. CREON *puts his hand on* PAGE's *shoulder.*] Would you be willing to die for me? Would you defy the Guard with your little shovel? [PAGE *looks up at* CREON.] Of course you would. You would do it, too. [A *pause.* CREON *looks away from* PAGE *and murmurs*] A child! [CREON *and* PAGE *go slowly up-stage center to top step.* PAGE *draws aside the curtain, through which exit* CREON *with* PAGE *behind him.*]

As soon as CREON *and* PAGE *have disappeared,* CHORUS *enters and leans against the upstage portal or arch, left. The lighting is brought up to its brightest point to suggest mid-afternoon.* CHORUS *allows a a pause to indicate that a crucial moment has been reached in the play, then moves slowly downstage, center. He stands for a moment silent, reflecting, and then smiles faintly.*

Chorus. The spring is wound up tight. It will uncoil of itself. That is what is so convenient in tragedy. The least little turn of the wrist will do the job. Anything will set it going: a glance at a girl who happens to be lifting her arms to her hair as you go by; a feeling when you wake up on a fine morning that you'd like a little respect paid to you today, as if it were as easy to order as a second cup of coffee; one question too many, idly thrown out over a friendly drink—and the tragedy is on.

The rest is automatic. You don't need to lift a finger. The machine is in perfect order; it has been oiled ever since time began, and it runs without friction. Death, treason, and sorrow are on the march; and they move in the wake of storm, of tears, of stillness. Every kind of stillness. The hush when the executioner's ax goes up at the end of the last act. The unbreathable silence when, at the beginning of the play, the two lovers, their hearts bared, their bodies naked, stand for the first time face to face in the darkened room, afraid to stir. The silence inside you when the roaring crowd acclaims the winner—so that you think of a film without a sound track, mouths agape and no sound coming out of them, a clamor that is no more than a picture; and you, the victor, already vanquished, alone in the desert of your silence. That is tragedy.

Tragedy is clean, it is restful, it is flawless. It has nothing to do with melodrama—with wicked villains, persecuted maidens, avengers, sudden revelations, and eleventh-hour repentances. Death, in a melodrama, is really horrible because it is never inevitable. The dear old father might so easily have been saved; the honest young man might so easily have brought in the police five minutes earlier.

In a tragedy, nothing is in doubt and everyone's destiny is known. That makes for tranquillity. There is a sort of fellow-feeling among characters in a tragedy: he who kills is as innocent as he who gets killed: it's all a matter of what part you are playing. Tragedy is restful; and the reason is that hope, that foul, deceitful thing, has no part in it. There isn't any hope. You're trapped. The whole sky has fallen on you, and all you can do about it is to shout.

Don't mistake me: I said "shout": I did not say groan, whimper, complain. That, you cannot do. But you can shout aloud; you can get all those things said that you never thought you'd be able to say—or never even knew you had it in you to say. And you don't say these things because it will do any good to say them: you know better than that. You say them for their own sake; you say them because you learn a lot from them.

In melodrama you argue and struggle in the hope of escape. That is vulgar; it's practical. But in tragedy, where there is no temptation to try to escape, argument is gratuitous: it's kingly.

Voices of the GUARDS *and scuffling sound heard through the archway.* CHORUS *looks in that direction; then, in a changed tone:*

The play is on. Antigone has been caught. For the first time in her life, little Antigone is going to be able to be herself.

Exit CHORUS *through arch. A pause, while the offstage voices rise in volume, then the* FIRST GUARD *enters, followed by* SECOND *and* THIRD GUARDS, *holding the arms of* ANTIGONE *and dragging her along. The* FIRST GUARD, *speaking as he enters, crosses swiftly to end of the table. The* TWO GUARDS *and* ANTIGONE *stop downstage.*

First Guard [*recovered from his fright*]. Come on, now, Miss, give it a rest. The chief will be here in a minute and you can tell him about it. All I know is my orders. I don't want to know what you were doing there. People always have excuses; but I can't afford to listen to them, see. Why, if we had to listen to all the people who want to tell us what's the matter with this country, we'd never get our work done. [*To the* Guards.] You keep hold of her and I'll see that she keeps her face shut.

Antigone. They are hurting me. Tell them to take their dirty hands off me.

First Guard. Dirty hands, eh? The least you can do is try to be polite, Miss. Look at me: I'm polite.

Antigone. Tell them to let me go. I shan't run away. My father was King Oedipus. I am Antigone.

First Guard. King Oedipus' little girl! Well, well, well! Listen, Miss, the night watch never picks up a lady but they say, you better be careful: I'm sleeping with the police commissioner.

The Guards *laugh.*

Antigone. I don't mind being killed, but I don't want them to touch me.

First Guard. And what about stiffs, and dirt, and such like? You wasn't afraid to touch them, was you? "Their dirty hands!" Take a look at your own hands. [Antigone, *handcuffed, smiles despite herself as she looks down at her hands. They are grubby.*] You must have lost your shovel, didn't you? Had to go at it with your fingernails the second time, I'll bet. By God, I never saw such nerve! I turn my back for about five seconds; I ask a pal for a chew; I say "thanks"; I get the tobacco stowed away in my cheek—the whole thing don't take ten seconds; and there she is, clawing away like a hyena. Right out in broad daylight! And did she scratch and kick when I grabbed her! Straight for my eyes with them nails she went. And yelling something fierce about, "I haven't finished yet; let me finish!" She ain't got all her marbles!

Second Guard. I pinched a nut like that the other day. Right on the main square she was, hoisting up her skirts and showing her behind to anybody that wanted to take a look.

First Guard. Listen, we're going to get a bonus out of this. What do you say we throw a party, the three of us?

Second Guard. At the old woman's? Behind Market Street?

Third Guard. Suits me. Sunday would be a good day. We're off duty Sunday. What do you say we bring our wives?

First Guard. No. Let's have some fun this time. Bring your wife, there's always something goes wrong. First place, what do you do with the kids? Bring them, they always want to go to the can just when you're right in the middle of a game of cards or something. Listen, who would have thought an hour ago that us three would be talking about throwing a party now? The way I felt when the old man was interrogating me, we'd be lucky if we got off with being docked a month's pay. I want to tell you, I was scared.

Second Guard. You sure we're going to get a bonus?

First Guard. Yes. Something tells me this is big stuff.

Third Guard [*to* SECOND GUARD]. What's-his-name, you know—in the Third Battalion? He got an extra month's pay for catching a firebug.

Second Guard. If we get an extra month's pay, I vote we throw the party at the Arabian's.

First Guard. You're crazy! He charges twice as much for liquor as anybody else in town. Unless you want to go upstairs, of course. Can't do that at the old woman's.

Third Guard. Well, we can't keep this from our wives, no matter how you work it out. You get an extra month's pay, and what happens? Everybody in the battalion knows it, and your wife knows it too. They might even line up the battalion and give it to you in front of everybody, so how could you keep your wife from finding out?

First Guard. Well, we'll see about that. If they do the job out in the barrack yard—of course that means women, kids, everything.

Antigone. I should like to sit down, if you please.

A pause, as the FIRST GUARD *thinks it over.*

First Guard. Let her sit down. But keep hold of her. [*The two* GUARDS *start to lead her toward the chair at end of table. The curtain upstage opens, and* CREON *enters, followed by his* PAGE. FIRST GUARD *turns and moves upstage a few steps, sees* CREON.] 'Tenshun! [*The three* GUARDS *salute.* CREON, *seeing* ANTIGONE *handcuffed to* THIRD GUARD, *stops on the top step, astonished.*]

Creon. Antigone! [*To the* FIRST GUARD.] Take off those handcuffs! [FIRST GUARD *crosses above table to left of* ANTIGONE.] What is this? [CREON *and his* PAGE *come down off the steps.*]

FIRST GUARD *takes key from his pocket and unlocks the* cuff *on* ANTIGONE'S *hand.* ANTIGONE *rubs her wrist as she crosses below table toward chair at end of table.* SECOND *and* THIRD GUARDS *step back to front of arch.* FIRST GUARD *turns upstage toward* CREON.

First Guard. The watch, sir. We all came this time.
Creon. Who is guarding the body?
First Guard. We sent for the relief.

CREON *comes down.*

Creon. But I gave orders that the relief was to go back to barracks and stay there! [ANTIGONE *sits on chair at left of table.*] I told you not to open your mouth about this!
First Guard. Nobody's said anything, sir. We made this arrest, and brought the party in, the way you said we should.
Creon [*to* ANTIGONE]. Where did these men find you?
First Guard. Right by the body.
Creon. What were you doing near your brother's body? You knew what my orders were.
First Guard. What was she doing? Sir, that's why we brought her in. She was digging up the dirt with her nails. She was trying to cover up the body all over again.
Creon. Do you realize what you are saying?
First Guard. Sir, ask these men here. After I reported to you, I went back, and first thing we did, we uncovered the body. The sun was coming up and it was beginning to smell, so we moved it up on a little rise to get him in the wind. Of course, you wouldn't expect any trouble in broad daylight. But just the same, we decided one of us had better keep his eye peeled all the time. About noon, what with the sun and the smell, and as the wind dropped and I wasn't feeling none too good, I went over to my pal to get a chew. I just had time to say "thanks" and stick it in my mouth, when I turned round and there she was, clawing away at the dirt with both hands. Right out in

broad daylight! Wouldn't you think when she saw me come running she'd stop and leg it out of there? Not her! She went right on digging as fast as she could, as if I wasn't there at all. And when I grabbed her, she scratched and bit and yelled to leave her alone, she hadn't finished yet, the body wasn't all covered yet, and the like of that.

Creon [*to* ANTIGONE]. Is this true?

Antigone. Yes, it is true.

First Guard. We scraped the dirt off as fast as we could, then we sent for the relief and we posted them. But we didn't tell them a thing, sir. And we brought in the party so's you could see her. And that's the truth, so help me God.

Creon [*to* ANTIGONE.] And was it you who covered the body the first time? In the night?

Antigone. Yes, it was. With a toy shovel we used to take to the seashore when we were children. It was Polynices' own shovel; he had cut his name in the handle. That was why I left it with him. But these men took it away; so the next time, I had to do it with my hands.

First Guard. Sir, she was clawing away like a wild animal. Matter of fact, first minute we saw her, what with the heat haze and everything, my pal says, "That must be a dog," he says. "Dog!" I says, "that's a girl, that is!" And it was.

Creon. Very well. [*Turns to the* PAGE.] Show these men to the anteroom. [*The* PAGE *crosses to the arch, stands there, waiting.* CREON *moves behind the table. To the* FIRST GUARD.] You three men will wait outside. I may want a report from you later.

First Guard. Do I put the cuffs back on her, sir?

Creon. No. [*The three* GUARDS *salute, do an about-turn, and exeunt through arch, right.* PAGE *follows them out. A pause.*] Had you told anybody what you meant to do?

Antigone. No.

Creon. Did you meet anyone on your way—coming or going?

Antigone. No, nobody.

Creon. Sure of that, are you?

Antigone. Perfectly sure.

Creon. Very well. Now listen to me. You will go straight to your room. When you get there, you will go to bed. You will say that your are not well and that you have not been out since yesterday. Your nurse will tell the same story. [*He looks toward arch, through which the* GUARDS *have gone out.*] And I'll get rid of those three men.

Antigone. Uncle Creon, you are going to a lot of trouble for no good reason. You must know that I'll do it all over again tonight.

A *pause. They look one another in the eye.*

Creon. Why did you try to bury your brother?

Antigone. I owed it to him.

Creon. I had forbidden it.

Antigone. I owed it to him. Those who are not buried wander eternally and find no rest. If my brother were alive, and he came home weary after a long day's hunting, I should kneel down and unlace his boots, I should fetch him food and drink, I should see that his bed was ready for him. Polynices is home from the hunt. I owe it to him to unlock the house of the dead in which my father and my mother are waiting to welcome him. Polynices has earned his rest.

Creon. Polynices was a rebel and a traitor, and you know it.

Antigone. He was my brother.

Creon. You heard my edict. It was proclaimed throughout Thebes. You read my edict. It was posted up on the city walls.

Antigone. Of course I did.

Creon. You knew the punishment I decreed for any person who attempted to give him burial.

Antigone. Yes, I knew the punishment.

Creon. Did you by any chance act on the assumption that a daughter of Oedipus, a daughter of Oedipus' stubborn pride, was above the law?

Antigone. No, I did not act on that assumption.

Creon. Because if you had acted on that assumption, Antigone, you would have been deeply wrong. Nobody has a more sacred obligation to obey the law than those who make the law. You are a daughter of lawmakers, a daughter of kings, Antigone. You must observe the law.

Antigone. Had I been a scullery maid washing my

dishes when that law was read aloud to me, I should have scrubbed the greasy water from my arms and gone out in my apron to bury my brother.

Creon. What nonsense! If you had been a scullery maid, there would have been no doubt in your mind about the seriousness of that edict. You would have known that it meant death; and you would have been satisfied to weep for your brother in your kitchen. But you! You thought that because you come of the royal line, because you were my niece and were going to marry my son, I shouldn't dare have you killed.

Antigone. You are mistaken. Quite the contrary. I never doubted for an instant that you would have me put to death.

A *pause, as* CREON *stares fixedly at her.*

Creon. The pride of Oedipus! Oedipus and his head-strong pride all over again. I can see your father in you—and I believe you. Of course you thought that I should have you killed! Proud as you are, it seemed to you a natural climax in your existence. Your father was like that. For him as for you human happiness was meaningless; and mere human misery was not enough to satisfy his passion for torment. [*He sits on stool behind the table.*] You come of people for whom the human vestment is a kind of straitjacket: it cracks at the seams. You spend your lives wriggling to get out of it. Nothing less than a cosy tea party with death and destiny will quench your thirst. The happiest hour of your father's life came when he listened greedily to the story of how, unknown to himself, he had killed his own father and dishonored the bed of his own mother. Drop by drop, word by word, he drank in the dark story that the gods had destined him first to live and then to hear. How avidly men and women drink the brew of such a tale when their names are Oedipus—and Antigone! And it is so simple, afterwards, to do what your father did, to put out one's eyes and take one's daughter begging on the highways.

Let me tell you, Antigone: those days are over for Thebes. Thebes has a right to a king without a past. My name, thank God, is only Creon. I stand here with both feet firm on the ground; with both hands in my pockets; and I have decided that so long as I am king—being less ambitious than your father was—I shall merely devote myself to introducing a little order into this absurd kingdom; if that is possible.

Don't think that being a king seems to me romantic. It is my trade; a trade a man has to work at every day; and like every other trade, it isn't all beer and skittles. But since it is my trade, I take it seriously. And if, tomorrow, some wild and bearded messenger walks in from some wild and distant valley—which is what happened to your dad—and tells me that he's not quite sure who my parents were, but thinks that my wife Eurydice is actually my mother, I shall ask him to do me the kindness to go back where he came from; and I shan't let a little matter like that persuade me to order my wife to take a blood test and the police to let me know whether or not my birth certificate was forged. Kings, my girl, have other things to do than to surrender themselves to their private feelings. [*He looks at her and, smiles.*] Hand *you* over to be killed! [*He rises, moves to end of table and sits on the top of table.*] I have other plans for you. You're going to marry Haemon; and I want you to fatten up a bit so that you can give him a sturdy boy. Let me assure you that Thebes needs that boy a good deal more than it needs your death. You will go to your room, now, and do as you have been told; and you won't say a word about this to anybody. Don't fret about the guards: I'll see that their mouths are shut. And don't annihilate me with those eyes. I know that you think I am a brute, and I'm sure you must consider me very prosaic. But the fact is, I have always been fond of you, stubborn though you always were. Don't forget that the first doll you ever had came from me. [*A pause.* ANTIGONE *says nothing, rises, and crosses slowly below the table toward the arch.* CREON *turns and watches her; then*] Where are you going?

Antigone [*stops downstage. Without any show of rebellion*]. You know very well where I am going.

Creon [*after a pause*]. What sort of game are you playing?

Antigone. I am not playing games.

Creon. Antigone, do you realize that if, apart from those three guards, a single soul finds out what you have tried to do, it will be impossible for me to avoid putting you to death? There is still a chance that I can save you;

but only if you keep this to yourself and give up your crazy purpose. Five minutes more, and it will be too late. You understand that?

Antigone. I must go and bury my brother. Those men uncovered him.

Creon. What good will it do? You know that there are other men standing guard over Polynices. And even if you did cover him over with earth again, the earth would again be removed.

Antigone. I know all that. I know it. But that much, at least, I can do. And what a person can do, a person ought to do.

Pause.

Creon. Tell me, Antigone, do you believe all that flummery about religious burial? Do you really believe that a so-called shade of your brother is condemned to wander for ever homeless if a little earth is not flung on his corpse to the accompaniment of some priestly abracadabra? Have you ever listened to the priests of Thebes when they were mumbling their formula? Have you ever watched those dreary bureaucrats while they were preparing the dead for burial—skipping half the gestures required by the ritual, swallowing half their words, hustling the dead into their graves out of fear that they might be late for lunch?

Antigone. Yes, I have seen all that.

Creon. And did you never say to yourself as you watched them, that if someone you really loved lay dead under the shuffling, mumbling ministrations of the priests, you would scream aloud and beg the priests to leave the dead in peace?

Antigone. Yes, I've thought all that.

Creon. And you still insist upon being put to death— merely because I refuse to let your brother go out with that grotesque passport; because I refuse his body the wretched consolation of that mass-production jibber-jabber, which you would have been the first to be embarrassed by if I had allowed it. The whole thing is absurd!

Antigone. Yes, it's absurd.

Creon. Then why, Antigone, why? For whose sake? For the sake of them that believe in it? To raise them against me?

Antigone. No.

Creon. For whom then if not for them and not for Polynices either?

Antigone. For nobody. For myself.

A pause as they stand looking at one another.

Creon. You must want very much to die. You look like a trapped animal.

Antigone. Stop feeling sorry for me. Do as I do. Do your job. But if you are a human being, do it quickly. That is all I ask of you. I'm not going to be able to hold out for ever.

Creon [*takes a step toward her*]. I want to save you, Antigone.

Antigone. You are the king, and you are all-powerful. But that you cannot do.

Creon. You think not?

Antigone. Neither save me nor stop me.

Creon. Prideful Antigone! Little Oedipus!

Antigone. Only this can you do: have me put to death.

Creon. Have you tortured, perhaps?

Antigone. Why would you do that? To see me cry? To hear me beg for mercy? Or swear whatever you wish, and then begin over again?

A pause.

Creon. You listen to me. You have cast me for the villain in this little play of yours, and yourself for the heroine. And you know it, you damned little mischief-maker! But don't you drive me too far! If I were one of your preposterous little tyrants that Greece is full of, you would be lying in a ditch this minute with your tongue pulled out and your body drawn and quartered. But you can see something in my face that makes me hesitate to send for the guards and turn you over to them. Instead, I let you go on arguing; and you taunt me, you take the offensive. [*He grasps her left wrist.*] What are you driving at, you she devil?

Antigone. Let me go. You are hurting my arm.

Creon [*gripping her tighter*]. I will not let you go.

Antigone [*moans*]. Oh!

Creon. I was a fool to waste words. I should have done this from the beginning. [*He looks at her.*] I may be your uncle—but we are not a particularly affectionate family. Are we, eh? [*Through his teeth, as he twists.*] Are we? [CREON *propels* ANTIGONE *round below him to his side.*] What fun for you, eh? To be able to spit in the face of a king who has all the power in the world; a man who has done his own killing in his day; who has killed people just as pitiable as you are—and who is still soft enough to go to all this trouble in order to keep you from being killed.

A pause.

Antigone. Now you are squeezing my arm too tightly. It doesn't hurt any more.

CREON *stares at her, then drops her arm.*

Creon. I shall save you yet. [*He goes below the table to the chair at end of table, takes off his coat, and places it on the chair.*] God knows, I have things enough to do today without wasting my time on an insect like you. There's plenty to do, I assure you, when you've just put down a revolution. But urgent things can wait. I am not going to let politics be the cause of your death. For it is a fact that this whole business is nothing but politics: the mournful shade of Polynices, the decomposing corpse, the sentimental weeping, and the hysteria that you mistake for heroism—nothing but politics.

Look here. I may not be soft, but I'm fastidious. I like things clean, shipshape, well scrubbed. Don't think that I am not just as offended as you are by the thought of that meat rotting in the sun. In the evening, when the breeze comes in off the sea, you can smell it in the palace, and it nauseates me. But I refuse even to shut my window. It's vile; and I can tell you what I wouldn't tell anybody else: it's stupid, monstrously stupid. But the people of Thebes have got to have their noses rubbed into it a little longer. My God! If it was up to me, I should have had them bury your brother long ago as a mere matter of public hygiene. I admit that what I am doing is childish. But if the featherheaded rabble I govern are to under-

stand what's what, that stench has got to fill the town
for a month!

Antigone [*turns to him*]. You are a loathsome man!

Creon. I agree. My trade forces me to be. We could
argue whether I ought or ought not to follow my trade;
but once I take on the job, I must do it properly.

Antigone. Why do you do it at all?

Creon. My dear, I woke up one morning and found
myself King of Thebes. God knows, there were other
things I loved in life more than power.

Antigone. Then you should have said no.

Creon. Yes, I could have done that. Only, I felt that it
would have been cowardly. I should have been like a
workman who turns down a job that has to be done. So
I said yes.

Antigone. So much the worse for you, then. I didn't
say yes. I can say no to anything I think vile, and I don't
have to count the cost. But because you said yes, all that
you can do, for all your crown and your trappings, and
your guards—all that you can do is to have me killed.

Creon. Listen to me.

Antigone. If I want to. I don't have to listen to you if
I don't want to. You've said your *yes*. There is nothing
more you can tell me that I don't know. You stand there,
drinking in my words. [*She moves behind chair.*] Why is
it that you don't call your guards? I'll tell you why? You
want to hear me out to the end; that's why.

Creon. You amuse me.

Antigone. Oh, no, I don't. I frighten you. That is why
you talk about saving me. Everything would be so much
easier if you had a docile, tongue-tied little Antigone living
in the palace. I'll tell you something, Uncle Creon: I'll
give you back one of your own words. You are too fastidious to make a good tyrant. But you are going to have to
put me to death today, and you know it. And that's what
frightens you. God! Is there anything uglier than a frightened man!

Creon. Very well. I am afraid, then. Does that satisfy
you? I am afraid that if you insist upon it, I shall have to
have you killed. And I don't want to.

Antigone. I don't have to do things that I think are
wrong. If it comes to that, you didn't really want to leave

my brother's body unburied, did you? Say it! Admit that you didn't.

Creon. I have said it already.

Antigone. But you did it just the same. And now, though you don't want to do it, you are going to have me killed. And you call that being a king!

Creon. Yes, I call that being a king.

Antigone. Poor Creon! My nails are broken, my fingers are bleeding, my arms are covered with the welts left by the paws of your guards—but I am a queen!

Creon. Then why not have pity on me, and live? Isn't your brother's corpse, rotting there under my windows, payment enough for peace and order in Thebes? My son loves you. Don't make me add your life to the payment. I've paid enough.

Antigone. No, Creon! You said yes, and made yourself king. Now you will never stop paying.

Creon. But God in heaven! Won't you try to understand me! I'm trying hard enough to understand you! There had to be one man who said yes. Somebody had to agree to captain the ship. She had sprung a hundred leaks; she was loaded to the water line with crime, ignorance, poverty. The wheel was swinging with the wind. The crew refused to work and were looting the cargo. The officers were building a raft, ready to slip overboard and desert the ship. The mast was splitting, the wind was howling, the sails were beginning to rip. Every man jack on board was about to drown—and only because the only thing they thought of was their own skins and their cheap little day-to-day traffic. Was that a time, do you think, for playing with words like yes and no? Was that a time for a man to be weighing the pros and cons, wondering if he wasn't going to pay too dearly later on; if he wasn't going to lose his life, or his family, or his touch with other men? You grab the wheel, you right the ship in the face of a mountain of water. You shout an order, and if one man refuses to obey, you shoot straight into the mob. Into the mob, I say! The beast as nameless as the wave that crashes down upon your deck; as nameless as the whipping wind. The thing that drops when you shoot may be someone who poured you a drink the night before; but it has no name. And you, braced at the wheel, you have no name, either. Nothing has a name—

except the ship, and the storm. [*A pause as he looks at her.*] Now do you understand?

Antigone. I am not here to understand. That's all very well for you. I am here to say no to you, and die.

Creon. It is easy to say no.

Antigone. Not always.

Creon. It is easy to say no. To say yes, you have to sweat and roll up your sleeves and plunge both hands into life up to the elbows. It is easy to say no, even if saying no means death. All you have to do is to sit still and wait. Wait to go on living; wait to be killed. That is the coward's part. No is one of your man-made words. Can you imagine a world in which trees say *no* to the sap? In which beasts say *no* to hunger or to propagation? Animals are good, simple, tough. They move in droves, nudging one another onwards, all traveling the same road. Some of them keel over, but the rest go on; and no matter how many may fall by the wayside, there are always those few left that go on bringing their young into the world, traveling the same road with the same obstinate will, unchanged from those who went before.

Antigone. Animals, eh, Creon! What a king you could be if only men were animals!

A pause. CREON *turns and looks at her.*

Creon. You despise me, don't you? [ANTIGONE *is silent.* CREON *goes on, as if to himself.*] Strange. Again and again, I have imagined myself holding this conversation with a pale young man I have never seen in the flesh. He would have come to assassinate me, and would have failed. I would be trying to find out from him why he wanted to kill me. But with all my logic and all my powers of debate, the only thing I could get out of him would be that he despised me. Who would have thought that the white-faced boy would turn out to be you? And that the debate would arise out of something so meaningless as the burial of your brother?

Antigone [*repeats contemptuously.*] Meaningless!

Creon [*earnestly, almost desperately*]. And yet, you must hear me out. My part is not an heroic one, but I shall play my part. I shall have you put to death. Only, before I do, I want to make one last appeal. I want to be sure that you know what you are doing as well as I know what I am doing. Antigone, do you know what you are dying for? Do you know the sordid story to which you are going to sign your name in blood, for all time to come?

Antigone. What story?

Creon. The story of Éteocles and Polynices, the story of your brothers. You think you know it, but you don't. Nobody in Thebes knows that story but me. And it seems to me, this afternoon, that you have a right to know it too. [*A pause as* ANTIGONE *moves to chair and sits.*] It's not a pretty story. [*He turns, gets stool from behind the table and places it between the table and the chair.*] You'll see. [*He looks at her for a moment.*] Tell me, first. What do you remember about your brothers? They were older than you, so they must have looked down on you. And I imagine that they tormented you— pulled your pigtails, broke your dolls, whispered secrets to each other to put you in a rage.

Antigone. They were big and I was little.

Creon. And later on, when they came home wearing evening clothes, smoking cigarettes, they would have nothing to do with you; and you thought they were wonderful.

Antigone. They were boys and I was a girl.

Creon. You didn't know why, exactly, but you knew that they were making your mother unhappy. You saw her in tears over them; and your father would fly into a rage because of them. You heard them come in, slamming doors, laughing noisily in the corridors—insolent, spineless, unruly, smelling of drink.

Antigone [*staring outward*]. Once, it was very early and we had just got up. I saw them coming home, and hid behind a door. Polynices was very pale and his eyes were shining. He was so handsome in his evening clothes. He saw me, and said: "Here, this is for you"; and he gave me a big paper flower that he had brought home from his night out.

Creon. And of course you still have that flower. Last night, before you crept out, you opened a drawer and looked at it for a time, to give yourself courage.

Antigone. Who told you so?

Creon. Poor Antigone! With her night club flower. Do you know what your brother was?

Antigone. Whatever he was, I know that you will say vile things about him.

Creon. A cheap, idiotic bounder, that is what he was. A cruel, vicious little voluptuary. A little beast with just wit enough to drive a car faster and throw more money away than any of his pals. I was with your father one day when Polynices, having lost a lot of money gambling, asked him to settle the debt; and when your father refused, the boy raised his hand against him and called him a vile name.

Antigone. That's a lie!

Creon. He struck your father in the face with his fist. It was pitiful. Your father sat at his desk with his head in his hands. His nose was bleeding. He was weeping with anguish. And in a corner of your father's study, Polynices stood sneering and lighting a cigarette.

Antigone. That's a lie.

A pause.

Creon. When did you last see Polynices alive? When you were twelve years old. *That's* true, isn't it?

Antigone. Yes, that's true.

Creon. Now you know why. Oedipus was too chicken-hearted to have the boy locked up. Polynices was allowed to go off and join the Argive army. And as soon as he reached Argos, the attempts upon your father's life began —upon the life of an old man who couldn't make up his mind to die, couldn't bear to be parted from his kingship. One after another, men slipped into Thebes from Argos for the purpose of assassinating him, and every killer we caught always ended by confessing who had put him up to it, who had paid him to try it. And it wasn't only Polynices. That is really what I am trying to tell you. I want you to know what went on in the back room, in the kitchen of politics; I want you to know what took place in the wings of this drama in which you are burning to play a part.

Yesterday, I gave Eteocles a State funeral, with pomp and honors. Today, Eteocles is a saint and a hero in the eyes of all Thebes. The whole city turned out to bury him. The schoolchildren emptied their saving boxes to buy wreaths for him. Old men, orating in quavering, hypocritical voices, glorified the virtues of the great-hearted brother, the devoted son, the loyal prince. I made a speech myself; and every temple priest was present with an appropriate show of sorrow and solemnity in his stupid face. And military honors were accorded the dead hero.

Well, what else could I have done? People had taken sides in the civil war. Both sides couldn't be wrong; that would be too much. I couldn't have made them swallow the truth. Two gangsters was more of a luxury than I could afford. [He pauses for a moment.] And this is the whole point of my story. Eteocles, that virtuous brother, was just as rotten as Polynices. That great-hearted son had done his best, too, to procure the assassination of his father. That loyal prince had also offered to sell out Thebes to the highest bidder.

Funny, isn't it? Polynices lies rotting in the sun while Eteocles is given a hero's funeral and will be housed in a marble vault. Yet I have absolute proof that everything that Polynices did, Eteocles had plotted to do. They were a pair of blackguards—both engaged in selling out Thebes, and both engaged in selling out each other; and they died like the cheap gangsters they were, over a division of the spoils.

But, as I told you a moment ago, I had to make a martyr of one of them. I sent out to the holocaust for their bodies; they were found clasped in one another's arms—for the first time in their lives, I imagine. Each had been spitted on the other's sword, and the Argive cavalry had trampled them down. They were mashed to a pulp, Antigone. I had the prettier of the two carcasses brought in and gave it a State funeral; and I left the other to rot. I don't know which was which. And I assure you, I don't care.

Long silence, neither looking at the other.

Antigone [*in a mild voice*]. Why do you tell me all this?

Creon. Would it have been better to let you die a victim to that obscene story?

Antigone. It might have been. I had my faith.

Creon. What are you going to do now?

Antigone [*rises to her feet in a daze*]. I shall go up to my room.

Creon. Don't stay alone. Go and find Haemon. And get married quickly.

Antigone [*in a whisper*]. Yes.

Creon. All this is really beside the point. You have your whole life ahead of you—and life is a treasure.

Antigone. Yes.

Creon. And you were about to throw it away. Don't think me fatuous if I say that I understand you; and that at your age I should have done the same thing. A moment ago, when we were quarreling, you said I was drinking in your words. I was. But it wasn't you I was listening to; it was a lad named Creon who lived here in Thebes many years ago. He was thin and pale, as you are. His mind, too, was filled with thoughts of self-sacrifice. Go and find Haemon. And get married quickly, Antigone. Be happy. Life flows like water, and you young people let it run away through your fingers. Shut your hands; hold on to it, Antigone. Life is not what you think it is. Life is a child playing around your feet, a tool you hold firmly in your grip, a bench you sit down upon in the evening, in your garden. People will tell you that that's not life, that life is something else. They will tell you that because they need your strength and your fire, and they will want to make use of you. Don't listen to them. Believe me, the only poor consolation that we have in our old age is to discover that what I have just said to you is true. Life is nothing more than the happiness that you get out of it.

Antigone [*murmurs, lost in thought*]. Happiness . . .

Creon [*suddenly a little self-conscious*]. Not much of a word, is it?

Antigone [*quietly*]. What kind of happiness do you foresee for me? Paint me the picture of your happy Antigone. What are the unimportant little sins that I shall have to commit before I am allowed to sink my teeth into life and tear happiness from it? Tell me: to whom shall I have to lie? Upon whom shall I have to fawn? To whom must I sell myself? Whom do you want me to leave dying, while I turn away my eyes?

Creon. Antigone, be quiet.

Antigone. Why do you tell me to be quiet when all I

want to know is what I have to do to be happy? This minute; since it is this very minute that I must make my choice. You tell me that life is so wonderful. I want to know what I have to do in order to be able to say that myself.

Creon. Do you love Haemon?

Antigone. Yes, I love Haemon. The Haemon I love is hard and young, faithful and difficult to satisfy, just as I am. But if what I love in Haemon is to be worn away like a stone step by the tread of the thing you call life, the thing you call happiness, if Haemon reaches the point where he stops growing pale with fear when I grow pale, stops thinking that I must have been killed in an accident when I am five minutes late, stops feeling that he is alone on earth when I laugh and he doesn't know why—if he too has to learn to say yes to everything—why, no, then, no! I do not love Haemon!

Creon. You don't know what you are talking about!

Antigone. I do know what I am talking about! Now it is you who have stopped understanding. I am too far away from you now, talking to you from a kingdom you can't get into, with your quick tongue and your hollow heart. [*Laughs.*] I laugh, Creon, because I see you suddenly as you must have been at fifteen: the same look of impotence in your face and the same inner conviction that there was nothing you couldn't do. What has life added to you, except those lines in your face, and that fat on your stomach?

Creon. Be quiet, I tell you!

Antigone. Why do you want me to be quiet? Because you know that I am right? Do you think I can't see in your face that what I am saying is true? You can't admit it, of course; you have to go on growling and defending the bone you call happiness.

Creon. It is your happiness, too, you little fool!

Antigone. I spit on your happiness! I spit on your idea of life—that life that must go on, come what may. You are all like dogs that lick everything they smell. You with your promise of a humdrum happiness—provided a person doesn't ask too much of life. I want everything of life, I do; and I want it now! I want it total, complete: otherwise I reject it! I will *not* be moderate. I will *not* be satisfied with the bit of cake you offer me if I promise to be a good little girl. I want to be sure of everything this very day; sure that everything will be as beautiful as when I was a little girl. If not, I want to die!

Creon. Scream on, daughter of Oedipus! Scream on, in your father's own voice!

Antigone. In my father's own voice, yes! We are of the tribe that asks questions, and we ask them to the bitter end. Until no tiniest chance of hope remains to be strangled by our hands. We are of the tribe that hates your filthy hope, your docile, female hope; hope, your whore——

Creon [*grasps her by her arms*]. Shut up! If you could see how ugly you are, shrieking those words!

Antigone. Yes, I am ugly! Father was ugly, too. [CREON *releases her arms, turns and moves away. Stands with his back to* ANTIGONE.] But Father became beautiful. And do you know when? [*She follows him to behind the table.*] At the very end. When all his questions had been answered. When he could no longer doubt that he *had* killed his own father; that he *had* gone to bed with his own mother. When all hope was gone, stamped out like a beetle. When it was absolutely certain that nothing, nothing could save him. Then he was at peace; then he could smile, almost; then he became beautiful. . . . Whereas you! Ah, those faces of yours, you candidates for election to happiness! It's you who are the ugly ones, even the handsomest of you—with that ugly glint in the corner of your eyes, that ugly crease at the corner of your mouths. Creon, you spoke the word a moment ago: the kitchen of politics. You look it and you smell of it.

Creon [*struggles to put his hand over her mouth*]. I order you to shut up! Do you hear me?

Antigone. You order me? Cook! Do you really believe that you can give me orders?

Creon. Antigone! The anteroom is full of people! Do you want them to hear you?

Antigone. Open the doors! Let us make sure that they can hear me!

Creon. By God! You shut up, I tell you!

ISMENE *enters through arch.*

Ismene [*distraught*]. Antigone!

Antigone [*turns to* ISMENE]. You, too? What do you want?

Ismene. Oh, forgive me, Antigone. I've come back. I'll be brave. I'll go with you now.

Antigone. Where will you go with me?

Ismene [*to* CREON]. Creon! If you kill her, you'll have to kill me too.

Antigone. Oh, no, Ismene. Not a bit of it. I die alone. You don't think I'm going to let you die with me after what I've been through? You don't deserve it.

Ismene. If you die, I don't want to live. I don't want to be left behind, alone.

Antigone. You chose life and I chose death. Now stop blubbering. You had your chance to come with me in the black night, creeping on your hands and knees. You had your chance to claw up the earth with your nails, as I did; to get yourself caught like a thief, as I did. And you refused it.

Ismene. Not any more. I'll do it alone tonight.

Antigone [*turns round toward* CREON]. You hear that, Creon? The thing is catching! Who knows but that lots of people will catch the disease from me! What are you waiting for? Call in your guards! Come on, Creon! Show a little courage! It only hurts for a minute! Come on, cook!

Creon [*turns toward arch and calls*]. Guard!

GUARDS *enter through arch.*

Antigone [*in a great cry of relief*]. At last, Creon!

CHORUS *enters through left arch.*

Creon [*to the* GUARDS]. Take her away! [CREON *goes up on top step.*]

GUARDS *grasp* ANTIGONE *by her arms, turn and hustle her toward the arch, right, and exeunt.* ISMENE *mimes horror, backs away toward the arch, left, then turns and runs out through the arch. A long pause, as* CREON *moves slowly downstage.*

Chorus [*behind* CREON. *Speaks in a deliberate voice*]. You are out of your mind, Creon. What have you done?

Creon [*his back to* CHORUS]. She had to die.

Chorus. You must not let Antigone die. We shall carry the scar of her death for centuries.

Creon. She insisted. No man on earth was strong enough to dissuade her. Death was her purpose, whether she knew it or not. Polynices was a mere pretext. When she had to give up that pretext, she found another one—that life and happiness were tawdry things and not worth possessing. She was bent upon only one thing: to reject life and to die.

Chorus. She is a mere child, Creon.

Creon. What do you want me to do for her? Condemn her to live?

Haemon [*calls from offstage*]. Father! [HAEMON *enters through arch, right.* CREON *turns toward him.*]

Creon. Haemon, forget Antigone. Forget her, my dearest boy.

Haemon. How can you talk like that?

Creon [*grasps* HAEMON *by the hands*]. I did everything I could to save her, Haemon. I used every argument. I swear I did. The girl doesn't love you. She could have gone on living for you; but she refused. She wanted it this way; she wanted to die.

Haemon. Father! The guards are dragging Antigone away! You've got to stop them! [*He breaks away from* CREON.]

Creon [*looks away from* HAEMON]. I can't stop them. It's too late. Antigone has spoken. The story is all over Thebes. I cannot save her now.

Chorus. Creon, you must find a way. Lock her up. Say that she has gone out of her mind.

Creon. Everybody will know it isn't so. The nation will say that I am making an exception of her because my son loves her. I cannot.

Chorus. You can still gain time, and get her out of Thebes.

Creon. The mob already knows the truth. It is howling for her blood. I can do nothing.

Haemon. But, Father, you are master in Thebes!

Creon. I am master under the law. Not above the law.

Haemon. You cannot let Antigone be taken from me. I am your son!

Creon. I cannot do anything else, my poor boy. She must die and you must live.

Haemon. Live, you say! Live a life without Antigone? A life in which I am to go on admiring you as you busy yourself about your kingdom, make your persuasive speeches, strike your attitudes? Not without Antigone. I love Antigone. I will not live without Antigone!

Creon. Haemon—you will have to resign yourself to life without Antigone. [*He moves to left of* HAEMON.] Sooner or later there comes a day of sorrow in each man's life when he must cease to be a child and take up the burden of manhood. That day has come for you.

Haemon [*backs away a step*]. That giant strength, that courage. That massive god who used to pick me up in his arms and shelter me from shadows and monsters—was that you, Father? Was it of you I stood in awe? Was that man you?

Creon. For God's sake, Haemon, do not judge me! Not you, too!

Haemon [*pleading now*]. This is all a bad dream, Father. You are not yourself. It isn't true that we have been backed up against a wall, forced to surrender. We don't have to say *yes* to this terrible thing. You are still king. You are still the father I revered. You have no right to desert me, to shrink into nothingness. The world will be too bare, I shall be too alone in the world, if you force me to disown you.

Creon. The world *is* bare, Haemon, and you *are* alone. You must cease to think your father all-powerful. Look straight at me. See your father as he is. That is what it means to grow up and be a man.

Haemon [*stares at* CREON *for a moment*]. I tell you that I will not live without Antigone. [*Turns and goes quickly out through arch.*]

Chorus. Creon, the boy will go mad.

Creon. Poor boy! He loves her.

Chorus. Creon, the boy is wounded to death.

Creon. We are all wounded to death.

FIRST GUARD *enters through arch, right, followed by* SECOND *and* THIRD GUARDS *pulling* ANTIGONE *along with them.*

First Guard. Sir, the people are crowding into the palace!

Antigone. Creon, I don't want to see their faces. I don't want to hear them howl. You are going to kill me; let that be enough. I want to be alone until it is over.

Creon. Empty the palace! Guards at the gates!

CREON *quickly crosses toward the arch; exit. Two* GUARDS *release* ANTIGONE; *exeunt behind* CREON. CHORUS *goes out through arch, left. The lighting dims so that only the area about the table is lighted. The cyclorama is covered with a dark blue color. The scene is intended to suggest a prison cell, filled with shadows and dimly lit.* ANTIGONE *moves to stool and sits. The* FIRST GUARD *stands upstage. He watches* ANTIGONE, *and as she sits, he begins pacing slowly downstage, then upstage. A pause.*

Antigone [*turns and looks at the* GUARD]. It's you, is it?

Guard. What do you mean, me?

Antigone. The last human face that I shall see. [*A pause as they look at each other, then* GUARD *paces upstage, turns, and crosses behind table.*] Was it you that arrested me this morning?

Guard. Yes, that was me.

Antigone. You hurt me. There was no need for you to hurt me. Did I act as if I was trying to escape?

Guard. Come on now, Miss. It was my business to bring you in. I did it. [*A pause. He paces to and fro upstage. Only the sound of his boots is heard.*]

Antigone. How old are you?

Guard. Thirty-nine.

Antigone. Have you any children?

Guard. Yes. Two.

Antigone. Do you love your children?

Guard. What's that got to with you? [*A pause. He paces upstage and downstage.*]

Antigone. How long have you been in the Guard?

Guard. Since the war. I was in the army. Sergeant. Then I joined the Guard.

Antigone. Does one have to have been an army sergeant to get into the Guard?

Guard. Supposed to be. Either that or on special detail. But when they make you a guard, you lose your stripes.

Antigone [*murmurs*]. I see.

Guard. Yes. Of course, if you're a guard, everybody knows you're something special; they know you're an old N.C.O. Take pay, for instance. When you're a guard you get your pay, and on top of that you get six months' extra pay, to make sure you don't lose anything by not being a sergeant any more. And of course you do better than that. You get a house, coal, rations, extras for the wife and kids. If you've got two kids, like me, you draw better than a sergeant.

Antigone [*barely audible*]. I see.

Guard. That's why sergeants, now, they don't like guards. Maybe you noticed they try to make out they're better than us? Promotion, that's what it is. In the army, anybody can get promoted. All you need is good conduct. Now in the Guard, it's slow, and you have to know your business—like how to make out a report and the like of that. But when you're an N.C.O. in the Guard, you've got something that even a sergeant-major ain't got. For instance——

Antigone [*breaking him off*]. Listen.

Guard. Yes, Miss.

Antigone. I'm going to die soon.

The GUARD *looks at her for a moment, then turns and moves away.*

Guard. For instance, people have a lot of respect for guards, they have. A guard may be a soldier, but he's kind of in the civil service, too.

Antigone. Do you think it hurts to die?

Guard. How would I know? Of course, if somebody sticks a saber in your guts and turns it round, it hurts.

Antigone. How are they going to put me to death?

Guard. Well, I'll tell you. I heard the proclamation all right. Wait a minute. How did it go now? [*He stares into space and recites from memory.*] "In order that our fair city shall not be pol-luted with her sinful blood, she shall be im-mured—immured." That means, they shove you in a cave and wall up the cave.

Antigone. Alive?

Guard. Yes. . . . [*He moves away a few steps.*]

Antigone [*murmurs*]. O tomb! O bridal bed! Alone! [ANTIGONE *sits there, a tiny figure in the middle of the stage. You would say she felt a little chilly. She wraps her arms round herself.*]

Guard. Yes! Outside the southeast gate of the town. In the Cave of Hades. In broad daylight. Some detail, eh, for them that's on the job! First they thought maybe it was a job for the army. Now it looks like it's going to be the Guard. There's an outfit for you! Nothing the Guard can't do. No wonder the army's jealous.

Antigone. A pair of animals.

Guard. What do you mean, a pair of animals?

Antigone. When the winds blow cold, all they need do is to press close against one another. I am all alone.

Guard. Is there anything you want? I can send out for it, you know.

Antigone. You are very kind. [*A pause.* ANTIGONE *looks up at the* GUARD.] Yes, there is something I want. I want you to give someone a letter from me, when I am dead.

Guard. How's that again? A letter?

Antigone. Yes, I want to write a letter; and I want you to give it to someone for me.

Guard [*straightens up*]. Now, wait a minute. Take it easy. It's as much as my job is worth to go handing out letters from prisoners.

Antigone [*removes a ring from her finger and holds it out toward him*]. I'll give you this ring if you will do it.

Guard. Is it gold? [*He takes the ring from her.*]

Antigone. Yes, it is gold.

Guard [*shakes his head*]. Uh-uh. No can do. Suppose they go through my pockets. I might get six months for a thing like that. [*He stares at the ring, then glances off right to make sure that he is not being watched.*] Listen, tell you what I'll do. You tell me what you want to say, and I'll write it down in my book. Then, afterwards, I'll tear out the pages and give them to the party, see? If it's in my handwriting, it's all right.

Antigone [*winces*]. In your handwriting? [*She shudders slightly.*] No. That would be awful. The poor darling! In your handwriting.

Guard [*offers back the ring*]. O.K. It's no skin off my nose.

Antigone [*quickly*]. Of course, of course. No, keep the ring. But hurry. Time is getting short. Where is your notebook? [*The* GUARD *pockets the ring, takes his notebook and pencil from his pocket, puts his foot up on chair, and rests the notebook on his knee, licks his pencil.*] Ready? [*He nods.*] Write, now. "My darling . . ."

Guard [*writes as he mutters*]. The boy friend, eh?

Antigone. "My darling. I wanted to die, and perhaps you will not love me any more . . ."

Guard [*mutters as he writes*] ". . . will not love me any more."

Antigone. "Creon was right. It is terrible to die."

Guard [*repeats as he writes*] ". . . terrible to die."

Antigone. "And I don't even know what I am dying for. I am afraid . . ."

Guard [*looks at her*]. Wait a minute! How fast do you think I can write?

Antigone [*takes hold of herself*]. Where are you?

Guard [*reads from his notebook*]. "And I don't even know what I am dying for."

Antigone. No. Scratch that out. Nobody must know that. They have no right to know. It's as if they saw me naked and touched me, after I was dead. Scratch it all out. Just write: "Forgive me."

Guard [*looks at* ANTIGONE]. I cut out everything you said there at the end, and I put down, "Forgive me"?

Antigone. Yes. "Forgive me, my darling. You would all have been so happy except for Antigone. I love you."

Guard [*finishes the letter*] ". . . I love you." [*He looks at her.*] Is that all?

Antigone. That's all.

Guard [*straightens up, looks at notebook*]. Damn funny letter.

Antigone. I know.

Guard [*looks at her*]. Who is it to? [*A sudden roll of drums begins and continues until after* ANTIGONE'S *exit. The* FIRST GUARD *pockets the notebook and shouts at* ANTIGONE.] O.K. That's enough out of you! Come on!

At the sound of the drum roll, SECOND *and* THIRD GUARDS *enter through the arch.* ANTIGONE *rises.* GUARDS *seize her and exeunt with her. The lighting moves up to suggest late afternoon.* CHORUS *enters.*

Chorus. And now it is Creon's turn.

MESSENGER *runs through the arch, right.*

Messenger. The Queen . . . the Queen! Where is the Queen?

Chorus. What do you want with the Queen? What have you to tell the Queen?

Messenger. News to break her heart. Antigone had just been thrust into the cave. They hadn't finished heaving the last block of stone into place when Creon and the rest heard a sudden moaning from the tomb. A hush fell over us all, for it was not the voice of Antigone. It was Haemon's voice that came forth from the tomb. Everybody looked at Creon; and he howled like a man demented: "Take away the stones! Take away the stones!" The slaves leaped at the wall of stones, and Creon worked with them, sweating and tearing at the blocks with his bleeding hands. Finally a narrow opening was forced, and into it slipped the smallest guard.

Antigone had hanged herself by the cord of her robe, by the red and golden twisted cord of her robe. The cord was round her neck like a child's collar. Haemon was on his knees, holding her in his arms and moaning, his face buried in her robe. More stones were removed, and Creon went into the tomb. He tried to raise Haemon to his feet. I could hear him begging Haemon to rise to his feet. Haemon was deaf to his father's voice, till suddenly he stood up of his own accord, his eyes dark and burning. Anguish was in his face, but it was the face of a little boy. He stared at his father. Then suddenly he struck him —hard; and he drew his sword. Creon leaped out of range. Haemon went on staring at him, his eyes full of contempt —a glance that was like a knife, and that Creon couldn't escape. The King stood trembling in the far corner of the tomb, and Haemon went on staring. Then, without a word, he stabbed himself and lay down beside Antigone, embracing her in a great pool of blood.

A *pause as* CREON *and* PAGE *enter through arch on the* MESSENGER'S *last words.* CHORUS *and the* MESSENGER *both turn to look at* CREON; *then exit the* MESSENGER *through curtain.*

Creon. I have had them laid out side by side. They are together at last, and at peace. Two lovers on the morrow of their bridal. Their work is done.

Chorus. But not yours, Creon. You have still one thing to learn. Eurydice, the Queen, your wife——

Creon. A good woman. Always busy with her garden, her preserves, her sweaters—those sweaters she never stopped knitting for the poor. Strange, how the poor never stop needing sweaters. One would almost think that was all they needed.

Chorus. The poor in Thebes are going to be cold this winter, Creon. When the Queen was told of her son's death, she waited carefully until she had finished her row, then put down her knitting calmly—as she did everything. She went up to her room, her lavender-scented room, with its embroidered doilies and its pictures framed in plush; and there, Creon, she cut her throat. She is laid out now in one of those two old-fashioned twin beds, exactly where you went to her one night when she was still a maiden. Her smile is still the same, scarcely a shade more melancholy. And if it were not for that great red blot on the bed linen by her neck, one might think she was asleep.

Creon [*in a dull voice*]. She, too. They are all asleep. [*Pause.*] It must be good to sleep.

Chorus. And now you are alone, Creon.

Creon. Yes, all alone. [*To* PAGE.] My lad.

Page. Sir?

Creon. Listen to me. They don't know it, but the truth is the work is there to be done, and a man can't fold his arms and refuse to do it. They say it's dirty work. But if we didn't do it, who would?

Page. I don't know, sir.

Creon. Of course you don't. You'll be lucky if you never find out. In a hurry to grow up, aren't you?

Page. Oh, yes, sir.

Creon. I shouldn't be if I were you. Never grow up if you can help it. [*He is lost in thought as the hour chimes.*] What time is it?

Page. Five o'clock, sir.

Creon. What have we on at five o'clock?

Page. Cabinet meeting, sir.

Creon. Cabinet meeting. Then we had better go along to it.

Exeunt CREON *and* PAGE *slowly through arch, left, and* CHORUS *moves downstage.*

Chorus. And there we are. It is quite true that if it had not been for Antigone they would all have been at peace. But that is over now. And they are all at peace. All those who were meant to die have died: those who believed one thing, those who believed the contrary thing, and even those who believed nothing at all, yet were caught up in the web without knowing why. All dead: stiff, useless, rotting. And those who have survived will now begin quietly to forget the dead: they won't remember who was who or which was which. It is all over. Antigone is calm tonight, and we shall never know the name of the fever that consumed her. She has played her part.

Three GUARDS *enter, resume their places on steps as at the rise of the curtain, and begin to play cards.*

A great melancholy wave of peace now settles down upon Thebes, upon the empty palace, upon Creon, who can now begin to wait for his own death.

Only the guards are left, and none of this matters to them. It's no skin off their noses. They go on playing cards.

CHORUS *walks toward the arch, left, as the curtain falls.*

EURYDICE

(LEGEND OF LOVERS)

Translated by

KITTY BLACK

CHARACTERS

FATHER
ORPHEUS
EURYDICE
MOTHER
STATION WAITER
VINCENT
MATHIAS
THE GIRL
DULAC
ANOTHER GIRL
THE YOUNG MAN (*Monsieur Henri*)
THE MANAGER
THE CASHIER
HOTEL WAITER
THE CLERK
LOUD-SPEAKER
VOICE

SCENES: The action of the play takes place in the refreshment room of a French provincial railway station and in a hotel bedroom in Marseilles.

EURYDICE

ACT ONE

The refreshment room of a provincial station. Overdecorated, worn, and dirty. Marble-topped tables, mirrors, benches covered with threadbare red velvet.

Seated at a too-high desk, like a Buddha on an altar, is the CASHIER, *with a large bun and enormous breasts. Aged* WAITERS, *bald and dignified, spittoons, and sawdust.*

Before the rise of the curtain we hear an accordion. It is ORPHEUS *playing quietly in the corner, beside his* FATHER, *absorbed in his miserable accounts in front of two empty glasses. In the background a single customer, a* YOUNG MAN *with his hat pulled down over his eyes, wearing a mackintosh, apparently lost in thought. Music for a moment, then the* FATHER *stops his additions and looks at* ORPHEUS.

FATHER. My boy?

Orpheus [*still playing*]. Father?

Father. You don't expect your poor old father to go round with the hat in a station restaurant?

Orpheus. I'm playing for my own pleasure.

Father [*continuing*]. A station restaurant with only one customer, who's pretending not to notice anyway. I know their little ways. They pretend not to be listening, and not to see the plate when you hold it out. But I pretend not to see they're pretending. [*Pause, while* ORPHEUS *continues to play.*] D'you enjoy playing as much as that? I can't imagine how you, a musician, can still manage to like music. When I've been twanging away for a bunch of idiots playing cards in a café, there's only one thing I want to do . . .

Orpheus [*without stopping*]. Go and play cards in another café.

Father [*surprised*]. Exactly. How did you know?

Orpheus. I guessed—nearly fifteen years ago.

Father. Fifteen years? Oh, come now! Fifteen years ago, I still had talent. . . . Fifteen years ago, when I played in the orchestra, who would have believed your old father would come down to playing his harp in the street? Who'd have thought he'd be reduced to going round afterward with a little saucer?

Orpheus. Mother would—every time you got yourself sacked from your current job. . . .

Father. Your mother never loved me. Neither do you. You spend all your time trying to humiliate me. But don't think I'll put up with it always. You know I was offered a job as harpist at the casino at Palavas-les-Flots?

Orpheus. Yes, father.

Father. And I refused because they had no vacancy for you?

Orpheus. Yes, father. Or rather, no, father.

Father. No, father? Why, no, father?

Orpheus. You refused because you know you play abominably and you'd be sacked the next morning.

Father [*turning away, hurt*]. I shan't even answer you. [ORPHEUS *goes back to his playing.*] Must you?

Orpheus. Yes. Does it bother you?

Father. I can't concentrate. Eight times seven?

Orpheus. Fifty-six.

Father. Are you sure?

Orpheus. Quite sure.

Father. Isn't it odd? I hoped it might be sixty-three. Still, eight times nine are obviously seventy-two. . . . You know we've very little money left, my boy.

Orpheus. Yes, father.

Father. Is that all you can say?

Orpheus. Yes, father.

Father. You're thinking of my white hairs?

Orpheus. No, father.

Father. I thought not. Oh, I'm used to it. [*He goes back to his additions.*] Eight times seven?

Orpheus. Fifty-six.

Father [*bitterly*]. Fifty-six. . . . You didn't have to remind me. [*He closes his notebook and gives up his accounts.*] That wasn't such a bad meal for twelve francs seventy-five. . . .

Orpheus. No, father.

Father. You shouldn't have ordered a vegetable. If you know how to do things, you get your vegetable with the main course and they let you have a second sweet instead. When you're having the set meal, it's always better to choose the two sweets. The Neapolitan ice was a dream.

. . . In one sense, we did better tonight for twelve francs seventy-five than yesterday for thirteen francs fifty à la carte at Montpellier. . . . You could say they had linen serviettes instead of paper ones. It was a place that gave itself airs, but fundamentally it was no better. And did you see they charged us three francs for the cheese? If they had at least brought the tray along like they do in proper restaurants! Once, my boy, I was taken to dine at Poccardi's, you know, in Paris. They brought the tray along. . . .

Orpheus. You've told me about it before, father.

Father [*hurt*]. All right—I don't want to bore you. [ORPHEUS *goes back to his playing. After a moment the* FATHER *is bored and decides to stop sulking.*] I say, my boy—that's horribly sad.

Orpheus. So is what I'm thinking.

Father. What are you thinking about?

Orpheus. About you, father.

Father. About me? Well, what is it now?

Orpheus. Or rather, you and me.

Father. The outlook isn't very promising, of course, but we're doing our best, my boy.

Orpheus. I'm thinking that ever since Mother died, I've followed you round the cafés with my accordion. I've watched you struggling with your accounts at night. I've listened to you discussing the menus of the set meals and then I've gone to bed. In the morning I get up again.

Father. When you get to my age, you'll see that that is life.

Orpheus. I'm thinking that if you were all alone, with your harp, you'd never be able to live.

Father [*worried suddenly*]. You don't want to leave me?

Orpheus. No. Probably I'll never be able to leave you. I'm a better musician than you are, I am young and I'm sure life has better things to offer; but I couldn't live if I knew you were starving somewhere else.

Father. That's good of you, my boy. Think of your old father.

Orpheus. Good, yes, but it's a big responsibility. Sometimes I dream something might come between us. . . .

Father. Now, now, we understand each other so well. . . .

Orpheus. There's the wonderful job where I earn

enough to make you an allowance. But it's a dream. A
musician never earns enough to pay for two rooms and
four meals a day.

Father. Oh, my needs are very small, you know. A meal
costing twelve francs seventy-five like today. A table at
the café. A small glass of something, a ten-centime cigar,
and I'm as happy as a sandboy. [*Pause, he adds.*] If I had
to, I could quite well do without the small something.

Orpheus [*going on with his dream*]. Then there's the
level crossing where one of us is knocked down by a
train. . . .

Father. Good heavens . . . which one?

Orpheus [*gently*]. Oh, it doesn't really matter. . . .

Father [*starting*]. How strange you are. I don't want to
die! You're full of gloom tonight, my boy. [*He burps
genteelly.*] That rabbit was really excellent. Good heavens,
you make me laugh! At your age, I thought life was wonderful. [*He suddenly studies the cashier.*] And what about
love? Had you thought you might fall in love?

Orpheus. What is love? Girls I might get to meet with
you?

Father. My dear boy, can any of us guess where and
how love will find us? [*He comes a little closer.*] Tell me,
you don't think I look rather too bald? She's quite charming, that girl. A little provincial, perhaps. More my type
than yours. What would you put her at? Forty? Forty-five?

Orpheus [*Gives a pale little smile. He claps his father
on the shoulder*]. I'm going outside for a bit. . . . We've
still got an hour before the train.

When he has gone, the FATHER rises, walks all round the
CASHIER, who blasts him with a look—the miserable customer. Suddenly, the FATHER feels he is old and ugly,
poor and bald. He rubs his hand over his head and goes
sadly back to pick up his instrument before going out.
                    Exit.

Outside on the platform a train arrives. The members
of Dulac's company are seen for a moment. Then EURY-
DICE enters and makes her way to a chair.

Eurydice's MOTHER enters in triumph. Boa and feather
hat. Ever since 1920 she has grown younger every day.

Mother. There you are, Eurydice. . . . This heat . . .

how I hate waiting at stations. The whole tour has been a disgrace—as usual. The manager ought to arrange that the leading actors don't spend all their time waiting for connections. When you've spent the whole day on a platform, how can you give your best in the evening?

Eurydice. There's only one train for the whole company and it's an hour late because of the storm yesterday. The manager can't help it.

Mother. You always find excuses for these incompetents!

The Waiter [*who has come up*]. May I take your orders, ladies?

Mother. Do you feel like something?

Eurydice. After that star entrance of yours, it's the least we can do.

Mother. Have you any really good peppermint? I'll have a peppermint. In Argentine, or in Brazil where the heat was really exhausting, I always used to take a peppermint just before making my first entrance. The divine Sarah gave me the tip. A peppermint.

The Waiter. And for mademoiselle?

Eurydice. Coffee, please.

Mother. Why aren't you with Mathias? He's wandering about like a soul in torment.

Eurydice. Don't worry about him.

Mother. It was very wrong of you to upset that boy. He adores you. It was your fault in the first place. You shouldn't have let him be your lover. I told you so at the time, but it's too late to worry about that now. Besides, we all begin and end with actors. When I was your age, I was much prettier than you. I could have been taken up by anyone I pleased. All I could do was waste my time with your father. . . . You see the charming results yourself.

Waiter [*who has brought the drinks*]. A little ice, madame?

Mother. Never—think of my voice! This peppermint is disgusting. I hate the provinces, I hate these second-rate tours. But in Paris nowadays, they only go mad over little idiots with no breasts, who can't say three words without fluffing. . . . What has the boy done to upset you? You didn't even get into the same compartment at Montélimar? My dear child, a mother is a girl's natural confidante, particularly when they're the same age—I mean, particularly when she's a very young mother. Come along, tell me. What has he done?

Eurydice. Nothing, mother.

Mother. Nothing, mother. That doesn't make sense. Only one thing is sure—he adores you madly. Maybe that's why you don't love him. We women are all the same. Nothing can make us change. How's your coffee?

Eurydice. You have it—I don't want it.

Mother. Thank you, darling. I like plenty of sugar. Waiter! Bring some more sugar for Mademoiselle. Don't you love him any more?

Eurydice. Who?

Mother. Mathias.

Eurydice. You're wasting your time, mother.

The WAITER, *sulking, has brought the sugar.*

Mother. Thank you. It's covered with flyblows! Charming. I, who have been round the world and stayed at all the best hotels—this is what I've come to. Oh, well, I suppose it will melt. . . . [*She drinks the coffee.*] I think you're absolutely right. You should always follow your instincts. I've always followed mine, like a thoroughgoing old pro. But then you're not really an actress by vocation. Do sit up! Ah, here's Vincent. Darling boy! He looks quite put out. Now do be nice to him. You know how fond of the boy I am.

VINCENT *enters, silver haired, handsome, and soft beneath a very energetic exterior. His gestures are ample, his smile full of bitterness. His eye a roving one. He kisses the* MOTHER'S *hand.*

Vincent. Ah, there you are! I've been looking for you everywhere.

Mother. I've been here, with Eurydice.

Vincent. This little manager is absolutely useless! Apparently we've got to wait here for more than an hour. We shan't have time for dinner again before the performance. I call it really annoying. We may all have the patience of angels, but you must admit it's really annoying!

Eurydice. It's not the manager's fault we had such a storm yesterday.

Mother. I wish I knew why you always stand up for the little idiot.

Vincent. He's an incompetent—a real incompetent! I can't think why Dulac keeps such a man in the job. The last thing I heard was that he's lost the basket with all the wigs. And tomorrow we've got a matinee of *The Burgomaster.* Can you imagine what it will be like?

Eurydice. I'm sure he'll find it again. It probably got left behind at Montélimar. . . .

Vincent. If it was, it'll probably arrive in time for tomorrow, but tonight—for *Guinevere's Disgrace*—what are we to do? He says it couldn't matter less because it's a modern play, but I've given Dulac my last word. I cannot play the doctor without my goatee.

Waiter [who has come up]. Can I take your order, sir?

Vincent [superb]. Nothing, thank you. A glass of water. [*The* WAITER *retreats, beaten.*] The first and second acts, perhaps, but I'm sure you'll agree with me, dear friend. With the best will in the world, how can I play the big scene in the last act without my goatee? What on earth should I look like?

EURYDICE *goes away bad temperedly.*

Mother. Where are you going, darling?
Eurydice. Just for a walk, mother.

She goes out abruptly.

Vincent [watches her departure, haughtily. When she has gone]. Dear friend, you know I'm not in the habit of getting on my high horse, but your daughter's attitude toward me is nothing short of scandalous.

Mother [simpering and trying to take his hand]. My big bear.

Vincent. Our relationship toward each other is perhaps a little delicate, I agree—although you're perfectly free to do as you please, you're separated from her father—but really, anyone would say she delights in aggravating it.

Mother. She's a silly girl. You know how she protects that fool, as she protects all the lame things in the world, God knows why—old cats, lost dogs, helpless drunkards. The thought that you might persuade Dulac to send him away was too much for her, that's all.

Vincent. It may have been too much for her, but there are ways of doing these things.

Mother. You know quite well that's what's wrong with her. . . . She's a good child, but she has no manners. [MATHIAS *enters abruptly. He is badly shaven, somber, on edge.*] Oh, hullo, Mathias.

Mathias. Excuse me, madame. Have you seen your daughter?

Mother. She's just gone down the platform.

MATHIAS *exits. The mother watches him go.*

Mother. Poor boy. He's mad about her. She's always been good to him until just lately and now I don't know what's come over her. These last two or three days it's as though she were looking for something, or someone. . . . What? I don't know. . . . [*Faraway the music of* OR-PHEUS.] Why must that man keep playing that thing? It's maddening.

Vincent. He's waiting for his train.

Mother. That's no reason. That music and the flies . . . it's so appallingly hot!

The music has come nearer. They listen. During the next scene, EURYDICE *walks across the back as though looking for the music.*

Mother [*abruptly, in a different voice*]. Remember the casino at Ostend?

Vincent. The year they launched the Mexican tango. . . .

Mother. How handsome you were!

Vincent. I still had my figure in those days. . . .

Mother. And such an air about you. . . . Remember the first day? "Madame, will you give me the pleasure of this dance?"

Vincent. "But, sir, I don't know how to dance the tango."

Mother. "Nothing simpler, madame. I hold you in my arms. You've only to let yourself go." The way you said that! Then you put your arms around me and everything swam together . . . the face of the old fool who was keeping me and was watching furiously . . . the barman

—he was making love to me, too, at the time. He was a Corsican, and he said he'd like to kill me—the waxed mustaches of the gypsies, the big mauve irises and pale green ranunculuses decorating the walls . . . ah! it was delicious. It was the year everyone wore *broderie anglaise.* . . . I had an exquisite white dress. . . .

Vincent. I wore a yellow carnation in my buttonhole, and a bird's-eye check in green and brown. . . .

Mother. When we danced you held me so tightly the pattern of my dress was driven right into my flesh. . . . The old fool noticed it and made a scene. I slapped his face and found myself in the street without a farthing. You hired a carriage with pink pompons and we drove all round the bay alone till it was dark. . . .

Vincent. Ah, the uncertainty, the delicious disturbance of that first day of days. The searching, the awareness, the groping toward the unknown. One does not yet know one's love and yet one knows it will last for the rest of one's life.

Mother [*suddenly with a change of voice*]. Why on earth did we quarrel a fortnight later?

Vincent. I don't know. I can't remember.

ORPHEUS *has stopped playing.* EURYDICE *is standing in front of him and they look at each other.*

Eurydice. Was it you playing just now?
Orpheus. Yes.
Eurydice. How beautifully you play!
Orpheus. Thank you.
Eurydice. What was it called—what you were playing?
Orpheus. I don't know. I was improvising. . . .
Eurydice [*in spite of herself*]. I'm sorry. . . .
Orpheus. Why?
Eurydice. I don't know. I would have liked it to have had a name.

A GIRL *passes along the platform, sees* EURYDICE *and calls.*

The Girl. Eurydice! Is that you?
Eurydice [*without taking her eyes off* ORPHEUS]. Yes.
The Girl. I've just seen Mathias. He's looking for you, darling. . . .

She disappears.

Eurydice. Yes. [*She looks at* Orpheus.] Your eyes are light blue.

Orpheus. Yes. I don't know how to describe yours.

Eurydice. They say it depends on what I'm thinking.

Orpheus. Just now they're dark green, like deep water beside the stone steps of a harbor.

Eurydice. They say that's when I'm happy.

Orpheus. Who's "they"?

Eurydice. The others.

The Girl [*coming back, calling from the platform*]. Eurydice!

Eurydice [*without turning round*]. Yes?

The Girl. Don't forget Mathias.

Eurydice. Yes. [*Suddenly she asks.*] D'you think you'll make me very unhappy?

Orpheus [*smiling gently*]. I don't think so.

Eurydice. I don't mean unhappy as I am at this moment. It's a sort of pain, but a sort of joy as well. What frightens me is being unhappy and lonely when you leave me.

Orpheus. I'll never leave you.

Eurydice. Will you swear that?

Orpheus. Yes.

Eurydice. On my head?

Orpheus [*smiling*]. Yes.

They look at each other. Suddenly she says gently.

Eurydice. I like it when you smile.

Orpheus. Don't you ever smile?

Eurydice. Never when I'm happy.

Orpheus. I thought you said you were unhappy.

Eurydice. Don't you understand? Are you a real man after all? How strange it is! Here we are, the two of us, standing face to face, with everything that's going to happen drawn up ready and waiting behind us. . . .

Orpheus. D'you think much is going to happen?

Eurydice [*gravely*]. Everything. All the things that happen to a man and woman on earth, one by one. . . .

Orpheus. Gay things, sweet things, terrible things?

Eurydice [*gently*]. Shameful things and filthy things. . . . We're going to be so unhappy.

Orpheus [*taking her in his arms*]. How wonderful!

VINCENT *and the* MOTHER, *dreaming cheek to cheek, continue softly.*

Vincent. Ah, *l'amour, l'amour!* You see my darling one, on this earth where all our hopes are shattered, where all is deception and pain and disappointment, it's a marvelous consolation to remember we still have our love. . . .

Mother. My big bear. . . .

Vincent. All men are liars, Lucienne, faithless, false, hypocritical, vainglorious, or cowards; all women are perfidious, artificial, vain, capricious, or depraved; the world is nothing but a bottomless sink where the most monstrous beasts disport and distort themselves through oceans of slime. But there is one holy and sublime hope left in the world—the union of these two imperfect and horrible beings!

Mother. Yes, my darling. Perdican's big speech.

Vincent [*stops, surprised*]. Is it? I've played it so often!

Mother. Remember? You played it that first evening at Ostend. I was in *The Foolish Virgin* at the *Kursaal,* but I was only in the first act. I waited for you in your dressing room. You came offstage still thrilling with the wonderful love scene you'd been playing and you took me there and then, in doublet and hose. . . .

Vincent. Ah, those nights, those nights! The fusion of body and heart! The moment, the unique moment when you no longer know if it's the flesh or the spirit fluttering. . . .

Mother. You're a wonderful lover, dear boy!

Vincent. And you, the most adorable of mistresses!

EURYDICE *and* ORPHEUS *have listened to them, pressed together as if afraid.*

Eurydice. Make them stop. Please, please, make them stop.

Orpheus [*going to the couple while* EURYDICE *hides*]. Monsieur, madame, you certainly won't understand my attitude. It will seem strange to you. Even very strange. But I'm afraid you must both get out of here.

Vincent. Out of here?

Orpheus. Yes, monsieur.

Vincent. Is it closing time?

Orpheus. Yes, monsieur. Closing time for you.

Vincent [rising]. Really, I. . . .

Mother [also rising]. But you don't belong here. I know you—you're the one who was playing. . . .

Orpheus. You must both go away at once. I promise if I could explain, I would, but I can't explain anything. You wouldn't understand. Something very important is happening here.

Mother. The boy's mad. . . .

Vincent. But good gracious, I mean to say, it doesn't make sense! This place is open to everyone!

Orpheus. Not any more.

Mother. Well, really! This is too much! [*She calls.*] Madame, please! Waiter!

Orpheus [pushing them toward the door]. No, don't call them, it's no use. Go away. I'll settle your bill myself.

Mother. But you can't be allowed to treat us like this!

Orpheus. I'm a peaceful soul, madame, very kind, very shy even. I promise you I'm very shy, madame, and until this minute I'd never have dared to do what I'm doing. . . .

Mother. I've never seen such a thing!

Orpheus. No, madame, you've never seen such a thing. Anyway, I've never seen such a thing.

Mother [to VINCENT*].* Can't you say something?

Vincent. Come away. You can see he's not in a normal condition.

Mother [disappears, calling]. I shall report you to the stationmaster.

Eurydice [coming out of hiding]. Ah! How horrible they were, weren't they? Horrible and stupid!

Orpheus [turning to her smiling]. Sh! Don't talk about them. How everything falls into place now that we are alone. How clear and simple everything has become. It's as though I were seeing the chandeliers and the palm . . . and the spittoons and the chairs for the first time. . . . Isn't a chair charming? You'd think it was an insect listening for the sound of our steps, ready to spring away on its four thin little legs. Careful! We mustn't move, or if we do, we must be very quick. . . . [*He makes a spring, dragging* EURYDICE.] Got it! Isn't a chair a clever invention. You can even sit on it. . . . [*He hands her to the chair with comical ceremony, then looks at her sadly.*]

What I don't understand, is why they invented the second chair. . . .

Eurydice [pulling him down and making room for him on her chair]. It was for people who didn't know each other. . . .

Orpheus [taking her in his arms and crying out]. But I know you! Just now as I was playing and you came along the platform and I didn't know you. . . . Now everything's changed, and it's wonderful! Everything round us has suddenly become extraordinary. Look . . . how beautiful the cashier is with her big bosom resting delicately on her counter. And the waiter! Look at the waiter! His long flat feet in his button boots, his distinguished mustache, and his noble, noble air. . . . This is an extraordinary evening; we were fated to meet each other, and to meet the noblest waiter in France. A waiter who might have been a governor, a colonel, a member of the *Comédie Française*. Waiter. . . .

Waiter [approaching]. Monsieur?

Orpheus. You are quite charming.

Waiter. But, monsieur. . . .

Orpheus. Yes, yes, don't protest. I'm very sincere, you know, and I'm not used to paying compliments. You're quite charming. And we shall always remember you and the cashier, Mademoiselle and I. You'll tell her so, won't you?

Waiter. Yes, monsieur.

Orpheus. Isn't it wonderful to be alive! I didn't know it was so exciting to breathe, to have blood rushing through your veins, muscles that can move. . . .

Eurydice. Am I heavy?

Orpheus. Oh, no! Just the right weight to keep me down to earth. Until now I was too light. I floated. I bumped into furniture and people. My arms were stretched too wide, my fingers were losing their grip. . . . How funny it is, and how lightly the experts make their calculations of weight! I've just realized I was short of exactly your weight to make me part of the atmosphere. . . .

Eurydice. Oh, my darling, you're frightening me! You really are part of it now? You'll never fly away again?

Orpheus. Never again.

Eurydice. What should I do, all alone on the earth, if you were to leave me? Swear you'll never leave me?

Orpheus. I swear.

Eurydice. That's so easy to say. I hope you don't really mean to leave me. If you really want to make me happy, swear you'll never even want to leave me, even for a minute, even if the prettiest girl in the world looked at you.

Orpheus. I swear that too.

Eurydice [*rising abruptly*]. You see how false you are! You swear that even if the prettiest girl in the world looked at you, you wouldn't want to leave me. But to know that she looked at you, you'd have to look at her. Oh, dear God, how unhappy I am! You've only just begun to love me, and already you're thinking of other women. Swear you wouldn't even see the idiot, my darling. . . .

Orpheus. I should be blind.

Eurydice. Even if you don't see her, people are so wicked, they'd tell you about her as quickly as they could, just so as they could hurt me. Swear you won't listen to them!

Orpheus. I should be deaf.

Eurydice. I know—there's something much simpler. Swear to me straightaway, sincerely, of your own free will and not just to please me, that you won't ever think another woman pretty. . . . Even the ones supposed to be beautiful. . . . It doesn't mean a thing, you know.

Orpheus. I swear it.

Eurydice [*suspiciously*]. Not even one who looked like me?

Orpheus. Even that one. I'll watch out for her.

Eurydice. You swear it of your own free will?

Orpheus. Of my own free will.

Eurydice. Good. And you know you've sworn it by my head?

Orpheus. By your head.

Eurydice. You know, don't you. that when you swear by someone's head, it means that person dies if you don't keep your word?

Orpheus. Yes, I know.

Eurydice [*going to him*]. Good. Now I'll tell you. I only wanted to test you. We haven't really sworn anything. To swear properly, it's not enough to lift your hand, a vague little gesture you can interpret how you like. You must stretch out your arm like this, spit on the ground—don't laugh. This is very serious. We must do it properly. Some people say that not only does the person die suddenly if you break your word, but that she suffers horribly as well.

Orpheus [*gravely*]. I've made a note of it.

Eurydice. Good. Now, you know what you'll make me risk if you lie, even a very little; you'll swear to me now, please, darling, stretching out your hand and spitting on the ground, that everything you've sworn was true.

Orpheus. I spit, I stretch out my hand, and I swear.

Eurydice [*with a great sigh*]. Good. I believe. Besides, it's so easy to deceive me, I'm very trusting. You're smiling. Are you laughing at me?

Orpheus. I'm looking at you. I've just realized I haven't had time to look at you before.

Eurydice. Am I ugly? Sometimes, when I've been crying, or laughing too much, I get a tiny red spot on the side of my nose. I'd rather tell you straightaway, so you don't get a shock later on.

Orpheus. I'll remember.

Eurydice. And I'm very thin. Not so thin as I look; when I'm in the bath, I don't think I'm too bad, but what I mean is, I'm not one of those women you can rest against comfortably.

Orpheus. I didn't expect to be very comfortable.

Eurydice. I can only give you what I've got, can't I? So you mustn't imagine things. . . . I'm very stupid too —I never know what to say and you mustn't rely on me too much to make conversation.

Orpheus [*smiling*]. You never stop talking!

Eurydice. I never stop talking, but I wouldn't know how to answer you. That's why I talk all the time, to prevent people asking me questions. It's my way of keeping quiet. You'll see you won't like anything about me.

Orpheus. You're quite wrong. I like it when you talk too much. It makes a little noise and it's very restful.

Eurydice. Really! I'm sure you like mysterious women. The Garbo type. Six feet high, huge eyes, big mouths, big feet, who spend the whole day smoking in the woods. I'm not like that at all. You must say good-by to that idea straightaway.

Orpheus. I have.

Eurydice. Yes, you say that, but I can see in your eyes. . . . [*She throws herself into his arms.*] Oh, darling, darling, it's too awful not to be the one you love! What can I do? Do you want me to grow? I'll try. I'll go in for exercises. Do you want me to look haggard? I'll put mascara on my eyelids, use much more make-up. I'll try and be somber, to smoke. . . .

Orpheus. Of course not!

Eurydice. Yes, yes, I'll even try to be mysterious. It's not so very complicated. All you have to do is think of nothing. Any woman can do it.

Orpheus. What a little lunatic you are!

Eurydice. I'll manage, you'll see! I'll be wise and extravagant and thrifty—sometimes—and obedient as a little odalisque, or terribly unjust the days you'd like to feel unhappy because of me. Oh, only those days, don't worry. . . . And then I'll make it up to you the days I'll be maternal—so maternal I'll be a little annoying—the days you'll have boils or toothache. Then on rainy days, I can still be bourgeois, badly brought up, prudish, ambitious, highly strung, or just plain boring.

Orpheus. D'you think you can play all those parts?

Eurydice. Of course, my darling, if I'm to keep you, I must be all the other women in one. . . .

Orpheus. And when will you be yourself?

Eurydice. In between. Whenever I've got the time— I'll manage.

Orpheus. It'll be a dog's life!

Eurydice. That's what love is! Anyway, it's easy for the lady dogs. All they have to do is let the other dogs sniff them a little, then trot along with a dreamy air, pretending they haven't noticed anything. Men are much more complicated!

Orpheus [*pulling her to him, laughing*]. I'm going to make you very unhappy!

Eurydice [*pressing herself to him*]. Oh, yes! I shall make myself so small, I shan't make any demands on you. All you'll need to do is let me sleep at night against your shoulder, hold my hand all day. . . .

Orpheus. I like sleeping on my back, diagonally across the bed. I like taking long walks by myself. . . .

Eurydice. We could both try and sleep across the bed, and when we go for walks, I'll walk a little behind you, if you like. Only a very little. Almost beside you all the same. But I shall love you so much, and I shall always be so true, so true. . . . Only you must always talk to me so I won't have time to think of stupid things. . . .

Orpheus [*dreams for a moment in silence with her in his arms; murmurs*]. Who are you? I feel I've known you always.

Eurydice. Why ask me who I am? It means so little. . . .

Orpheus. Who are you? It's too late, I know quite well, I could never leave you now. You appeared quite suddenly in this station. I stopped playing my accordion, and now you're in my arms. Who are you?

Eurydice. I don't know who you are, either. And yet I don't want you to explain. I'm happy. That's enough.

Orpheus. I don't know why I'm suddenly afraid of being hurt.

The Girl [*passing on the platform*]. What? Still there? Mathias is expecting you in the third-class waiting room. If you don't want a whole new series of rows, darling, you'd better go to him straightaway. . . . [*She has gone.*]

Orpheus [*who has let* EURYDICE *go*]. Who is this Mathias?

Eurydice [*quickly*]. No one, darling.

Orpheus. This is the third time someone's said he's looking for you.

Eurydice. He's one of the boys in the company. No one at all. He's looking for me. All right. He's probably got something to say.

Orpheus. Who is this Mathias?

Eurydice [*crying out*]. I don't love him, darling, I've never loved him!

Orpheus. Is he your lover?

Eurydice. These things are so quickly said, it's so easy to call everything by the same name. I'd rather tell you the truth at once, and tell you myself. Everything must be clear between us. Yes. He is my lover. [ORPHEUS *falls back a step.*] No, don't leave me. I so much wanted to be able to say, I'm only a girl. I've been waiting for you. Yours will be the first hand to touch me. I so much wanted to be able to tell you that—isn't it stupid?—it seemed to me it was true.

Orpheus. Has he been your lover long?

Eurydice. I don't know. Six months perhaps. I've never loved him.

Orpheus. Then why?

Eurydice. Why? Oh, don't keep asking me questions. When we don't know each other very well, when we don't know everything about each other, questions can become the most terrible weapons. . . .

Orpheus. Why? I want to know.

Eurydice. Why? Because he was unhappy, I suppose, and I was tired. And lonely. He was in love with me.

Orpheus. And before?

Eurydice. Before, my darling?

Orpheus. Before him?

Eurydice. Before him?

Orpheus. You've never had another lover?

Eurydice [*after imperceptible hesitation*]. No. Never.

Orpheus. Then he taught you how to make love? Answer me. Why don't you say something? You said you only wanted the truth to be between us.

Eurydice [*crying out in despair*]. Yes, but, my darling, I'm trying to decide what will hurt you least! If it was him, whom you'll probably see, or someone else, a long time ago, whom you'll never see. . . .

Orpheus. It's not a question of what hurts me least, but the truth!

Eurydice. Well, when I was very young, a man, a stranger, took me, almost by force. . . . It lasted for a few weeks, and then he went away.

Orpheus. Did you love him?

Eurydice. He hurt me, I was afraid. I was ashamed.

Orpheus [*after pause*]. Is that all?

Eurydice. Yes, my darling. You see, it was very stupid, very sad, but very simple.

Orpheus [*in a low voice*]. I'll try never to think of them.

Eurydice. Yes, darling.

Orpheus. I'll try never to think of their faces close to yours, their eyes upon you, their hands touching you.

Eurydice. Yes, darling.

Orpheus. I'll try not to think they've already held you close. [*Takes her in his arms again.*] There, now it's all begun again. I'm the one who's holding you.

Eurydice [*very gently*]. It's wonderful in your arms. Like a tiny house, snug and secure, in the middle of the world. A tiny house where no one can ever come. [*They kiss for the first time.*] Here? In this café?

Orpheus. In this café. I, who always feel embarrassed when people look at me. I wish it could be full of people

. . . it will be a beautiful wedding! For witnesses we shall have had the cashier, the noblest waiter in France, and a shy little man in a mackintosh who pretends not to see us, though I'm sure he can. . . .

He kisses her. The YOUNG MAN *in the mackintosh who has been sitting silently in the background from the beginning of the act, looks at them, then gets up noiselessly and comes to lean against a column nearer to them. They haven't seen him.*

Eurydice [freeing herself suddenly]. Now, you must leave me. There's something I must do. No, don't ask me. Go out for a moment, I'll call you back. [*She goes with him to the door, then goes back to the door that opens on to the platform; she stops and stands motionless for a moment on the threshold. One realizes she is looking at someone invisible who is also staring at her. Suddenly she says in a hard voice.*] Come in.[MATHIAS *enters slowly without taking his eyes off her. He stops on the threshold.*] You saw? I kissed him. I love him. What do you want?

Mathias. Who is he?

Eurydice. I don't know.

Mathias. You're mad.

Eurydice. Yes.

Mathias. For a week now, you've been avoiding me.

Eurydice. For a week, yes, but it wasn't because of him. I've only known him for an hour.

Mathias [looks at her in sudden fear]. What did you say? [*He draws back.*]

Eurydice. You know, Mathias.

Mathias. Eurydice, you know I cannot live without you.

Eurydice. Yes, Mathias. I love him.

Mathias. You know I'd rather die at once than go on living alone, now that I've had you with me. I don't ask anything of you, Eurydice, nothing except not to be left alone. . . .

Eurydice. I love him, Mathias.

Mathias. Is that the only thing you can say?

Eurydice [softly, pitilessly]. I love him.

Mathias [going out suddenly]. Very well. If that's the way you want it.

Eurydice [running after him]. Listen, Mathias, try to understand. I like you very much, only—I love him. . . .

They have gone. The YOUNG MAN *in the mackintosh watches them go. He goes out slowly after them. The stage is empty for a moment. We hear a bell ringing, then the whistle of a train in the distance.* ORPHEUS *comes in slowly, watching* EURYDICE *and* MATHIAS *disappear. Behind him his* FATHER *bursts in with his harp, while the train whistles and the bell becomes more insistent.*

Father. The train's coming, my boy. Platform two. Are you ready? [*Takes a step, suddenly becomes absent-minded.*] Er . . . have you paid? I think you said it was your turn?

Orpheus [*gently, without looking at him*]. I'm not going, father.

Father. Why always wait until the last minute? The train will be in in two minutes and we've got to take the subway. With the harp, we've only just got time.

Orpheus. I'm not taking this train.

Father. What? You aren't taking this train? Why aren't you taking this train? We want to get to Palavas tonight, it's the only one.

Orpheus. Then take it. I'm not going.

Father. This is something new! What's the matter with you?

Orpheus. Listen, father. I'm very fond of you. I know you need me, that it'll be terrible, but it had to happen one day. I'm going to leave you. . . .

Father [*a man fallen from the clouds*]. What are you saying?

Orpheus [*crying out suddenly*]. You heard me quite well! Don't make me say it again to give you a lead into a pathetic scene. Don't hold your breath so that you can turn pale; don't pretend to tremble and tear your hair! I know all your tricks. It was all right when I was little. They don't impress me now. [*He repeats, in a low voice.*] I'm going to leave you, father.

Father [*changing his tactics suddenly and wrapping himself in an exaggerated dignity*]. I refuse to listen to you. You're not in your right mind. Come along.

Orpheus. Dignity doesn't work either. I told you I knew all your tricks.

Father [*hurt*]. Forget my white hairs—forget my white

hairs! I'm used to it. . . . But I repeat, I refuse to listen to you. That's clear enough, isn't it?

Orpheus. You must listen to me because you've only two minutes to understand. Your train's whistling already.

Father [sneering nobly]. Ah! Ah!

Orpheus. Don't sneer nobly, I beg you! Listen to me. You've got to catch that train, and catch it alone. It's your only hope of arriving at Palavas-les-Flots in time to get the job as harpist.

Father [babbling]. But I refused the job! I refused it on your account!

Orpheus. You can say you've thought it over, that you're deserting me, that you accept. Tortoni has probably not had time to find another harpist. He's your friend. He'll do his best for you.

Father. But I refused his offer. He's drunk his shame to the very dregs. You mustn't forget he's an Italian. Those people never forgive an insult.

Orpheus. Take the train, father. As soon as you've gone, I'll telephone to Palavas, I swear I'll make him forget you refused.

Father [shouts in a voice the power of which is unsuspected in his frail body]. Never!

Orpheus. Don't shout! He's not such a bad chap. I'm sure he will listen to me.

Father. Never, do you hear? Your father will never abase himself.

Orpheus. But I'm the one who's going to be abased! I'll say it was all my fault. I'll telephone Tortoni straightaway. [*Goes to desk.*] Madame, can I telephone from here?

Father [catching him back]. Listen, my boy. Don't telephone that animal. I'd rather tell you straightaway. The harpist's job. . . .

Orpheus. Well?

Father. Well—he never offered it to me.

Orpheus. What?

Father. I said it to make you think better of me. I got wind of the job and begged him to have me. He refused.

Orpheus [after short pause]. I see. . . . [*Says gently.*] I thought you could have had that job. It's a pity. It would have settled so many things.

Pause.

Father [*gently*]. I am old, Orpheus. . . .

The train whistles.

Orpheus [*suddenly, in a sort of fever*]. Take the train all the same, please, please, father; go to Palavas-les-Flots; there are plenty of cafés there. It's the height of the season, I promise you you'll be able to earn your living!

Father. With nothing but the harp . . . you're joking!

Orpheus. But that's what people like—they always noticed the harp. You see so few about. Every beggar plays the accordion in the street. But the harp—you've said it often enough yourself—that was what made us both look like artists.

Father. Yes, but you play extremely well, and the women thought you were young and charming. They dug their elbows into their escorts and made them put two francs into the plate. When I'm alone, they'll keep their elbows to themselves.

Orpheus [*trying to laugh*]. Of course they won't, father —the more mature ones. You're an old Don Juan still!

Father [*throwing a glance at the cashier who humiliated him earlier, and stroking his beard*]. Between ourselves, an old Don Juan for chambermaids in cheap hotels —and only ugly chambermaids. . . .

Orpheus. You're exaggerating, father—you're still successful when you choose!

Father. So I tell you, but it doesn't always happen as I say. Besides, I've never told you this, my boy. I brought you up, I had my paternal pride—I don't know if you've noticed . . . I . . . I play the harp very badly.

There is a terrible silence; ORPHEUS *hangs his head; he cannot help smiling a little.*

Orpheus. I couldn't help noticing, father.

Father. You see, you say so yourself. . . .

Another pause. The train whistles very close.

Orpheus [*shaking him suddenly*]. Father, I can't do anything more for you. If I were rich, I'd give you some money. But I haven't any. Go and take your train. Keep everything we've got, and good luck.

Father. Just now you said you couldn't leave me!
Orpheus. Just now, yes. Now I can.

The train is heard coming into the station.

Orpheus. Here's your train. Hurry, pick up the harp.
Father [*still struggling*]. You've met someone, haven't you?
Orpheus. Yes, father.
Father. The girl who came in just now?
Orpheus [*kneeling in front of the suitcases*]. Yes, father.

Takes some things from one case, puts them into the other.

Father. I talked a little with those people. She's an actress, you know, a tenth-rate company that plays in flea pits. She's no better than she ought to be.
Orpheus. Yes, father. We really must hurry. . . .
Father. I shall curse you! This will cost you dear!
Orpheus. Yes, father.
Father [*rising*]. Laugh away. I've still got a few hundred francs. I can earn my living from day to day, you'll have nothing.
Orpheus [*laughing, in spite of himself, and catching him by the shoulders*]. My father, my dear old father, my terrible father. I'm very fond of you, but I can do nothing more for you.
Loudspeaker [*outside*]. Passengers for Béziers, Montpellier, Sète, Palavas-les-Flots.
Orpheus. Quick, you're going to miss it. You've got the harp, the big suitcase? I've got two hundred francs, keep the rest.
Father. Don't be so generous!
Loudspeaker. Passengers for Béziers, Montpellier, Sète, Palavas-les-Flots!
Father [*suddenly*]. Do you think I could get a rebate on your ticket?
Orpheus [*embracing him*]. I don't know. I'm so happy, father. I love her. I'll write to you. You ought to be a little pleased to see me happy. I so much want to live!
Father [*loading himself up*]. I'll never be able to manage alone.

Orpheus. I'll help you. You must get a porter at the other end.

Father [*crying from the doorway like a ridiculous curse, and dropping some of his parcels in the process*]. You're deserting your father for a woman! A woman who probably doesn't love you in return!

Orpheus [*crying out, following him*]. I'm so happy, father. . . .

Voice [*outside*]. Mind the doors!

Father [*before going out*]. You're sending me away to die!

Orpheus [*pushing him*]. Hurry, father, hurry!

Whistles, noise of the porters, steam. Suddenly, the train is heard starting up. EURYDICE *enters with a small suitcase and sits in a corner, making herself very inconspicuous.* ORPHEUS *comes back; he goes to her. She looks at him.*

Orpheus. It's all over.

Eurydice [*comically*]. It's all over with me, too.

Orpheus [*kissing her head*]. Forgive me. He's rather ridiculous. He's my father.

Eurydice. You mustn't ask me to forgive you. The woman talking about love just now, with all those noises, was my mother. I didn't dare tell you.

They are facing each other, smiling gently. A bell rings, then the whistle of an approaching train.

Loudspeaker. Passengers for Toulouse, Béziers, Carcassonne, platform seven. The train arriving now.

Another Loudspeaker [*farther away*]. Passengers for Toulouse, Béziers, Carcassonne, platform seven. The train arriving now.

Through the door opening on to the platform, the members of the company pass with their baggage.

The Girl. Quickly, darling, or we'll have to stand all the way again. Naturally, the stars are traveling second. Who's paying the extra, I ask you? Who's paying the extra?

Another Girl [continuing a story]. Then, d'you know what she said to me? She said, I don't give a damn. I've my position to consider. . . .

They have gone. The MOTHER *and* VINCENT *pass, overloaded with hatboxes, enormous suitcases.*

Mother. Vincent, darling boy, the big case and the green box?

Vincent. I've got them both. Off we go!

Mother. Be very careful. The handle's not very secure. It reminds me of one day at Buenos Aires. Sarah's hatbox burst open in the middle of the station. There were ostrich feathers all over the track. . . .

They have gone. A fat man passes, puffing, behind them.

Dulac. Quickly, for God's sake, quickly! And check that the trunks have been loaded. Then get in the back. The rest of us will be up front.

Eurydice [gently]. All the people in my life. . . .

Running, and unable to run, comic, lamentable, absurd, the little MANAGER *comes last, tripping over too many suitcases, too many parcels slipping from his grasp. All in the midst of distant cries and the approaching whistles of the train.*

Eurydice [gently, to ORPHEUS*].* Close the door. [ORPHEUS *closes the door. A sudden silence covers them.*] There. Now we're alone in the world.

Loudspeaker [farther away]. Passengers for Toulouse, Béziers, Carcassonne, platform seven. The train arriving now.

ORPHEUS *has gently come back to her. Noise of train reaching the station and a cry, a cry that becomes a noise that swells and stops suddenly, giving place to a terrible silence. The* CASHIER *has stood up and tried to see. The* WAITER *runs across the stage, calling to them as he passes.*

Waiter. Someone's thrown himself in front of the express—a young man!

People pass, running along the platform. ORPHEUS *and*
EURYDICE *are facing each other, unable to look at one
another. They say nothing. The* YOUNG MAN *in the
mackintosh appears on the platform. He comes in, then
shuts the door and looks at them.*

Eurydice [*gently*]. I couldn't help it. I love you and I
didn't love him.

*There is a pause. Each stares straight ahead without look-
ing at the other. The* YOUNG MAN *in the mackintosh
comes up to them.*

The Young Man [*in an expressionless voice, without
taking his eyes off them*]. He threw himself in front of the
engine. The shock itself must have killed him.
Orpheus. How horrible!
The Young Man. No. He chose a fairly good method.
Poison is very slow, and causes so much suffering. One
vomits, and twists about, and it is all disgusting. It's the
same with sleeping draughts. People think they'll go to
sleep, but it's a death in the midst of hiccups and bad
smells. [*He has come nearer, calm and smiling.*] Believe
me . . . the easiest way when you're very tired, when
you've nursed that same idea for a long time is to slip
into the water as if it were a bed. . . . You stifle for a
moment, with a magnificent succession of visions . . .
then you go to sleep. That's all!
Eurydice. You don't think it hurt him to die?
The Young Man [*gently*]. It never hurts to die. Death
never hurts anybody. Death is gentle. . . . What makes
you suffer when you take certain poisons, or give yourself a clumsy wound, is life itself.

ORPHEUS *and* EURYDICE *are pressed against each other.*

Eurydice [*gently, like an explanation*]. We couldn't
help ourselves. We love each other.
The Young Man. Yes, I know. I've been listening to
you. A fine young man, and a pretty girl. Two courageous
little animals, with supple limbs and sharp white teeth,
ready to fight till dawn, as they should, and fall together,
mortally wounded.

Eurydice [*murmuring*]. We don't even know you. . . .
The Young Man. But I know you. I'm very glad to have met you both. You're leaving here together? There's only one more train tonight. The train for Marseilles. Perhaps you'll be taking it?
Orpheus. Perhaps.
The Young Man. I'm going there myself. I hope I'll have the pleasure of meeting you again?

He bows and exits. ORPHEUS *and* EURYDICE *turn to each other. They are standing, looking very small, in the middle of the empty hall.*

Orpheus [*gently*]. My love.
Eurydice. My dear love.
Orpheus. Our story is beginning. . . .
Eurydice. I'm a little afraid. . . . Are you good, or wicked? What's your name?
Orpheus. It's Orpheus. What's yours?
Eurydice. Eurydice.

Curtain.

ACT TWO

A room in a provincial hotel—huge, somber, and dirty. The ceilings are too high, lost in shadow, dusty double curtains, a big iron bed, a screen, a miserable light.

ORPHEUS *and* EURYDICE *are lying on the bed, fully dressed.*

ORPHEUS. To think everything might have gone wrong. . . . Supposing you'd turned to the right, I to the left, not even that. Nothing more important than the flight of a bird, a child's cry, to make you turn your head for a second. I'd be playing my accordion on the terraces at Perpignan with father.
Eurydice. And I'd be playing *The Orphans of the Storm* at the municipal theater of Avignon. Mother and I play the two orphans.
Orpheus. Last night I thought of all the luck that

brought us together. To think we might never have met; that we might have mistaken the day or the station.

Eurydice. Or met while we were still too young.

Orpheus. But we didn't mistake the day, or the minute. We never missed a step during the whole eventful journey. We're very clever.

Eurydice. Yes, my darling.

Orpheus [*powerful and gay*]. We're much stronger than the whole world, both of us.

Eurydice [*looking at him with a little smile*]. My hero! All the same you were very frightened yesterday when we came into this room.

Orpheus. Yesterday we weren't stronger than all the people in the world. Now, at least, we know each other. We know how heavy a sleeping head feels, the sound of our laughter. Now we have our memories to protect us.

Eurydice. A whole evening, a whole night, a whole day —how rich we are!

Orpheus. Yesterday, we had nothing. We knew nothing, and we came into this room by chance, under the eye of that terrible waiter with the mustache who was sure we were going to make love. We began to undress, quickly, standing, face to face. . . .

Eurydice. You threw your clothes like a madman into the four corners of the room. . . .

Orpheus. You were shaking all over. You couldn't undo the little buttons of your dress and I watched you pull them off without making a movement to help you. And then, when you were naked, suddenly you were ashamed.

Eurydice [*hanging her head*]. I thought I ought to be beautiful as well, and I wasn't sure. . . .

Orpheus. We stood like that for a long time, face to face, without speaking, without daring to speak. . . . Oh, we were too poor, too naked, and it was too unjust to have to risk everything like that on a single throw. Then suddenly a wave of tenderness took me by the throat because I saw you had a tiny red spot on your shoulder.

Eurydice. Then afterward, it all became so simple. . . .

Orpheus. You laid your head against me and fell asleep. You said things in your dreams I couldn't answer. . . .

Eurydice. Did I? I often talk in my sleep. I hope you didn't listen.

Orpheus. Of course I did.

Eurydice. I call that very mean of you! Instead of sleeping honestly, you spy on me. How do you think I can know what I say when I'm asleep?

Orpheus. I only understood three words. You sighed a terrible deep sigh. Your lips trembled a little, and then you said, "It's so difficult."

Eurydice [*repeating*]. It's so difficult.

Orpheus. What was so difficult?

Eurydice [*stays for a moment without answering, then shakes her head and says in a little voice*]. I don't know, my darling. I was dreaming.

Knock at the door. It is the WAITER, *who enters immediately. He has big gray mustaches, and a strange air.*

Waiter. Did you ring, sir?

Orpheus. No.

Waiter. Oh! I thought you did. [*Hesitates for moment, then goes out, saying.*] Excuse me, sir.

Eurydice [*as soon as he has gone*]. D'you think they're real?

Orpheus. What?

Eurydice. His mustaches.

Orpheus. Of course. They don't look real. It's only false ones that look real—everyone knows that.

Eurydice. He doesn't look as noble as the waiter at the station.

Orpheus. The one from the *Comédie Française*? He may have been noble, but he was very conventional. Under his imposing façade, I think he was a weakling. This one has more mystery about him.

Eurydice. Yes. Too much. I don't like people with too much mystery. They frighten me a little. Don't they you?

Orpheus. A little, but I didn't like to tell you.

Eurydice [*pressing herself to him*]. Oh, my darling, hold me very tight. How lucky it is that there are two of us.

Orpheus. There are so many characters in our story already—two waiters, a noble weaking, a strange mustache, the lovely cashier and her enormous breasts. . . .

Eurydice. Such a pity she never said anything to us!

Orpheus. In all stories there are silent characters like her. She didn't say anything, but she watched us all the time. If she hadn't been silent all the time, what a lot of stories she could tell about us. . . .

Eurydice. And the porter?

Orpheus. The one who stammered?

Eurydice. Yes, my darling. Wasn't he sweet? I'd have liked to put him in a box and keep him, with his fat watch chain and brand-new cap.

Orpheus. Remember how he told us the names of all the stations where we didn't have to change, to make us remember, without any possible doubt, the name of the station where we really had to change!

Eurydice. He was quite enchanting. I'm sure he brought us luck. But the other one, the brute, the conductor. . . .

Orpheus. That fool! The one who couldn't understand we had a third-class ticket for Perpignan and another for Avignon, so what we wanted was to pay the difference on two second-class tickets to Marseilles?

Eurydice. Yes, that one. Wasn't he ugly and stupid with his greasy uniform, his self-importance, and his oily fat cheeks?

Orpheus. He is our first ignoble character. There'll be others, you'll see. . . . All happy stories are full of despicable characters.

Eurydice. Oh, but I refuse to keep him. I'll send him away. You must tell him I don't want him any more. I won't have such an idiot in my memories of you.

Orpheus. It's too late, my darling, we have no right to reject anyone.

Eurydice. Then, all our lives, this dirty, self-satisfied man will be a part of our first day together?

Orpheus. All our lives.

Eurydice. Are you sure we couldn't just forget the bad ones and only keep the good?

Orpheus. Out of the question. They have happened now, the good with the evil. They've danced their little pirouettes, said their three words in your life . . . and there they are, inside you, as they are, forever.

Eurydice [*suddenly*]. Then, you mean, if you've seen a lot of ugly things in your life, they stay inside you too?

Orpheus. Yes.

Eurydice. And everything you've ever done, does one's body remember that too, d'you think?

Orpheus. Yes.

Eurydice. You're sure that even the words we said without meaning them, the ones we can't recall, are still inside us when we talk?

Orpheus [*trying to kiss her*]. Of course, darling fool.

Eurydice [*freeing herself*]. Wait, don't kiss me. Explain. Are you sure what you've just told me is true, or is it only what you think? Do other people say it too?

Orpheus. Of course.

Eurydice. Clever people? I mean, people who ought to know, people one ought to believe?

Orpheus. Of course.

Eurydice. Then we can never really be alone, with all that around us. We can never be sincere, even when we mean what we say with all our strength. . . . If all the words are there, all the filthy bursts of laughter, if all the hands that have ever touched you are still sticking to your flesh, none of us can really change?

Orpheus. What are you talking about?

Eurydice [*after a pause*]. Do you think we'd do the same, if when we were little, we knew that one day it would be vitally important to be clean and pure? And when we say these things—when we say, "I made that movement, I said those words, I listened to that sentence, I deserted that man. . . ." [*She stops.*] When one says those same things to someone else—to the man you love, for instance—do they think that kills all your memories around you?

Orpheus. Yes. They call that confessing yourself. Afterward, they say that we are washed clean again, shining and pure. . . .

Eurydice. Oh! Are they very sure of that?

Orpheus. So they say.

Eurydice [*after thinking for a little*]. Yes, yes, but if ever they were wrong, or if they just said that for the effect; supposing they go on living twice as strong, twice as powerful, for having been repeated; if ever the other person began to remember, for always. . . . You can tell your clever people I don't trust them, and I think it's better not to say a word. . . . [ORPHEUS *looks at her, she sees this and adds quickly, pressing herself against him.*] Or else, my darling, when it's simple, as it was for us two yesterday, to tell everything, like me.

The WAITER *knocks and enters.*

Waiter. Did you ring, sir?

Orpheus. No.

Waiter. Oh! Sorry I disturbed you. [*Turns to go, then adds.*] I ought to tell you, sir, the bell is out of order. If you want me at any time, it's better if you call.

Orpheus. Thank you.

They think the WAITER *is going, but he changes his mind, crosses room and goes to double curtains; he opens and closes them again.*

Waiter. The curtains work.

Orpheus. So we see.

Waiter. In some rooms it's the opposite. The bell works and the curtains don't. [*Starts to go, then says again.*] Still, if monsieur tries to make them work later, and they don't, you've only to ring. . . . [*Stops.*] I mean, call, because, as I said before, the bell. . . .

Makes a gesture and exits.

Orpheus. He's our first eccentric. We'll have lots of others. I should think he's really a very good man, entirely without malice.

Eurydice. Oh, no. He looked at me all the time. Didn't you see how he kept looking at me?

Orpheus. You're dreaming.

Eurydice. Oh, I like the other much better—the nice one from the *Comédie Française*. . . . You could feel that even in a tragedy he wouldn't be very dangerous. . . .

The WAITER *knocks and enters again. He gives very clearly the impression of having been behind the door.*

Waiter. Excuse me, sir. I forgot to tell you, madame asks if you'll be good enough to go downstairs. There's something missing on your form. Madame must send it in tonight and it isn't complete.

Orpheus. Does she want me right away?

Waiter. Yes, sir, if you'll be so kind.

Orpheus. All right, I'll come with you. [*To* EURYDICE.] Get dressed while I'm gone, then we'll go out for dinner.

The WAITER *opens the door for* ORPHEUS *and goes out*

after him. He comes back almost at once and goes to
EURYDICE, *who has raised herself on the bed.*

Waiter [*holding out an envelope*]. Here's a letter for
you. I was told to give it to you when you were alone.
Madame isn't in her office. I was lying. There's only one
floor to go. You have thirty seconds to read it.

He remains standing in front of her. EURYDICE *has taken
the letter, trembling a little. She opens it, reads it, tears
it into tiny pieces without moving a muscle of her face.
Then she makes to throw away the bits.*

Waiter. Never use the basket. [*He goes to the basket,
kneels down, and begins to pick up the pieces, which he
stuffs into the pocket of his apron.*] Have you known each
other long?
Eurydice. One whole day.
Waiter. Then everything should still be fine.
Eurydice [*gently*]. Yes, it should be.
Waiter. The numbers I've seen passing through this
room lying on the bed, just like you. And not only good-
looking ones. Some were too fat, or too thin, or real
monsters. All using their saliva to say "our love." Sometimes, when it's getting dark, as it is now, I seem to see
them all again—all together. The room is humming with
them. Ah, love isn't very pretty.
Eurydice [*hardly audible*]. No.
Orpheus [*entering*]. You still here?
Waiter. Just going, sir.
Orpheus. The manageress wasn't there.
Waiter. I must have taken too long coming up. I suppose she couldn't wait. It doesn't matter, sir, it will do
this evening.

Looks at them both again and goes out.

Orpheus. What was he doing here?
Eurydice. Nothing. He was describing all the other
lovers he's seen passing through this room.
Orpheus. Very amusing!
Eurydice. He says sometimes he seems to see them all
together. The whole room is humming with them.
Orpheus. And you listened to such stupidity?

Eurydice. Perhaps it wasn't so stupid. You, who know everything, said that all the people one had ever met go on living in our memories. Perhaps a room remembers too. . . . All the people who have been here are around us, coupled together, the fat ones, the thin ones, real monsters.

Orpheus. Little lunatic!

Eurydice. The bed is full of them. How ugly love can be.

Orpheus [*dragging her away*]. Let's go out to dinner. The streets are flushing with the first lamps of evening. We'll go and dine in a little restaurant smelling of garlic. You'll drink from a glass a thousand lips have touched, and the thousand fat behinds that have hollowed out the leather bench will make a tiny place for you where you'll be very comfortable. Come, let's go.

Eurydice [*resisting*]. You're laughing—you're always laughing. You're so strong.

Orpheus. Ever since yesterday! A hero! You said so yourself.

Eurydice. Yes, yes, a hero who understands nothing, who feels nothing, who is so sure of himself he goes straight forward. Ah, you can take things lightly, you others—yes—now that you have made me so heavy. . . . You say things the moment you least expect them, you bring to life all the dirty lovers who have done things between these four walls, and then you don't give it another thought. You go out to dinner, saying, it's a fine day, the lamps are shining, and the restaurant smells of garlic.

Orpheus. So will you, in a minute. Come, let's get out of here.

Eurydice. It isn't nice here any more. It doesn't feel nice. How brief it was. . . .

Orpheus. What's the matter? You're trembling.

Eurydice. Yes.

Orpheus. You're quite pale.

Eurydice. Yes.

Orpheus. How strange you look. I've never seen you look like this.

He tries to make her follow him; she turns away.

Eurydice. Don't look at me. When you look at me, I can feel it. It's as if you had put your two hands on my back, and entered, burning, into me. Don't look at me.

Orpheus. I've been looking at you since yesterday.

He draws her away; she lets herself go.

Eurydice [*murmuring, beaten*]. You are strong, you know. . . . You look such a thin little boy and you are stronger than anyone. When you play your accordion, like yesterday in the station, or when you talk, I turn into a little snake. . . . There's nothing I can do except crawl along slowly toward you.

Orpheus. Then you say, "It's so difficult."

Eurydice [*crying out suddenly and freeing herself*]. Darling!

Orpheus. Yes.

Eurydice. I'm so afraid it may be too difficult.

Orpheus. What?

Eurydice. The first day, everything seems so easy. The first day all you have to do is invent. You're sure we haven't invented everything?

Orpheus [*taking her head in his hands*]. I'm sure I love you, and you love me. Sure as the stones, sure as the things made of wood and iron.

Eurydice. Yes, but perhaps you thought I was someone else. And when you see me as I am. . . .

Orpheus. Since yesterday I've been looking at you. I've heard you talking in your sleep.

Eurydice. Yes, but I didn't say much. Supposing I go to sleep tonight and tell you everything?

Orpheus. Everything? What's everything?

Eurydice. Or if someone, one of our characters, came and told you. . . .

Orpheus. What could they come and tell me about you, I know you better than they do, now.

Eurydice. Are you sure?

She lifts her head and looks at ORPHEUS, *who continues with joyous strength.*

Orpheus. Sure. I haven't thanked you either for your courage. . . . For the days that will soon be here when we'll go without our dinner, smoking our last cigarette, one puff in turn. For the dresses you'll pretend not to see in the windows; for the beds made up, the rooms swept out, your reddened hands and the kitchen smell still caught up in your hair. Everything you gave when you agreed to follow me. [EURYDICE's *head is lowered. He looks at her in silence.*] I didn't think it would be possible to meet a comrade who would go with you, a little silent companion who takes on all the chores and at night is warm and beautiful beside you. Tender and secret, a woman for you alone. I woke last night to ask myself if I really did deserve to have you.

EURYDICE *has raised her head and stares at him in the growing darkness.*

Eurydice. You really think all that of me?
Orpheus. Yes, my love.
Eurydice [*thinks a little, then says*]. It's true. She'd be a very charming Eurydice: the very wife for you. Mademoiselle Eurydice—your wife!
Orpheus [*putting his arms round her*]. Are you happy, little serpent? [*They remain embraced for a moment, then he springs up, strong and joyful.*] And now, will you come and eat? The snake charmer can't blow his flute any longer—he's dying of hunger.
Eurydice [*in a different voice*]. Put on the lights.
Orpheus. There's a sensible thing to say! Lights up everywhere. Floods of light. Drive away the phantoms.

ORPHEUS *turns on the switch. A hard light fills the room, making it ugly.* EURYDICE *has risen.*

Eurydice. Darling, I don't want to go to a restaurant, with all those people. If you like, I'll go downstairs, I'll buy something, and we can eat it here.
Orpheus. In the room humming with noises?
Eurydice. Yes. It doesn't matter any more.
Orpheus [*moving*]. It'll be great fun. I'll come down with you.
Eurydice [*quickly*]. No, let me go alone. [*He stops.*] I'd like to do your shopping for you, just this once, like a respectable married woman.
Orpheus. All right. Buy all sorts of things.
Eurydice. Yes.

Orpheus. We must have a real party.

Eurydice. Yes, darling.

Orpheus. Exactly as if we had plenty of money. It's a miracle the rich can never understand. . . . Buy a pine-apple—a real one, just as the good Lord made it, not a sad American pineapple in a can. We haven't got a knife. We'll never be able to eat it. But that's the way pineapples protect themselves.

Eurydice [*with a little laugh, her eyes filled with tears*]. Yes, my darling.

Orpheus. Buy some flowers too—lots and lots of flowers. . . .

Eurydice [*falteringly, with her poor little smile*]. You can't eat flowers.

Orpheus. Nor can you. We'll put them on the table. [*Looks round.*] We haven't got a table. Never mind, buy lots of flowers all the same. And buy some fruit. Peaches, fat hothouse peaches, apricots, golden pears. A little bread to demonstrate the serious side of our nature, and a bottle of white wine we can drink out of the tooth glass. Hurry, hurry! I'm dying of hunger. [EURYDICE *fetches her little hat and puts it on in front of the mirror.*] You're putting on your hat?

Eurydice. Yes. [*Turns round suddenly and says in a strange hoarse voice.*] Adieu, my darling.

Orpheus [*cries to her, laughing*]. But you're saying good-by!

Eurydice [*from the doorway*]. Yes.

She looks at him for a second longer, smilingly and pity-ingly, and goes out abruptly. ORPHEUS *stays for a moment without moving, smiling at the absent Eurydice. Sud-denly his smile disappears, his face looks drawn, a vague fear seizes him, he runs to the door, calling.*

Orpheus. Eurydice!

He opens the door, and recoils, stupefied. The YOUNG MAN *who spoke to them at the station is on the threshold, smiling.*

The Young Man. She's just gone downstairs. [ORPHEUS *retreats, surprised, hesitating to recognize him.*] Don't you remember me? We met yesterday in the station restaurant, just after the accident. . . . You know, the young man who threw himself under the train. I've taken the liberty of coming to say good evening. I liked you both so much. We're neighbors. I'm in room eleven. [*Takes a step into the room, holding out a packet of cigarettes.*] Smoke? [ORPHEUS *takes a cigarette mechanically.*] I don't myself. [*Takes out a box of matches and lights one.*] Light?

Orpheus. Thanks. [*He closes the door again and asks mechanically.*] May I ask your name?

The Young Man. When you meet people on journeys, half the charm is to know as little as possible about them. My name won't mean anything to you. Call me Monsieur Henri. [*He has come right into the room. He looks at* ORPHEUS *and smiles.* ORPHEUS *looks at him as if hypnotized.*] A fine town, Marseilles. This human ant heap, this collection of riffraff, this filth. There aren't as many suicides in the old port as they say, but all the same, it's a fine town. Do you expect to stay here long?

Orpheus. I don't know.

M. Henri. I didn't wait to be introduced before speaking to you yesterday. But you were so touching, the two of you, holding each other so closely in the middle of that huge hall. . . . A beautiful setting, wasn't it? Somber and red, with the night falling and the station noises in the background. . . . [*Looks at* ORPHEUS *for a long time, smiling.*] Little Orpheus and Mademoiselle Eurydice. . . . One doesn't get such a stroke of luck every day. . . . I shouldn't have spoken to you. . . . Normally, I never speak to people. What's the good? But I couldn't resist the urge to know you better—I don't know why. You're a musician?

Orpheus. Yes.

M. Henri. I like music. I like everything that is sweet and happy. To tell the truth, I like happiness. But let's talk about you. It's of no interest to talk about me. But first let's have something to drink. It helps the conversation. [*Rises and rings the bell. He looks at* ORPHEUS *and smiles during the short wait.*] It gives me a great deal of pleasure to talk to you like this. [*The* WAITER *has entered.*] What'll you have? Whisky? Brandy?

Orpheus. If you like.

M. Henri. Some brandy, please.

Waiter. Just one?

M. Henri. Yes. [*To* ORPHEUS.] Forgive me, won't you. I never drink. [*The* WAITER *has gone out. He still watches* ORPHEUS, *smiling.*] I'm really delighted to have met you.

Orpheus [*embarrassed*]. It's kind of you to say so.

M. Henri. You must be wondering why I take such an interest in you. [ORPHEUS *makes a movement.*] I was at the back of the restaurant yesterday when she came to you, as if called by your music. These moments when we catch a glimpse of Fate laying her snares are very exciting, aren't they? [*The* WAITER *has returned.*] Ah, your brandy.

Waiter. Here you are, sir. One brandy.

Orpheus. Thank you.

The WAITER *goes out.*

M. Henri [*who has watched him*]. Did you notice how slowly and insolently the waiter went out of the room?

Orpheus. No.

M. Henri [*going to listen at the door*]. He's certainly gone back to his post behind the door. [*Comes back to* ORPHEUS.] I'm sure he's been in here on several different occasions with different excuses; I'm sure he's tried to speak to you?

Orpheus. Yes.

M. Henri. You see, I'm not the only one to take an interest in you. . . . Haven't shopkeepers, porters, little girls in the streets smiled at you oddly since yesterday. . . .

Orpheus. Everyone is kind to lovers.

M. Henri. It isn't only kindness. Don't you think they look at you a little too closely?

Orpheus. No. Why?

M. Henri [*smiling*]. No reason. [*Dreams for a moment, then suddenly takes his arm.*] Listen, my friend, there are two races of beings. The masses, teeming and happy— common clay, if you like—eating, breeding, working, counting their pennies; people who just live; ordinary people; people you can't imagine dead. And then, there are the others—the noble ones, the heroes. The ones you can quite well imagine lying shot, pale and tragic: one minute triumphant with a guard of honor, and the next being marched away between two gendarmes. Hasn't that sort of thing ever attracted you?

Orpheus. Never; and this evening less than usual.

M. Henri [*going to him and laying his hand on his shoulder; looking at him, almost tenderly*]. It's a pity. You shouldn't believe too blindly in happiness. Particularly not when you belong to the good race. You're only laying up disappointments for yourself.

The WAITER *knocks and enters.*

Waiter. There's a young lady here asking for Mademoiselle Eurydice. I told her she had gone out, but she doesn't seem to believe me. She insists on seeing you. May I ask her to come up?

The Girl [*entering and pushing the* WAITER *aside*]. I've already come. Where's Eurydice?

Orpheus. She's gone out, mademoiselle. Who are you?

The Girl. One of her friends from the company. I must talk to her at once.

Orpheus. I tell you she's gone out. Besides, I don't think she has anything to say to you.

The Girl. You're wrong. She's got plenty to say. How long ago did she go out? Did she take her suitcase with her?

Orpheus. Her suitcase? Why should she take her suitcase? She's gone out to buy our dinner.

The Girl. She may have gone out to buy your dinner, but she had very good reasons for taking her suitcase. She was supposed to meet us at the station to catch the eight-twelve train.

Orpheus [*crying out*]. Meet who?

Waiter [*who has pulled out a fat copper watch*]. It's ten minutes and forty seconds past eight now. . . .

The Girl [*as if to herself*]. She must be on the platform with him already. Thank you.

She turns to go.

Orpheus [*catches her up in front of the door*]. On the platform with who?

The Girl. Let me go. You're hurting me. You'll make me miss the train.

Waiter [*still looking at his watch*]. Exactly eleven minutes past eight.

Dulac [*appearing in the doorway, to the* WAITER]. It's eight-thirteen. Your watch is slow. The train has gone. [*To* ORPHEUS.] Let the girl go. I can answer you. On the platform with me.

Orpheus [*retreating*]. Who are you?

Dulac. Alfredo Dulac. Eurydice's impresario. Where is she?

Orpheus. What do you want her for?

Dulac [*walking calmly into room, chewing his cigar*]. What do you want her for?

Orpheus. Eurydice is my mistress.

Dulac. Since when?

Orpheus. Since yesterday.

Dulac. She also happens to be mine. And has been, for a year.

Orpheus. You're lying!

Dulac [*smiling*]. Because she forgot to tell you? Because the child was in this bed last night instead of mine? You're a child, too, my boy. A girl like Eurydice has to be humored in her little caprices. She slept with the fool who killed himself yesterday too. I can understand her liking you. You're good looking, young. . . .

Orpheus [*crying out*]. I love Eurydice and she loves me!

Dulac. Did she tell you so?

Orpheus. Yes.

Dulac [*sitting calmly in armchair*]. She's an extraordinary girl. Luckily, I know her so well.

Orpheus. Supposing I know her better than you?

Dulac. Since yesterday?

Orpheus. Yes, since yesterday.

Dulac. I don't pretend to be an expert. If it were a question of anything else—you look much more intelligent than I am—I'd probably say "Good" but there are two things I really understand. First my job. . . .

Orpheus. And then, Eurydice?

Dulac. No, I don't make any such claims. I was going to use a much more modest expression: women. I've been an impresario for twenty years. I sell women, my boy, by the gross, to kick up their heels in provincial revues, or massacre the big arias from *La Tosca* in a casino. I don't give a damn—besides, I love them. That makes at least one good reason out of two for pretending to understand them. Eurydice is perhaps an odd little girl—I'm the first to ad-

mit it—but considering the opportunities we've both had
to see, you'll agree with me that she is a woman. . . .

Orpheus. No.

Dulac. How do you mean, no? She seemed to be an
angel, did she? Look at me squarely, my boy. Eurydice
belonged to me for over a year. Do I look as though I
could seduce an angel?

Orpheus. You're lying. Eurydice could never have belonged to you.

Dulac. You're her lover, so am I. Would you like me
to describe her to you?

Orpheus [*recoiling*]. No.

Dulac [*advancing, ignoble*]. What's she like, your Eurydice? How do you get her out of bed in the morning? Can
you drag her away from her thrillers and her cigarettes?
Have you ever seen her for a moment without a scowl on
her face like a little criminal? And her stockings? Could
she find them when she once got up? Be frank with me.
Admit her petticoat was hanging from the top of the
cupboard, her shoes in the bathroom, her hat under the
chair, and her bag completely lost. I've already bought
her seven.

Orpheus. It isn't true.

Dulac. How do you mean, it isn't true? Is yours a tidy
Eurydice? I'm beginning to think we're not talking of the
same person, or else she thought it wouldn't last for long.
. . . She told you it would be for life? I'm sure she must
have been sincere. She thought: "It'll be for all my life,
if he's strong enough to keep me, if Papa Dulac doesn't
find my tracks again, if he doesn't want to take me back."
And at the bottom of her heart, she must have known
quite well that Papa Dulac would find her out. It's only
what I would have expected of her.

Orpheus. No.

Dulac. Of course, my boy, of course . . . Eurydice is
a girl in a million, but her mentality is exactly the same as
any other girl of that sort.

Orpheus. It isn't true!

Dulac. You won't admit anything's true! You're very
odd. How long ago did she go downstairs?

Orpheus. Twenty minutes.

Dulac. Good. Is that true?

Orpheus. Yes.

Dulac. She insisted on going alone, didn't she?

Orpheus. Yes. She said it would be fun to buy our dinner alone.

Dulac. Is that true, too?

Orpheus. Yes.

Dulac. Very well, listen to me. Five minutes before, I had a letter given to her, asking her to meet me on the platform.

Orpheus. No one brought her a letter. I haven't left her for an instant since yesterday.

Dulac. Are you sure?

He looks at the WAITER; ORPHEUS *also looks at the* WAITER *without knowing why.*

Waiter [*suddenly worried*]. Excuse me, I think I'm being called.

He disappears.

Orpheus. I did leave her for a moment, yes. That man came and told me I was wanted in the office.

Dulac. I told him to give my note to Eurydice when she was alone. He gave it to her while you were downstairs.

Orpheus [*going to him*]. What did you say in your letter?

Dulac. I said I was expecting her on the eight-twelve train. I didn't have to say anything else . . . because Fate had knocked on her door and said, "Eurydice, it's over." I was sure she would obey me. It's only men who jump out of windows.

Orpheus. All the same, she didn't join you!

Dulac. That's true. She didn't come. But my Eurydice is always late. I'm not very worried. Did you ask yours to buy a lot of things?

Orpheus. Some bread and fruit.

Dulac. And you say she went out twenty minutes ago? It seems a long time to me to buy bread and fruit. The street is full of shops. Maybe your Eurydice is unpunctual too? [*To the* GIRL.] She must be at the station looking for us. Go and see.

Orpheus. I'm going with you!

Dulac. You're beginning to think she may have gone to meet us after all? I'm staying here.

Orpheus [stops and cries to the GIRL]. If you see her, tell her. . . .

Dulac. Quite useless. If she finds her at the station, then I'm right. Your faithful and tidy Eurydice was only a dream. And in that case, you have nothing more to say to her.

Orpheus [calling to the GIRL]. Tell her I love her!

Dulac. She may perhaps shed a tear; she's very sentimental. That's all.

Orpheus [still calling]. Tell her she isn't what the others think her. She is as I know her to be!

Dulac. Too complicated to explain at a railway station. Hurry along, and listen—I'm a sportsman—bring her here. In one minute she may be able to tell us herself what she is.

The GIRL *goes out, bumping into the* WAITER.

Waiter [appearing in doorway]. Excuse me, sir. . . .

Orpheus. What is it?

Waiter. There's an officer with a police van. . . .

Orpheus. What does he want?

Waiter. He's asking if there's anyone here related to the young lady. She's had an accident, sir—in the bus for Toulon. . . .

Orpheus [crying like a madman]. Is she hurt? Eurydice!

He hurls himself out into the corridor. DULAC *follows him, throwing away his cigar with a stifled oath. The* GIRL *disappears as well.*

Dulac [as he goes out]. What the devil was she doing in the bus for Toulon?

The WAITER *is left facing* MONSIEUR HENRI, *who hasn't moved.*

Waiter. They'll never know what she was doing . . . she isn't hurt, she's dead. As they drove out of Marseilles the bus crashed into a gasoline truck. The other passengers were only cut by the glass. She's the only one . . . I saw her. They've laid her out in the police van. There's a tiny mark on her temple. You'd say she was asleep.

M. Henri [*does not seem to have heard; his hands driven into the pockets of his coat, he walks past the* WAITER; *in the doorway he turns round*]. Make out my bill. I'm leaving.

He goes out.
Curtain.

ACT THREE

The Station restaurant in shadow. It is night. A vague light only comes from the platform where only the signal lamps are lit. There is a strange humming noise coming from faraway. The restaurant is empty. The chairs are piled on the tables. The stage is empty for a moment.

Then one of the doors from the platform opens slightly. M. HENRI enters, bringing ORPHEUS behind him, hatless, wearing a mackintosh. He is haggard, exhausted.

ORPHEUS [*looking round without understanding*]. Where are we?

M. Henri. Don't you know?

Orpheus. I can't walk any farther.

M. Henri. You can rest now. [*Picks a chair off a table.*] Have a chair.

Orpheus [*sitting down*]. Where are we? What did I have to drink? Everything's been turning round and round. What's been happening since yesterday?

M. Henri. It's still yesterday.

Orpheus [*realizing suddenly and crying out, trying to rise*]. You promised.

M. Henri [*laying his hand on his shoulder*]. Yes, I promised. Keep still. Relax. Have a cigarette?

He holds out a cigarette, which ORPHEUS *takes mechanically.*

Orpheus [*still looking round while the match burns*]. Where are we?

M. Henri. Guess.

Orpheus. I want to know where we are.

M. Henri. You told me you wouldn't be frightened.

Orpheus. I'm not frightened. All I want to know is if we've arrived at last.

M. Henri. Yes, we've arrived.

Orpheus. Where?

M. Henri. Just a little patience. [*He strikes another match, follows the wall round until he finds the electric light. A tiny noise in the shadows, and a bracket lights up on the back wall, throwing out a meager light.*] D'you know now?

Orpheus. It's the station restaurant. . . .

M. Henri. Yes.

Orpheus [*rising*]. You were lying, weren't you?

M. Henri [*pushing him back in the chair*]. No. I never lie. Keep still. Don't make a noise.

Orpheus. Why did you come into my room just now? I was lying on that tumbled bed. Utterly wretched. I was almost happy, shut up in my misery.

M. Henri [*in a low voice*]. I couldn't bear to see you suffer.

Orpheus. What difference could it make to you if I were suffering?

M. Henri. I don't know. It's the first time it's happened. Something strange began to fail inside me. If you had gone on weeping, suffering, it would have begun to bleed like a wound. . . . I was almost leaving the hotel. I put down my suitcase and came back again to comfort you. Then, as you wouldn't be comforted, I made you that promise to keep you quiet.

Orpheus [*taking his head in his hands*]. I want to believe you with all my strength, but I don't believe you, no.

M. Henri [*laughs a little silently, then he pulls* ORPHEUS' *hair*]. Stubborn as a mule, aren't you? You're crying, and groaning and suffering, but you don't want to believe me. I like you very much. If I hadn't liked you so much, I'd have gone away yesterday as I always do. I wouldn't have gone into that room where you were sobbing. I can't bear grief. [*He pulls his hair again with a strange sort of tenderness.*] Soon you won't be weeping any more—you won't have to ask yourself if you should or should not believe me.

Orpheus. Is she coming?

M. Henri. She is already here.

Orpheus. Here? [*Crying out suddenly.*] But she's dead. I saw them carry her away.

M. Henri. You want to understand, don't you? It's not enough that fate is making an enormous exception for you. You took my hand without a tremor, you followed me without even asking who I was, without slackening speed the whole night through, but on top of everything, you want to understand.

Orpheus. No. I want to see her again. That's all.

M. Henri. You aren't more curious than that? I bring you to the doors of death, and you think of nothing but your little friend. . . . You're perfectly right—death deserves nothing but your scorn. She throws out her huge nets, grotesque, enormous. An idiot, a clumsy reaper, capable of chopping off her own limbs with the rest. [*He has sat down near* ORPHEUS, *a little tired.*] I'm going to tell you a secret, just for yourself, because I'm fond of you. There's just one thing about death no one knows. She's very kindhearted, horribly kindhearted. She's afraid of tears and grief. Every time she can, whenever life allows her, she does it quickly . . . she unties, relaxes, while life persists, clutching blindly, even if the game is lost, even if the man cannot move, if he is disfigured, even if he might suffer always. Death alone is a friend. With the tip of her finger she can give the monster back his face, soothe the soul in torment she delivers.

Orpheus. She has stolen Eurydice! This friend of yours! With her finger she has destroyed the young Eurydice, the gay Eurydice, the smiling Eurydice.

M. Henri [*rising suddenly as if he has had too much, then brusquely*]. She's giving her back to you.

Orpheus. When?

M. Henri. At once. But listen carefully. Your happiness was over anyway. Those twenty-four hours, that pitiful little day, was all life had in store for you—your life— your cherished life. Today you wouldn't have been weeping because she was dead, but because she'd left you.

Orpheus. That's not true! She never went to meet that horrible man!

M. Henri. No. But she didn't come back to you either. She took the bus for Toulon alone, without money, without baggage. Where was she flying to? What was she exactly, this little Eurydice you thought you could love?

Orpheus. Whatever she is, I love her still. I want to see her again. Ah, I beg you, give her back to me, however imperfect. I want to suffer and be ashamed because of her.

I want to lose her, and find her again. I want to hate her, and rock her gently afterward, like a little child. I want to struggle, to suffer, to accept . . . I want to live

M. Henri [annoyed]. Of course you'll live. . . .

Orpheus. With the mistakes, the failures, the despair, the fresh starts . . . the shame.

M. Henri [looks at him, scornful and tender; murmurs]. Poor boy. . . . [He goes to him, and says in a different voice.] Good-by. The moment has come. She's out there, on the platform, standing on the same spot where you saw her yesterday for the first time—waiting for you, eternally. Do you remember the condition?

Orpheus [already looking at the door]. Yes.

M. Henri. Say it out loud. If you forget, I can do nothing more for you.

Orpheus. I mustn't look at her.

M. Henri. It won't be easy.

Orpheus. If I look at her just once before the dawn, I lose her again forever.

M. Henri [stops, smiling]. You don't ask me why or how any more?

Orpheus [still looking at the door]. No.

M. Henri [still smiling]. Fine. Good-by. You can start again from the beginning. Don't try and thank me. I'll see you later.

He goes out. ORPHEUS stands for a moment without moving, then goes to the door and opens it on the deserted platform. First he says nothing, then in a low voice, he asks without looking.

Orpheus. Are you there?

Eurydice. Yes, my darling. What a long time you've been.

Orpheus. I've been allowed to come back and fetch you. . . . Only I mustn't look at you before the morning.

Eurydice [appearing]. Yes, I know. They told me.

Orpheus [taking her hand and pulling her along without looking at her; they cross the stage in silence until they reach a bench]. Come. We can wait for morning here. When the waiters arrive for the first train, at dawn, we shall be free. We'll ask them for some nice hot coffee and something to eat. You'll be alive. You haven't been too cold?

Eurydice. Yes. That's the worst part. The terrible cold. But I've been forbidden to talk about anything. I can only tell you what happened up to the moment when the driver smiled into his little mirror and the gasoline truck fell on us like a mad beast. [*Pause. She adds in a little voice.*] After that I can't tell you anything.

Orpheus. Are you comfortable?

Eurydice. Oh yes—here against you.

Orpheus. Put my coat around your shoulders.

Puts his coat round her; pause; they are happy.

Eurydice. Remember the waiter from the *Comédie Française?*

Orpheus. We'll see him again tomorrow.

Eurydice. And the beautiful silent cashier? Maybe we'll know what she thought of us at last? It's so convenient to be alive again. . . . As if we'd just met for the first time. [*She asks him as she did that first time.*] Are you good, or wicked? What's your name?

Orpheus [*entering into the game and smiling*]. It's Orpheus. What's yours?

Eurydice. Eurydice. . . . [*Then gently she adds.*] Only this time we've been warned. [*She hangs her head, then says after a tiny pause.*] Please forgive me. You must have been so afraid. . . .

Orpheus. Yes. When I saw you downstairs, lying in the van, it all stopped. I wasn't afraid any more.

Eurydice. Did they put me in a van?

Orpheus. A police van. They laid you out on a bench at the back, with a policeman sitting beside you, like a little thief who had been arrested.

Eurydice. Was I ugly?

Orpheus. There was a little blood on your temple. That's all. You seemed to be asleep.

Eurydice. Asleep? If you knew how I was running. I was running as fast as I could go, like a mad thing. [*She stops; there is a tiny pause; she asks.*] You must have suffered horribly?

Orpheus. Yes.

Eurydice. Please forgive me.

Orpheus [*in a low voice*]. There's no need.

Eurydice [*after another pause*]. If they brought me back to the hotel it must have been because I was still holding my letter. I had written to you in the bus before we started. Did they give it to you?

Orpheus. No. They must have kept it at the police station.

Eurydice. Ah! [*She asks, worried suddenly.*] Do you think they'll read it?

Orpheus. They may.

Eurydice. D'you think we could stop them reading it? Couldn't we do something straightaway? Send someone there, telephone them, tell them they have no right?

Orpheus. It's too late.

Eurydice. But I wrote that letter to you! What I said was only for you. How could anyone else possibly read it? How could anyone else say those words? A fat man, with a dirty mind, perhaps, an ugly, self-satisfied, fat old man? He'll laugh, he'll surely laugh when he reads my agony. Oh, stop him, stop him, please—please stop him reading it! It makes me feel as if I were naked in front of a stranger.

Orpheus. They may not even have opened the envelope.

Eurydice. I hadn't time to close it! I was just going to when the truck crashed into us. Probably that's why the driver looked at me in the glass. I put my tongue out, it made him smile, and I smiled too.

Orpheus. You smiled. You could still smile?

Eurydice. Of course not. I couldn't smile. You don't understand! I had just written you this letter where I told you I loved you, that I was suffering, but I had to go away. . . . I put out my tongue to lick the envelope, he made a crack as all those boys do, and everyone smiled. [*She stops, discouraged.*] Ah, It's not the same when you describe it. It's difficult. You see, it's too difficult.

Orpheus [*in a low voice*]. What were you doing in the bus for Toulon?

Eurydice. I was running away.

Orpheus. You had the letter from Dulac?

Eurydice. Yes, that's why.

Orpheus. Why didn't you show me the letter when I came back?

Eurydice. I couldn't.

Orpheus. What did he say in the letter?

Eurydice. To meet him on the eight-twelve train, or else he'd come and fetch me.

Orpheus. Is that why you ran away?

Eurydice. Yes. I didn't want you to see him

Orpheus. You didn't think he might come and I'd see him just the same?

Eurydice. Yes, but I was a coward. I didn't want to be there.

Orpheus. You've been his mistress?

Eurydice [*crying out*]. No! Is that what he told you? I knew he would, and you'd believe him! He's been chasing me for a long time, he hates me. I knew he'd tell you about me. I was afraid.

Orpheus. Why didn't you tell me yesterday, when I asked you to tell me everything? Why didn't you tell me you'd been his mistress?

Eurydice. I wasn't.

Orpheus. Eurydice, now it would be better to tell me everything. No matter what happens, we are two poor wounded beings sitting on this bench, two poor souls talking without daring to look at each other—

Eurydice. What must I say to make you believe me?

Orpheus. I don't know. That's what's so terrible. . . . I don't know how I'm ever going to believe you. . . . [*Pause; he asks, gently, humbly.*] Eurydice, so I won't have to worry afterward, when you tell me the simplest things—tell me the truth now, even if it is terrible. Even if it will hurt me horribly. It can't hurt any more than the air I haven't been able to breathe since I've known you lied to me. . . . If it's too difficult to say, don't answer me, but please don't lie. Did that man tell the truth?

Eurydice [*after an imperceptible pause*]. No. He was lying.

Orpheus. You've never belonged to him?

Eurydice. Never.

There is a pause.

Orpheus [*in a low voice, staring straight in front of him*]. If you're telling me the truth, it should be easy to see. Your eyes are as clear as a pool of water. If you're lying, or if you aren't sure of yourself, a dark green circle forms and shrinks around the pupil. . . .

Eurydice. The dawn will soon be here, my darling, and

you can look at me. . . . [*Gently.*] Don't talk any more.
Don't think. Let your hand wander over me. Let it be
happy all alone. Everything will become so simple if you
just let your hand love me alone. Without saying anything
more.

Orpheus. D'you think that's what they call happiness?

Eurydice. Yes. Your hand is happy at this moment. It
doesn't ask anything more of me than to be there, obedient and warm beneath it. Don't ask anything more of me,
either. We love each other, we are young; we're going to
live. Agree to be happy, please. . . .

Orpheus [*rising*]. I can't.

Eurydice. If you love me. . . .

Orpheus. I can't.

Eurydice. Be quiet, then, at least.

Orpheus. I can't do that either! All the words haven't
yet been said. And we must say them all, one after the
other. We must go now to the very end, word by word.
And there are plenty of them!

Eurydice. My darling, be quiet, I beg you!

Orpheus. Can't you hear? A swarm of them has been
around us ever since yesterday. Dulac's words, my words,
your words, all the words that brought us here. And the
words of all the people who looked at us as if we were
two animals being led along. The ones that haven't been
spoken yet, but which are there, attracted by the aroma
of the rest; the most conventional, the most vulgar, the
ones we hate the most. We're going to say them; we're
surely going to say them. They must always be said.

Eurydice [*rises, crying out*]. My darling!

Orpheus. Ah, no! I want no more words—enough!
We've choked ourselves with words since yesterday. Now
I've got to look at you.

Eurydice [*throwing herself against him, holding him
close to her with her arms round his waist*]. Wait, wait,
please wait. What we must do is get through the night.
It will soon be morning. Wait. Everything will be simple
again. They'll bring us coffee, rolls and butter. . . .

Orpheus. I can't wait till morning. It's too long to wait
until we're old. . . .

Eurydice [*still holding him, her head pressed to his
back, imploringly*]. Oh, please, please, don't look at me,
my darling, don't look at me just yet. . . . Maybe I'm

not the person you wanted me to be. The one you invented in the happiness of the very first day. . . . But you can feel me, can't you, here against you? I'm here, I'm warm, I'm sweet, and I love you. I'll give you all the happiness that is in me. But don't ask more of me than I can give. . . . Don't look at me. Let me live. . . . I so much want to live. . . .

Orpheus. Live! Live! Like your mother and her lover, perhaps, with baby talk, smiles, and indulgences, and then a good meal, a little love-making, and everything's all right. Ah, no! I love you too much to live! [*He has turned round and looked at her. They are standing face to face, separated by an appalling silence; suddenly he asks, in a low voice.*] Did he hold you to him, that horrible man? Did he touch you with those hands all covered with rings?

Eurydice. Yes.

Orpheus. How long have you been his mistress?

Eurydice [*replying to him now with the same eagerness to lacerate herself*]. For a year.

Orpheus. Is it true you were with him two days ago?

Eurydice. Yes, the night before I met you; he called for me after the performance. He made a scene. He made a scene every time.

Orpheus. What scene?

The little MANAGER *appears, in agony, awkward, clumsy. He raises his little hat before speaking.*

Manager. He threatened to send me away, monsieur. I'm his company manager, and each time he threatened to dismiss me.

Dulac [*entering, and exploding when he see the* MANAGER]. He's a fool! He loses everything! I won't keep such an idiot in my company.

Manager. Oh, Monsieur Dulac, I have to look after all the trunks, all the scenery, and I'm alone. I'll never manage! I'll never manage!

Dulac. He's a half-wit, I tell you. He's a half-wit!

Eurydice. It's your fault—you're always shouting at him. I'm sure if you talked to him gently, he'd understand. Listen, Louis darling. . . .

Manager. I'm listening, Eurydice. . . .

Eurydice. Listen, darling Louis, it's really very simple. You get to the station where we have to change. You get out of the train very quickly. You run to the baggage car. You count the trunks to make sure they haven't forgotten one. . . .

Manager. Yes, but the others put their suitcases down beside me and tell me to look after them and go away. And the platform is full of people hurrying along. . . .

Eurydice. You mustn't let them go away! You must run after them!

Manager. I can't watch the trunks if I'm running after them! I'll never be able to manage, I tell you, I'll never be able to manage. I'd much better go away. . . .

Dulac [*roaring*]. He's a fool! A fool, I tell you! This time it's settled. He leaves at Châtellerault!

Eurydice. Don't shout at him all the time. If you do, how can you expect him to understand?

Dulac. He'll never understand. I tell you he's an incompetent. He leaves the company at Châtellerault, and that's my final word!

Manager. Monsieur Dulac, if you fire me, I don't know what I shall do. I promise you I'll be very careful, Monsieur Dulac!

Dulac. You're fired! You're fired, I tell you!

Eurydice. I'll help you! I promise I'll manage so that he doesn't lose anything. . . .

Dulac. I know what your promises are worth! No, no, he's quite useless. Sacked, fired! Get out! [*And he pushes the little* MANAGER *out into the darkness.*]

Eurydice [*she fastens on to him, imploringly*]. I promise you he'll be careful. Dulac, I promise. . . .

Dulac [*looking at her*]. Oh, you're always promising, but you don't always keep your word.

Eurydice [*in a lower voice*]. Yes.

Dulac [*going to her, softly*]. If I keep him just once more, you'll be good to me?

Eurydice [*hanging her head*]. Yes.

DULAC *embraces her roughly.*

Dulac. Admit that that time you came with me because you wanted to, you little liar.

Eurydice [*pulling herself away from him*]. Because I wanted to? I spat every time you kissed me.

Dulac [*calmly*]. Yes, my dove.

Eurydice. As soon as you left me, I ran away. I undressed completely. I washed all over—changed my clothes. You never knew that, did you? [DULAC *laughs.*] Oh, I know you, my darling—you can laugh, but it's out of the wrong side of your face.

Dulac. You aren't going to tell me you believed in that scene for a whole year?

Eurydice. Don't pretend to be so damn clever!

Dulac. Don't pretend to be stupid, Eurydice. You aren't stupid at all. Did you, yourself, believe in that scene for a whole year?

Eurydice. What!

Dulac. It had become a mere formality, that threat. I made it so that you could save your dirty pride, and pretend you had a reason which forced you to follow me without admitting you enjoyed it.

Eurydice. You mean, it wasn't true, you wouldn't really have fired him?

Dulac. Of course not. [*And he laughs again, as he disappears into the shadows.*]

Eurydice. That's what happened every time. Forgive me, my darling.

Orpheus [*who has recoiled, in a low voice*]. I shall always see you with that man's hands on you. I shall always see you as he described you in that room.

Eurydice [*humbly*]. Yes, my darling.

Orpheus. He wasn't even jealous when he came to fetch you. He even knew you were a coward. That if he came to fetch you, you wouldn't stay with me. Because you are a coward, aren't you? He knows you better than I do.

Eurydice. Yes, my darling.

Orpheus. Explain, can't you? Why don't you try and explain?

Eurydice. How can I explain? Do you want me to lie to you? I am untidy, I am a coward. Ah, it's too difficult.

There is a pause. ORPHEUS *raises his head. He looks at* EURYDICE *who is standing humbly before him.*

Orpheus. If you loved me, why were you going away?

Eurydice. I thought I'd never be able to make you understand.

Mother [*exclaiming suddenly*]. What I don't understand is why everything seems so terribly sad to these children!

Vincent. I've always said: a little love, a little money, a little success, and life is wonderful!

Mother. A little love? A great deal of love! That child thinks she's invented the whole thing with her little musician. We've adored each other too, haven't we? We've often wanted to kill ourselves for each other's sake. Remember the time I tried to swallow vinegar? I took the wrong bottle. It was wine.

Vincent. Anyway, the details don't matter. What matters is that we've also loved each other passionately enough to die for it.

Mother. Well, are we dead?

Eurydice [*As the* MOTHER *and* VINCENT *fade out of sight*]. No, Mother. [*To* ORPHEUS.] You see, darling, we mustn't complain too much. . . . You were right. In trying to be happy, we might perhaps have become like them. . . .

Orpheus. Why didn't you tell me everything the first day? The first day I might have been able to understand. . . .

Eurydice. There's no more time. . . . [*She runs up the steps at the back, turns to take him in her arms, then tears herself away. A figure appears in the light, and she turns toward him.*] The waiter from the *Comédie Française!* Our very first character. How are you?

Waiter [*with an overelaborate gesture*]. Farewell, mademoiselle!

Eurydice [*smiling in spite of herself*]. You're very noble, very charming, you know. Good-by, good-by. [*The* WAITER *disappears. The* CASHIER *takes his place.*] Oh, you're the lovely silent cashier. I've always felt you had something to say to us.

Cashier. How beautiful you were when you came together through the music. Beautiful, innocent and terrible —like love itself.

Eurydice [*smiles at her and turns to go*]. Thank you, madame.

A young man appears and calls after her urgently.

The Young Man. Mademoiselle! Mademoiselle!

Eurydice. I think you're mistaken. I don't remember you at all.

The Young Man. I'm a clerk at the police station, mademoiselle. You have never seen me.

Eurydice. Ah! Then you must be the one who has my letter. Give it back to me, please, monsieur. Give it back.

The Young Man. I'm afraid that's impossible, mademoiselle.

Eurydice. I don't want that big, fat, dirty man to read it!

The Young Man. I can promise you the Inspector won't read it, mademoiselle. I realized at once it would be impossible for a man such as the Inspector to read that letter. I took it out of the file. The case is closed, no one will ever notice. I have it with me. I read it every day when I am alone. . . . But it's different for me. [*He bows, noble and sad, takes the letter from his pocket, and after putting on his spectacles, begins to read in his somewhat flat voice.*] "My darling, I'm in this bus, and you're waiting for me. I know I'm never coming back to you, and I'm miserable, miserable on your account. The people in the bus are looking at me. They think it's sad because I'm crying. I hate tears. They're such stupid things. For the sorrow I feel now, I would have liked not to cry. I'm much too miserable to cry. [*He resettles his voice, turns the page and continues.*] "I'm going away, my darling. Ever since yesterday I've been afraid, and when I was asleep you heard me say, 'It's so difficult.' A man is coming. He has had a letter given to me. I've never talked to you about this man, but he has been my lover too. Don't believe I loved him—you'll see him, no one could love him. But I thought so little of myself, and I didn't love you then, my darling. That's the whole secret. I didn't love you then. That's the only reason I'm going away. Not only because I'm afraid he'll tell you I belonged to him, not only because I'm afraid you may stop loving me. . . . I don't know if you'll ever understand, but I'm going away because I'm red with shame. . . ."

Orpheus. Forgive me, Eurydice.

Eurydice [*tenderly*]. There's no need, my darling. It's I who ask you to forgive me. I must go. [*And she disappears into the shadows.*]

Orpheus. Eurydice!

He runs to the back like a madman. She has disappeared.
ORPHEUS *is alone. He does not move. The morning*
breaks. A train whistles faraway. When the light of day
is almost real, the WAITER *enters, looking very much*
alive.

Waiter. Good morning, sir. Bitterly cold day. Can I get
you some coffee, sir?

ORPHEUS *does not reply. The* WAITER *takes this for a sign*
of assent, and begins to lift the chairs down from the
tables. A TRAVELER *passes on the platform, hesitates, then*
enters timidly. He is overloaded with suitcases and musical
instruments. It is Orpheus' FATHER.

Father. Oh, is that you, my boy? I didn't take the train
to Palavas, after all. Full. Full to bursting, my boy. And
those swine wanted me to pay the difference to travel
second. I got out. I'll complain to the management. A
traveler is entitled to a seat in all classes. They should
have let me travel second for nothing. Are you having
some coffee? [ORPHEUS *seems not to see him.*] I could
do with some myself. I spent the night in the waiting
room. I was anything but warm. [*He whispers in*
ORPHEUS' *ear.*] To tell you the truth, I slipped into the
first class. An excellent leather sofa, my dear. I slept like
a prince. [*The* CASHIER *enters and goes across the restau-*
rant, humming a traditional sentimental song. She sees
the father, and stops in her tracks, then tosses her head
and hurries away.] She loses a lot by daylight, that woman.
She's got a fine figure, but she looks extremely common. . . . Well, my boy, what are you going to do?
Night brings good counsel. Are you coming with me after
all?

Orpheus [*with an effort*]. Yes, father.

Father. I knew you'd never desert your old father!
We'll celebrate by having a good dinner at Perpignan. I
know of a wonderful restaurant, the Bouillon Jeanne-
Hachette, where for fifteen francs seventy-five, you can
have hors-d'oeuvres (including wine) or lobster, if you
pay an extra four francs; main dish—very generous, veg-
etables, cheese, sweet, fruit or pastries—wait, wait—
coffee and brandy, or sweet liqueurs for the ladies. The

little menu at the Jeanne-Hachette used to include a good cigar. . . .

During this speech, M. HENRI has come in quietly, and at this point, he advances on the FATHER, holding out a cigar.

M. Henri. Allow me?

Father [*looking at the cigar, and at MONSIEUR HENRI*]. What, what? Oh, thanks very much. [*He accepts the cigar, and the light offered by M. HENRI.*] Ah, delicious. A Merveillitas, isn't it?

M. Henri. Yes.

Father. Must have cost a packet, a cigar like that.

M. Henri. Yes.

Father. Don't you smoke?

M. Henri. No.

Father. I don't understand why you carry such expensive cigars if you don't smoke yourself. Maybe you're a traveling salesman?

M. Henri. That's it.

Father. Big business, probably?

M. Henri. Yes.

Father. Then I understand. You've got to soften up the customers. At the right moment, you pull out a Merveillitas. You ask him if he'll smoke? He accepts, of course. And bingo! it's in the bag. You're all so clever. I'd have adored to have been in business. Wouldn't you, my boy? [*ORPHEUS doesn't answer. He looks at him.*] You must snap out of it, my boy. Look, give him a Merveillitas too. If he doesn't finish it, I will. When I'm down in the mouth, a good cigar. . . . [*Neither ORPHEUS nor MONSIEUR HENRI gives any sign of having registered this remark. The FATHER sighs and adds more timidly.*] Well, we all have our tastes.

He goes back to smoking, with a glance now and then at the two silent men. The WAITER brings the coffee and sets it down on one of the tables.

M. Henri [*gently, after a pause*]. You must go back with your father, Orpheus.

Father [*helping himself to coffee*]. Of course he must. I've just been telling him so. . . .

M. Henri. You ought to listen to your father.

Father. I know how sad it is. I've suffered too. I lost a girl once I adored. A girl from Toulouse, a creature made of fire. Carried off in a week. Bronchitis. I sobbed like a child during the funeral. They had to take me into a café to recover. It hurts at first. Naturally. But one fine day—it took me like that—you have a bath, do up your tie, the sun is shining, you go into the street, and suddenly, bingo! you see the girls are pretty again. We're terrible, my boy, all the same, terrible scoundrels.

M. Henri. Listen carefully, Orpheus. . . .

Father. I don't say you take the first one who comes along. No. We aren't animals after all, and you're bound to feel a little awkward when you open the conversation. You say how lonely you are, how lost. And it's true, it's sincere. Ah, you can imagine how much that sort of talk can influence a woman! You'll say, of course, that I'm an old rogue, but I was still using the same technique ten years afterward.

Orpheus. Be quiet, Father.

M. Henri. Why should you want him to be quiet? He's talking to you as life will talk to you through every mouth; he's saying what you'll see tomorrow in every eye, if you get up and try to start life again. . . . But Eurydice can be given back to you forever. The Eurydice of your first meeting, eternally pure and young, eternally herself.

Orpheus [*looks at him, after a pause, shaking his head*]. No.

M. Henri [*smiling*]. Why not?

Orpheus. I hate death.

M. Henri [*gently*]. You're unfair. Why should you hate death? She alone can create the proper setting for love. You heard your father talking about life just now. It was grotesque, wasn't it, but that's what it is like. Go and wander round life's side shows with your little Eurydice, and you'd meet her at the exit with her dress covered with finger marks. Life would never have allowed you to keep Eurydice.

Orpheus. I don't want to die.

M. Henri. Then listen to your father, Orpheus. He can tell you about life.

Father [*who has been replenishing his coffee cup,*

turns at this]. Life? But life is wonderful, my boy. When you have your health and strength, it's all so simple. The whole secret—daily exercise. Ten minutes every morning. You don't need more, but it's those ten minutes that count. [*He gets up, and with the butt of his cigar between his teeth, begins to go through a ridiculous form of Swedish drill.*] One, two, three, four. One, two, three, four. One, two, three, four. One, two. One, two. One, two. One, two. If you do that you'll never have a sagging stomach, or varicose veins. Health through joy, joy through health, and vice versa.

M. Henri. You see, Orpheus. It's very simple!

Father [*sitting down again, puffing like a grampus*]. It's a question of will power. Everything in life is a question of will power. Now, you're unhappy, but you're young. I like a young man to be ambitious. Don't you want to be a millionaire? Oh, money, money! But that is life, my boy! Think that you might become very rich. Think of the women, my boy, think of love! Blondes, brunettes, redheads, peroxides! Such variety, such choice! And all for you. You're the sultan, you lift your finger. That one! She comes to you. And then it's a succession of enchanted nights. . . . Passion, cries, bites, mad kisses. . . . Or else on the divans of secret boudoirs, from five to seven, wrapped in rich furs. . . . I've no need to tell you more, my boy! Sensations! Every possible sensation. A lifetime of sensations. And where's your grief? Gone up in smoke. [*He makes a gesture, and becomes serious.*] That is not the whole of life. There's respectability, a social life. You're strong and powerful, a captain of industry. Board meetings with brilliant minds. You juggle with the economic safety of Europe. Then the strike. The armed workmen. Violence. You appear alone before the factory. A shot is fired and misses you. You don't move. In a voice of thunder, you speak to them. You castigate them. They hang their heads, go back to work. Beaten! It's magnificent. Then, on the advice of your best friends, you go in for politics. Honored, powerful, decorated, a senator. Always in the forefront. National funeral, flowers, a million flowers, muffled drums, long speeches. And I, modestly in a corner—a distinguished old man, but mastering my grief, erect and at attention. [*He declaims.*] "Let us pay the homage due to a father's grief!" [*It is too beautiful. He breaks down.*] Ah, my boy, my boy, life is wonderful.

M. Henri. You see, Orpheus.

Father. The man talking to you has suffered. He has drunk his cup to the very dregs. You wonder sometimes at my bent back, my premature white hairs, my child. If you knew how heavy is the weight of a lifetime on the shoulders of a man. . . .

He pulls in vain on the butt of his cigar. He looks at it, annoyed, then reaches for a match. M. HENRI goes to him, holding out his case.

M. Henri. Another cigar?

Father. Thank you. I'm embarrassed. Yes, yes, embarrassed. What an aroma! Tell me, have you heard it said that the girls who make these roll them on their thighs? [*He sighs.*] Their thighs. . . . [*He lights the cigar.*] What was I saying?

M. Henri. The weight of a lifetime. . . .

Father [*who has lost his lyric fervor*]. How do you mean, the weight of a lifetime?

M. Henri. If you knew how heavy the weight of a lifetime can be on a man's shoulders.

Father. Ah! That's right. If you knew how heavy the weight of a lifetime can be. . . . [*He stops, takes a pull at his cigar, and concludes simply.*] Well, it's heavy, my boy. Extremely heavy. [*He inhales a deep breath with delight.*] Marvelous. [*He winks at M. Henri.*] I feel as if I'm smoking the thigh itself! [*He starts to laugh and chokes in the smoke. M. HENRI returns to Orpheus.*]

M. Henri. You've listened to your father, Orpheus? Fathers are always right. Even the foolish ones. Life is made in such a way that foolish fathers know as much, sometimes more than clever fathers. [*He moves away for a moment, then suddenly comes back to Orpheus.*] Supposing life had held in store for you a day when you would have found yourself alone beside your living Eurydice.

Orpheus. No.

M. Henri. Yes. One day or the next, in a year, in five years, in ten, if you like, without stopping loving her, perhaps, you might have realized you didn't want Eurydice any more, that Eurydice didn't want you either.

Orpheus. No.

M. *Henri.* Yes. It might have been as stupid as that. You'd have become the man who'd been unfaithful to Eurydice.

Orpheus [*crying out*]. Never!

M. *Henri.* Why do you protest so loudly? For my benefit, or for yours? [*He makes a gesture*]. In any case, Eurydice might already have abandoned you.

Orpheus [*plaintively this time*]. No.

M. *Henri.* Why not? Because she loved you yesterday?

Orpheus. We could never have stopped loving each other.

M. *Henri.* Maybe she wouldn't have stopped loving you. It's not so easy to stop loving someone. Tenderness is a stubborn emotion, you know. She might perhaps have had a way of giving herself to you, before going to meet her lover, so humbly, so gently, that you might almost have known a little of the old happiness.

Orpheus. No! Her love for me would have lasted forever, until she was old beside me, and I was old beside her.

M. *Henri.* No, little man. You're all the same. You thirst for eternity, and after the first kiss you're green with fear because you have a vague feeling it can never last. Vows are soon exhausted. Then you build houses, because stones at least will endure. You have a child. You lightly stake the happiness of that tiny, innocent recruit to this uncertain battle on the most fragile thing in the world— your love of man and woman. And it dissolves and crumbles. It falls to pieces exactly as if you'd made no vows at all. [*The* FATHER *has fallen asleep. He begins to snore gently.*] Your father's snoring, Orpheus. Look at him. He's ugly. And pitiful. He has lived. Who knows? Maybe he hasn't been as stupid as he seemed just now. Maybe there has been a moment when he touched the heights of love and beauty. Look at him now, clinging to existence, with his poor snoring carcass sprawled over there. Look at him well. People believe that the wear and tear on a face is the fear of death. What a mistake! It's the fear of life. Take a good look at your father, Orpheus, and remember Eurydice is waiting.

Orpheus [*suddenly, after a pause*]. Where? What must I do?

M. *Henri.* Put on your coat, it's cold this morning.

Walk out of the station. Follow the main road. You'll see a little wood of olives That's the place.

Orpheus. What place?

M. Henri. Your rendezvous with death. At seven o'clock. It's nearly that now. Don't keep her waiting.

Orpheus. I'll see Eurydice again?

M. Henri. Immediately.

Orpheus. Very well. [*He crosses to the door, then turns and hesitates, looking at his father. He bends down and kisses the sleeping old man, then turns back to the door, with a last look at M. HENRI.*] Good-by.

M. Henri. Au revoir, my friend.

ORPHEUS *has gone. Suddenly the lights change, leaving the station in darkness, and M. HENRI standing quite still, his hands in his pockets. He calls softly and urgently.*

Eurydice! [*She enters, and stands in a shaft of light.*]

Eurydice. He's agreed?

M. Henri. Yes, he's agreed.

Eurydice. Will he be able to look at me?

M. Henri. Yes. Without ever being afraid of losing you.

Eurydice. Oh, my darling, come quickly, quickly.

In the distance a clock begins to strike. With the last strokes, the music begins to build to a crescendo, and ORPHEUS *appears, hesitating, as if dazzled by the light. She turns, to take him in her arms.*

My darling, what a long time you've been!

M. HENRI *turns and walks away into the darkness, leaving the two lovers clasped in a long embrace.*

Curtain.

THE ERMINE

(L'HERMINE)

Translated by

MIRIAM JOHN

CHARACTERS

Mr. Bentz
Frantz
Monime
Philippe
Florentine
Mrs. Bentz
Marie-Anne
Maid to Mrs. Bentz
La Duchesse de Granat
Her Maid
Urbain
Joseph
First Police Officer
Second Police Officer
Third Police Officer

THE ERMINE

ACT ONE

SCENE—*The hall of a country house, with windows open wide onto a garden.*

TIME: Evening.

MR. BENTZ *and* FRANTZ *stand facing each other.*

BENTZ [*extending a hand*]. Well, Monsieur Frantz, it was nice seeing you. And I thought your friends were quite charming.

Frantz. Mr. Bentz, you can't let me go like this!

Bentz. That little cousin of yours is delightful. Gentle, too, I should imagine. I always longed to have a gentle wife; Mrs. Bentz is a demon.

Frantz. If I still haven't got the money by the day after tomorrow, the business will fold up. This is my last chance. I can't let it slip through my fingers.

Bentz. You're young.

Frantz. Not any longer.

Bentz. Bit of a romanticist, I guess. [*Pause. Sounds as of a vain effort to start up a car.*] What are they up to, those friends of yours? Still trying to start the car? What's the idea of having such an old crock?

Frantz. We're poor!

Bentz. I haven't got a car at all. [FRANTZ *shrugs.*] Oh, it isn't that I want to be a miser. I know very well I could have several cars if I wanted them; but to reach that happy state I've had to build up scores of businesses and watch them all collapse; I've had to make scores of fresh starts, my friend.

Frantz. I haven't got time to make scores of fresh starts. I've got to save this business, and to do that I must have money right away.

Bentz. I know how you feel. But you must have patience, too. Why always resort to me, instead of to patience?

Frantz. You've been saying that over and over again

for the last two years. But don't you realize I'm at the end of my tether now—I just can't go on any longer!

Bentz. All young men say that.

Frantz. Very well.

Silence.

Bentz. You're going to sell?

Frantz. Yes. Tomorrow.

Bentz. I'm not the monster you think me, you know. I like helping people. I might buy, if that would be any use to you. Oh, I don't say I could give you much for it. You won't get a great price for the business anyway, you know. Probably not even as much as you put into it. In fact, I'm very much afraid that all you'll get out of it in the end will be debts.

Frantz [*looks at him and murmurs*]. Swine!

Bentz. Tut-tut! Cigarette?

Frantz. Mr. Bentz, you're a rich man. All I want is enough money—just enough to live on and be happy.

Bentz. You're a sentimentalist, you know.

Frantz. All I know is that I'm a young man wanting to buy a little happiness. It would be so easy for you to put that happiness within my reach. All it needs is a——

Bentz. I have visits like yours every week.

Frantz. But you said I was your friend. . . .

Bentz. You are my friend, Monsieur Frantz. Both my wife and I think a great deal of you. Why the devil do we always have to be talking about money? You're the one that makes it difficult for us to be friends. [*He helps himself to a drink.*] Why can't we just quietly enjoy the pleasure of a good drink and intelligent conversation? I like talking to you.

Frantz. How I detest you.

Bentz. You shouldn't. Someone like me could be very useful to you—help you to give of your best.

Frantz. I don't want to give of my best. I want to be happy. For that, I need money.

Bentz. Would it be a girl friend, I wonder? You can confide in me. I might be able to help you. I have a very wide experience in such matters.

Frantz. I'm asking you for money, not advice.

Bentz. How extraordinarily tactless you are. First of all

you appeal to our friendship—you want me to part with a sizable sum of money for purely sentimental reasons—and then a while later you talk to me as though I were some petty pawnbroker about to snatch your watch from you.

Pause.

Frantz. I lost my temper. . . .
Bentz. Right. I'll prove to you that I have better manners than you. Maybe the well-bred Frenchman can take a lesson from the self-made Yankee. I'll save you the humiliation of apologizing by warning you right away that there's no point in it. I can't do anything about your business. But I'm still your friend.

He holds out his hand. Enter MONIME.

Ah! The little cousin.
Monime. Frantz, something awful has happened. Philippe says he'll never be able to get the car to go. Could you go and help him?

Exit FRANTZ, *muttering "Oh, all right," etc.*

Bentz. You don't smoke, mademoiselle?
Monime. I try. But I don't really like it much.

Silence.

Bentz. This must have been very jolly for you and your friends, this little moonlight treasure hunt. Frantz has some charming ideas. . . . You're quite a happy little band, by the look of it.
Monime. Yes. Philippe and Florentine are great fun. Florentine is a friend of mine. She came with us from Granat.
Bentz. I thought you were all at Vichy?
Monime. No, Granat. At my aunt's château.
Bentz. I had some business dealings with a Duc de Granat some time ago—a long time ago, in fact.
Monime. That must have been my uncle. He got killed in a riding accident.

Bentz. And the Duchess—is she related to Monsieur Frantz?

Monime. No, she's my aunt, not his. As a matter of fact we're not really cousins. Frantz is the son of a friend of my aunt's and was brought up with me.

Bentz. I see. And of course she always treated him like one of the family.

Monime. Well, not really. . . . He always wanted to go his own way . . . and when she tried to arrange a marriage for him, he wouldn't have anything to do with it.

Bentz. I see. . . . Your aunt was anxious to get him settled, then?

Monime. Yes, but it was a very bad match. She wanted him to marry the local miller's daughter. A great, tall, skinny girl who puts on the most awful airs just because she's got a bit of money. Oh, it was stupid! Besides, Frantz doesn't want to marry.

Bentz. He doesn't? All the same, his affairs are in a bit of a mess at the moment—I suppose you know—and it would be a way out. I rather gather that Madame de Granat has never thought of supporting him herself? [MONIME *looks hard at him.*] I must apologize for asking such a question, mademoiselle, but the fact is I seem to be getting myself mixed up in business discussions with Monsieur Frantz; he came to see me this evening to ask me to help him—financially. He was extremely pressing.

Pause. Enter FRANTZ. *He stands looking at them.*

Frantz. Were you requiring any more information, Mr. Bentz?

Bentz. I was simply expressing my surprise to this charming young lady at the fact that the Duchess is making no attempt to help you out of this spot you're in.

Frantz. You don't need to express surprise to anyone about what Madame de Granat does or does not do.

Bentz. How very quick-tempered you are—and tactless as usual!

The whole party comes in. FLORENTINE, *fair and laughing.* PHILIPPE, *obviously glad to be alive.* MARIE-ANNE, *an elderly companion, apparently frightened out of her wits. And* MRS. BENTZ.

Philippe. I think the old bus really *has* had it now. We might as well chuck it.

Florentine. This is *the* very end.

Mrs. Bentz. I must say I'm rather glad about it. It means that you'll all have to stay the night.

Marie-Anne. Oh, but that's quite impossible. Think of it, madame. Her Grace is expecting us. Eleven o'clock already! We should be back by now, and there are still sixty miles to go.

Philippe. On foot, too!

FLORENTINE *bursts out laughing.*

Florentine. Idiot!

Marie-Anne. What are we going to do, Monsieur Frantz? Whatever will Madame de Granat think?

Frantz. Isn't there a garage anywhere?

Mrs. Bentz. There is one on the way to Moulins, about six miles from here, but you'll never get a mechanic in the middle of the night. No, my snare is well and truly laid. I'm going to keep you all here.

Marie-Anne. Oh, this is really most unfortunate! The Duchess is waiting up for us. . . .

Florentine. I think it's wonderful, don't you?

Philippe. Terrific.

Florentine. We shall all sleep in the same room. . . .

Mrs. Bentz. Never fear, my dear. I have three rooms upstairs and you can have one each. As for your men friends, they can take potluck. One of them can shake down here on the divan. I'll have it made up. And the other can sleep in the summer house—tnere's a divan there too. My husband will be delighted to lend them some pajamas. Don't pull such a face, Frantz, Mr. Bentz has some very fine pajamas.

Marie-Anne. I'm sorry, Mrs. Bentz, it really isn't possible. We really must get back. The Duchess would never forgive me. . . .

Mrs. Bentz. But how can you possibly expect to get back?

Frantz. Isn't there at least a bicycle? I'm going to try to get to that garage.

Mrs. Bentz. No, there is *not* a bicycle. And the mechanic wouldn't come anyway. I know him. He's a lout.

You may as well resign yourself, my dear Frantz. Now don't make those cat's eyes of yours. Give in with a good grace, there's a dear boy.

Florentine. That's very good—he *does* make cat's eyes!

Monime. Cat's eyes?

Mrs. Bentz. My dear young lady, you don't mean to tell me that you're his cousin and you didn't know that he makes cat's eyes when he's angry? [MONIME *gives him a long look.*] But why are we all standing up? At least let's make ourselves comfortable.

Marie-Anne. Oh, dear me, this is most unsettling. Her Grace will simply not speak to me tomorrow. . . . She made me responsible for these young people, Mrs. Bentz. . . .

Mrs. Bentz. I promise you to return them unscathed.

Bentz. Too bad I haven't a car. But there is at least a telephone. I have to have that, to keep in touch with the stock market. Couldn't they phone to Granat?

Mrs. Bentz. Toby, you're the only one with any sense. You see, now everything can be arranged. The Duchess will forgive you, after all.

Marie-Anne. I wonder whether it is really advisable to tell her this way. . . .

Mrs. Bentz. We have no choice. I shall go and prepare the rooms. [*Exit.*]

Bentz. What number is it?

Monime. Granat 5.

Bentz. Give me Granat 5, please.

Florentine. Oh, Mr. Bentz, would you please ask for 7 as well, so that I can warn my mother?

Bentz. Hullo! Hullo! Give me Granat 7 as well. Thanks. [*He leaves the telephone and comes back to the others.*] Now, in a few minutes from now we shall all have our minds at rest and be able to enjoy the charm of this little unexpected party in peace, eh, Monsieur Frantz?

Frantz. Yes.

Silence for a while. BENTZ *hands round cigarettes.*

Marie-Anne. Monsieur Frantz, do you think the Duchess will ever forgive me?

Frantz. What else could we do? You don't think I want to stay here, do you?

Bentz. As I was saying, your cousin is charming, but you will have to teach her to enjoy smoking. There is no moment at which a woman is more seductive than when she is smoking a cigarette. Properly, of course.

Florentine. Do you find me attractive when I smoke, Mr. Bentz?

Bentz. Enormously.

Florentine. You see, Philippe? Please note that I can be enormously attractive.

Philippe. Duly noted.

Bentz. I should like to see my friend Frantz and his cousin in the same good spirits. Would they be hiding some secret grief, I wonder? Aha! If my wife were here, she'd say you were making your cat's eyes, young man. . . .

MONIME *looks furiously at* BENTZ, *who bursts out laughing.*

Philippe. Mr. Bentz, you mustn't forget that when Monime's about, Frantz is labeled "Please do not touch."

Marie-Anne. These children must be wondering what sort of welcome we shall have from the Duchess tomorrow, Mr. Bentz. That is if it is a welcome. I must say I wonder too. . . .

Bentz. This woman seems to be an ogress. [*Telephone rings.*] Ah, you see? . . . Hullo! Hullo! Granat 5? Hold on a moment, please. Now, which of you is going to take it?

Monime [*getting up*]. Is that you, Urbain? . . . It's Mademoiselle Monime. Is Madame de Granat in her room? Oh, she can't sleep . . . she was worrying . . . oh . . . would you please ask her if she could come to the phone, Urbain?

Marie-Anne. You see, Mr. Bentz, she's still up! Oh, good gracious me, what a state of affairs!

Bentz. Please don't get upset. Everything will be all right.

Monime. Is that you, Aunt? . . . Yes, it's Monime.

Florentine. Now for it!

Monime. No, Aunt, I'm dreadfully sorry . . . we're with Mr. and Mrs. Bentz. Frantz had some business to discuss here this evening. . . . We thought we should be back by eleven, but Philippe's car broke down. . . .

Philippe Luc . . . We can't possibly get back. . . . No,
I'm afraid not. There's no one to repair it. Mrs. Bentz
has very kindly said we can stay here for the night. . . .
We can get it repaired tomorrow. . . . But Aunt . . .
no, but really, Aunt . . . Well, if you wish, then, Aunt,
send Albert. But we're more than sixty miles away and he
wouldn't get here before two in the morning . . . we
shan't be home before four and we shall be terribly tired.
. . . Yes, really, Aunt . . . Very well, let him leave early
in the morning . . . we shall go to bed soon, and we'll
expect your call. . . . Yes, I think that really would be
better. Yes, Aunt, Marie-Anne is here. I'll put you on to
her.

Marie-Anne. It's all my fault . . . I know it only too
well, it's all my fault. . . . Good evening, your Grace.
But, your Grace . . . but your Grace . . . but your
Grace . . . Yes, I'll ask him to come to the telephone,
your Grace. . . .

She holds out the receiver to FRANTZ. FLORENTINE *blows
out her cheeks with laughter.*

Bentz. She certainly seems to be a fierce lady.

FRANTZ *listens respectfully, then hangs up.*

Marie-Anne. Oh, Monsieur Frantz, you hung up!
Frantz [*shrugging*]. So did she.
Bentz [*moving close*]. Tact, my boy, tact. Why kill the
goose that lays the golden eggs?
Mrs. Bentz [*reappearing*]. The rooms are ready. Has
everything been settled?
Monime. Not very satisfactorily, I'm afraid, Mrs. Bentz.
We're being called for at five o'clock. I do hope that's all
right for you. It seems awful to abuse your hospitality like
this.
Mrs. Bentz. Five o'clock? Madame de Granat seems
very anxious not to leave you at my mercy any longer than
she can help.
Marie-Anne. You must admit, Mrs. Bentz, that it is a
little unusual for a young lady of noble birth to spend the
night at a strange house.
Mrs. Bentz. But you are here, too, mademoiselle. Young
girls go anywhere with a chaperon, even in France.

Marie-Anne. I quite realize that, Mrs. Bentz. But for a great lady such as her Grace, there is always tradition to think of.

Bentz. Now that's the sort of thing we Yankees find quite fascinating, isn't it, darling?

The telephone rings.

Bentz. Here's the other number, laughing lady!

Florentine. Hullo! Is that Emile! Would you ask my mother to come to the phone, please? Hullo . . . is that you, Mummy? . . . Oh, Mummy, such an upheaval . . . we've had a breakdown about sixty miles away. There's Monime, Marie-Anne, Frantz, and another young man—rather charming. We're spending the night with some awfully nice people Frantz came to see. Yes . . . yes, I shall be home at about six in the morning. Yes, six. 'By then, Mummy. [*To the others.*] Well, that's that.

Bentz. Nice work.

Florentine. Oh, I'm used to this sort of thing.

Bentz. And how about Mademoiselle Monime—is she used to it?

Monime. I don't go out very much.

Marie-Anne. It is evident that you do not know her Grace, Mr. Bentz! Oh, I am not looking forward to our return!

Bentz [*to his wife*]. You know, I figure, my dear, that we've become unwilling accomplices in some sort of family drama. Mademoiselle Florentine, you don't seem to me to be the timid type. . . . Does the lady really deserve this baleful reputation?

Marie-Anne. Oh, Mr. Bentz!

Florentine. You couldn't imagine a sweeter old lady!

Marie-Anne. But, Mademoiselle Florentine, that's absurd. . . .

Everyone laughs, except FRANTZ *and* MARIE-ANNE.

Bentz. I can't help feeling relations must be extremely strained between the Duchess and our moody young friend here, who loses his temper so easily.

Philippe. You should see them together—it's too absurd for words. The Duchess fixes Frantz with a stony stare from behind her fan, and Frantz just sits there and scowls back at her. They hardly ever speak to each other, or, if one of them does say something, the other never answers.

Monime. My aunt treats Frantz very badly. When he is at Granat, hardly a day passes without her finding some way or another of annoying him.

Bentz. Looks like Granat is steeped in melodrama. How very fortunate that you are there to console him, mademoiselle.

Monime. Oh, yes. . . .

They all smile.

Frantz [rising abruptly]. Mrs. Bentz, please forgive me —but it's past midnight, and we have to leave very early. May I ask you to show Monime her room—she'll be very tired in the morning. . . .

Monime. Frantz! You must be mad! I'm perfectly capable of sitting up like everyone else. . . . Oh, now I feel embarrassed. You make me look an idiot.

Bentz. Be assured we understand everything, mademoiselle. You were treating us to some charming details, and I guess our friend Frantz was afraid they might become a little embarrassing for him.

Monime. What on earth is the matter, Frantz? I don't want to go to bed. . . .

Marie-Anne. It is true that at Granat her Grace insists that everyone should retire at eleven o'clock.

Monime. But we're not at Granat.

Frantz [gently]. Please, little one, for my sake . . . go to bed. You'll be tired in the morning.

Monime [who has been looking at him]. Yes . . . I'll say good night then, Mrs. Bentz . . . if you'll excuse me. . . .

Bentz. How docile the little cousin is. . . . Courage, mademoiselle. He looks very frightening, but I know him . . . his bark is worse than his bite. . . .

Mrs. Bentz. Do be quiet, Toby; you're being very silly. Frantz is quite right. We shouldn't be keeping them here talking when they have to get up so early. . . .

Florentine. Oh, we're used to it.

Mrs. Bentz. No . . . you'll be dead tired tomorrow and the journey will be dreadful for you. No, I should never forgive myself for enjoying your charming company at that price. [*She rings.*] Good night, monsieur, we shall meet again tomorrow morning. At five, I shall be out in the garden in overalls, cutting roses. You'll be sleeping, I suppose, won't you, Toby?

Bentz. Definitely. [*He shakes hands with* MARIE-ANNE *and* PHILIPPE. *To* FLORENTINE.] Good-by for the present, mademoiselle. You know, I really do find you very attractive when you smoke; and when you smile, too.

Florentine. Thank you. I'll try to do both at once.

Bentz [*to* MONIME]. Good night, mademoiselle. You'll never be happy if you let him frighten you.

Mrs. Bentz [*to the* Maid]. Louise, show Monsieur the room you have prepared in the summer house and make up the divan here for Monsieur Frantz. Now [*to* FLOREN-TINE *and* MONIME] if you will follow me, I will show you your rooms.

Farewells all round. FRANTZ *is left alone with* BENTZ.

Bentz. You're in love with Mademoiselle Monime, aren't you—and you need money so that you can marry her?

Frantz [*making toward him*]. Mind your own damned business! You say I'm tactless with the people who could help me—well, so I am!

Bentz. You seem to be furious. Maybe I hit the nail on the head? [*Pause, while they stare at each other.*] I think it's charming.

Frantz. If you've kept me here to talk about that after refusing me the money, you really are a skunk.

Bentz. A-ah! May I point out that the only reason you are here is that your car broke down. Just that. Perhaps I might also point out that I don't have to be a skunk, as you put it, just because, having refused you money, I want to talk to you about yourself. In the eyes of the world we're friends, and that sort of conversation is quite usual among friends.

Frantz. It's what is known as a confidence. That's something that's given, not asked for.

Bentz. As opposed to money, which is asked for, but not always given.

Frantz. Quite so—as opposed to money. In other words, it's a subject you're not qualified to discuss.

Bentz. Come now, we're getting things mixed up and expressing ourselves clumsily as usual. Just now you were talking business. You asked me for money. I replied in kind. Now I've lost interest in your enterprise—I want nothing further to do with it. Right. But there's nothing to prevent our discussing personal matters, is there?

Frantz. What are you driving at?

Bentz. I am your friend, young man, and yet you won't confide in me.

Frantz. Your use of the word "friend" doesn't deceive either of us.

Enter MRS. BENTZ.

Bentz. Isn't that so, darling? I was telling him he is our friend.

Mrs. Bentz [*taking* FRANTZ *by the hand*]. Did he dare to doubt it?

Bentz. Yes. And he keeps on making those cat's eyes.

Mrs. Bentz. We must make him sit down and talk to us.

Bentz. We must. [*He serves drinks and passes them cigarettes.*] You see, my dear, I've guessed everything. This attachment of our young friend to that hopeless business of his, that he keeps on wanting money for, amounts to something much more than the vanity and greed that usually prompt people in such matters. . . . This will appeal to you, my dear—you're a sentimentalist. . . . As I say, it was more than that. It was in order to achieve the conquest of Mademoiselle Monime that the young man has been making such desperate efforts these past two years.

Mrs. Bentz. Oh! Frantz, dear, is that true?

Pause. FRANTZ *lowers his eyes and remains silent.*

Bentz. Come now, my boy, answer the lady.

Frantz [*who has got up abruptly and walked away from them*]. You said I was to sleep in this room, didn't you, Mrs. Bentz? Do you think your maid could please prepare my bed? I'm tired.

Mrs. Bentz. Toby, you are an idiot. . . . Frantz . . . Frantz, dear, you know what a terrible tease my husband is. He just couldn't resist the desire to pull your leg. Frantz, I do apologize for him. I'm sure he's sorry.

Bentz. I beg you not to be angry with me.

Mrs. Bentz. It's going to cost him a lot of dollars to buy his pardon. Come back, Frantz dear, I promise you he'll help you. [*They all sit down again.* Mrs. Bentz *continues after a silence.*] I'm your friend, Frantz. You can talk to me, absolutely frankly. Give me your hand. Now, tell me honestly, do you really love Monime, and is it for her you're working so hard?

Frantz. Yes, I love her.

Mrs. Bentz. How thrilling! They make such a delicious couple, don't you think, Toby?

Bentz. Yes. Does she love you?

Pause.

Mrs. Bentz. Oh! Could anyone not love the dear boy?

Frantz. Yes. She loves me.

Bentz. Fine. But—do forgive the question—does she love you the way little girls love the first young man that talks to them one fine evening at some party or other— you understand me?

Mrs. Bentz. Toby! I won't let you be stupid tonight! One doesn't love Frantz that way. . . .

Bentz. I ask you that as a father might ask it. I don't believe it can ever be a good thing to encourage a union based on a little girl's whim.

Frantz. Monime loves me. I know.

Bentz. That's better. Said like that, it's believable. I know you're too intelligent to be mistaken about it. Now, can you tell me exactly what relation you are to the Duchess?

Frantz. I'm not any relation to her. My father was her doctor for twenty years. She helped me finish my studies when he died.

Bentz. U-huh. I didn't know how you stood. So Madame de Granat isn't expecting her niece to marry money?

Frantz. No. She's rich.

Bentz. I see. So obviously she's on the lookout for titles?

Frantz. Yes.

Bentz. Which you, as obviously, don't possess.

Frantz. No. [*He puts his head in his hands.*]

Mrs. Bentz. Frantz darling, don't be sad. Everything will be all right. We'll help you.

Bentz. One more thing. Has Mademoiselle Monime much influence on her aunt?

Frantz. No. What are you driving at?

Bentz. I've got a shrewd idea that, even if you have the money, you'll never get the Duchess's consent to the marriage. Is your cousin under age?

Frantz. Yes.

Bentz. Are you sure the money is hers and not her aunt's?

Frantz. Oh, Monime hasn't any money. Her father went bankrupt and killed himself. The fact is, all the money belongs to her aunt.

Bentz. I see. Well, of course that makes the whole thing impossible!

Frantz. But when I have money I shall take Monime away, and then when she comes of age, we can get married!

Bentz. But her aunt won't give her a sou.

Frantz. No, but if my business goes well, I shall have enough.

Bentz. Yes.

Frantz. Don't you see that patience is just not enough? I must have money right away. The business isn't too bad, you know, Mr. Bentz. It's already doing better this year. If I can clear off this payment the day after tomorrow, I shall be able to make some money.

Bentz. No, Monsieur Frantz. That business of yours is no good.

Frantz. But you were saying just now——

Bentz. Oh, you might have been able to flog the dead horse for a bit, and keep up the appearances of a large income. But what's the good, since you admit yourself that nothing will persuade the Duchess to accept you?

Frantz. But it doesn't matter to me whether she accepts me or not!

Bentz. I beg your pardon. It does to me. I can't put into this thing the considerable sums of money that are needed, with no other guarantee than your possible future success. I should have a lot more confidence in the nephew by marriage of the Duchess de Granat. Even though he may not possess your personal qualities.

Frantz. Then . . . you still refuse to help me out?

Bentz. I'm sorry. I thought you were going to reveal a more or less official romance—something it would have been possible to risk money on. But as things are, your situation is extremely tricky. In fact, if you ask my advice as a friend, I'd say give the girl up.

Frantz. Oh! I hate you. . . .

He hurls himself at BENTZ, *but* MRS. BENTZ *holds him back.*

Mrs. Bentz. Frantz, darling . . .

Frantz. Let go of me!

Mrs. Bentz. Frantz, I don't want—— Go away, Toby, leave him alone . . . he's beside himself. . . .

Bentz. I'm sorry.

Frantz. You . . . scum! To think I've told you everything—things I've never said to anyone else. It hurt too, but I thought you were going to pay for it in good hard cash. . . . And now you refuse me money . . . you . . . you . . . thieves! Let me go! Do you think you'd have got all this out of me if you hadn't promised me money? I've told you everything. . . . You've got to pay now . . . thieves!

Mrs. Bentz. Get out, Toby. . . . Please, Frantz. . . .

Bentz. You forget yourself. You are under my roof. I shall refrain from taking the obvious course.

He bows and leaves.

Frantz. Thief . . . thief . . .

Mrs. Bentz. Frantz, my little one . . .

Frantz. Leave me alone . . . you disgust me too.

There is a knock. It is the Maid *with the sheets and blankets.* MRS. BENTZ *helps her to make up the divan. She glances at* FRANTZ *from time to time, secretly. When the* Maid *leaves, she goes up to him.*

Mrs. Bentz. You mustn't harbor these hard feelings against me, darling. You can count on me as a friend. My husband is a businessman, and you know what they are—they only understand money. I'm a sentimentalist. I get very upset about his way of doing things.

Frantz. Go away.

Mrs. Bentz. I don't want to leave you in this state. Oh! you're feverish! Lie down on the bed—you'll feel better. [*He throws himself down on the bed.*] There . . . I'll stay at your bedside, like a nurse. . . . You mustn't give up hope. His bark is worse than his bite. He's really very weak. I can do just what I like with him. When I go to him for money to help some young man I'm truly fond of, he always gives it me. He says he's buying his freedom. I make it very expensive sometimes. How much do you need to clear off your debt, Frantz?

Frantz. A thousand dollars.

Mrs. Bentz. Really? Do you mean to say it's for that that you and my husband have been hurling insults at each other for the past hour? Toby really is unforgivable. But you know what businessmen are like. Money is money, no matter how much or how little. In private life it's quite different. He sometimes gives me checks for larger amounts than that without even asking me what I'm going to do with it. . . . I can't understand why you bother with these stupid business matters that bring you in so little money. That sort of thing's all right for Toby, but you're worth something much better. The idea of you scribbling away at figures and screaming your head off at the stock exchange—it's repellent! You should always be as you are now—lying there, with your arms behind your head, looking like a sulky child . . . you're adorable like that, darling. [*She sits down close to him and touches a stray lock of hair on his forehead.*] I'll help you myself, if you like, and you can give up that silly old business.

Frantz [*sitting up and looking at her. She also gets up*]. Get out.

Mrs. Bentz. What's the matter, Frantz? What have I said to hurt you?

Frantz. I said, get out.

Mrs. Bentz [*going toward the door*]. Sweet little idiot. Come back and see me when the megrims have gone. I'll always be happy to take an interest in you.

She goes out. FRANTZ *stays motionless for a while. Enter* PHILIPPE.

Philippe. Aren't you asleep yet?

Frantz. No, what about you?

Philippe. Your little Florentine's got under my skin.

Frantz. Go and find her then, she's bound to be waiting for you.

Philippe. You think so?

Frantz. Yes. Don't be shy—she sleeps with everybody.

Philippe. I'll stay and talk a bit.

Frantz. That's very decent of you. But you go on and find her.

Philippe. You look fed up. What did Bentz say?

Frantz. He refused.

Philippe. Refused? [*Silence.*] You're going to have to sell?

Frantz. Yes.

Philippe. Oh, I'm sorry, old man . . .

Frantz. Two years. This farce has been dragging on for two years. And all for this.

Philippe. What are you going to do? [FRANTZ *shrugs his shoulders.*] I told you when you first plunged into this thing that you weren't cut out to be a businessman.

Frantz. I knew it, too. But I can't just be content to earn a few thousand francs a month on a newspaper the way you do. I must have money.

Philippe. Who mustn't?

Frantz. I know, but for you it's just something to make jokes about. I haven't the strength to laugh about it any more. What a sinister sort of farce life is when you're young and poor!

Philippe. To be young and rich is a farce, too.

Frantz. I know, I know. No contact with life. Poor people have to invent that sort of myth to console themselves. But they don't mention what it's like to be the sort of young man that women don't smile at—that doesn't know how to behave with waiters and whose every gesture is studied and calculated. . . . Oh, yes, we've had contact with life all right! It's taught us not to be careless or wasteful. To be rational, sober, prudent. . . . Coming back from my father's funeral, I knew the whole business had been more than my family could afford. . . . Since then . . .

Philippe. I know something about that, too.

Frantz. Less than I do, it seems, since you're not prepared to do anything about it.

Philippe. "Do anything about it." . . . There's nothing

one can do. I want to be happy, too. Meanwhile I shall make the best of what I've got.

Frantz. Not me. . . .

Silence for a while.

Philippe. When we were studying, two years ago, you were the cheery one.

Frantz. Life is easy when you only talk about it in cafés. . . . But you have to face the real thing sooner or later.

Philippe. You're not really unhappy, though, are you?

Frantz. I'm poor.

Philippe. All the same, you've got a bit of money. And you have girl friends and men friends. . . .

Frantz. Do you really believe that's enough? [*Pause.*] When every day, at every single turn, you knock your head against the same old brick wall: poverty! When you know there's no way out. That you've got to choose between either the sort of upright, straightforward youth who brings up his brothers and sisters and maintains his old mother and gets pushed around by all and sundry, or else becoming a sort of travesty—like a draper's assistant on holiday. Imagination, idleness, generosity are vices for us, Philippe. We're specimens of "the poor." The sort they write books on morality for.

Philippe. Frantz, what's got into you? I've never seen you like this.

Frantz. I've been holding myself in for two years. Two whole years I've waited patiently. . . . I've clothed myself in all their virtues—put them all on as a worker puts on his overalls. I've been economical, prudent, practical. I've been lying for two years. I've cheated myself for two years and this is where it gets me.

Philippe. Why didn't you stay with us?

Frantz. The very reason I want money is to get away from you.

Philippe. Come back. We manage to be happy enough.

Frantz. Back to Lili, for instance, to the occasional round of drinks, sparkling conversation over coffee, earnest political discussions, the flicks. . . . No thanks.

Philippe. Not only that. There is such a thing as friendship.

Frantz. With you, perhaps . . . to some extent . . .

in so far as you are sane and fabulously good-humored. But as for the others—now be honest.

Philippe. You've been growing away from us for quite a while, now. But you'd soon take up the threads again.

Frantz. I'd rather leave the threads where they are. What am I missing? That great bore Martial, for instance, always wanting to drag you off to a brothel. Clement babbling politics all the time. And Jacques, with his lectures on literature. You certainly have to gird up your loins to resist that bunch. I couldn't do it any more.

Philippe. What are you going to do?

Frantz. Keep going. Live alone, I suppose.

Philippe. What will you do about money?

Frantz. What is there to do?

Philippe. Frantz! It's not as bad as that.

Frantz. It is.

Philippe. You haven't any money? Look at us. None of us has any money.

Frantz. You don't even begin to understand. You're still living the life of Boulevard Saint Michel and the Quartier Latin! Or else you've become resigned. I've been struggling for two years, understand? Two years, at a dead loss. I know what's what. And I'm not resigned.

Philippe. Well, then, there's nothing lost, my dear old chap. [*He stops short at a look from* FRANTZ.]

Frantz. Because I'm not resigned?

Philippe. The way you say that! [A *gesture from* FRANTZ.] Frantz!

Frantz. I can't stand it any more.

Philippe. Well, then, you must take some sort of action.

Frantz. Ah! These good friends who give encouraging advice. . . . What sort of action?

Philippe. My dear chap, you're not twenty-five; at our age there's a solution to everything. Work . . .

Frantz. I've tried to believe in that one for two years.

Philippe. I don't mean that sort of work. There's all your ideas. Your novel—what about that?

Frantz. Oh, I've said good-by to those illusions long ago. I haven't any talent. You're barking up the wrong tree, Philippe. You seem to think I'm suffering from some sort of belated *mal du siècle*—that I'm just looking for something to keep me employed. But I'm not. I'm the sort that wants to live and be happy. I need money to build up the kind of happiness I'm aiming at, and I know now that there is no way of getting it.

Philippe. And yet you were jolly near success. . . . If Bentz hadn't refused his help at the last minute.

Frantz. Any failure could tell you how many times he very nearly succeeded. But for me it'll be only once.

Philippe. You can't just cave in like that, old man.

Frantz. I just haven't any guts left, Philippe—can't you understand the feeling? This was a last chance, and it slipped through my fingers. It's all up now. It's harder this time because it's the last. That's all there is to it.

Philippe. How could you *not* succeed, with all the wealthy people you know?

Frantz. Another little illusion you'd better discard. Rich people never lend their friends money. They only offer them cups of tea and dainty sandwiches.

Philippe. Get married then.

Frantz. Why do you say that?

Philippe. It'd be a solution.

Frantz. To whom, for instance?

Philippe. A wealthy heiress!

Frantz. Look, I've no name, no looks to speak of, I'm not famous. . . . Besides, I should despise myself for the rest of my life if I were to go about it that way. Making love to a woman who doesn't attract you is as sordid as working.

Philippe. All the same, Charles got himself out of the same sort of mess by marrying that Argentinian.

Frantz. Mrs. Bentz has just given me to understand that if I were to sleep with her she would make her husband advance the money I need.

Philippe. And you refused? I'd have thought you'd take any chance that came.

Frantz. This isn't so much a chance as a superstition. In any case, I'm having nothing to do with it for the moment.

Philippe. Is it your little cousin that's having this effect on you?

Frantz. Possibly.

Silence.

Philippe. Frantz, do you realize that for two years we haven't talked about ourselves to each other at all?

Frantz. I know.

Philippe. It's you who've forced our friendship into this conspiracy of silence that'll probably be the death of it.

Frantz. Yes, it's me. [*Long silence, which* FRANTZ *eventually breaks, in formal conversational tones.*] Have you got a good story to cover at the moment?

Philippe. Yes. Two kids who've murdered an old woman, the grandmother of one of them, to get the money for a trip to Paris.

Frantz. What are they getting?

Philippe. Reform school. The older one may get a spot of jail.

Frantz. How old is he?

Philippe. Sixteen.

Frantz. Poor, I suppose? Will he stay there?

Silence.

Philippe. Pretty sure to.

Frantz. If I landed in jail one day, would you do anything about it?

Philippe. If I happened to have any money at the time, yes.

Frantz. Do people get very miserable in prison, I wonder?

Philippe. Our sort does, I imagine. Inside, as in the army, there are no pips for intelligence.

Frantz [*absently*]. Their grandmother. She'd probably been good to them when they were little. What did they say when the judge expressed the usual indignation?

Philippe. That an old woman isn't any use anyway.

Frantz. You know, one can admire that, Philippe! To kill your grandmother because you want to go to Paris. Don't you feel how terribly simple it is?—so much simpler than we imagine.

Philippe. Are you crazy?

Frantz. Not crazy enough, I'm afraid. However, that is one solution that's still open to me. If only my childhood were not so smothered in priests, and pious books, and mother love. . . .

Philippe. Are you trying to be funny, Frantz?

Frantz. Yes, I'm trying to be funny. I'm trying to live. Suppose I were to kill someone, too, in order to get my happiness? Do you think I could commit a crime,

Philippe? Seriously. Don't answer right away, and don't joke about it. You know me very well. Think, and then look me straight in the eye and tell me. Do you think I could commit a crime?

Philippe. No, Frantz.

Frantz. You mean from the moral point of view. Do you think that would stop me?

Philippe. No. Don't be angry, Frantz, but I simply think you wouldn't have the guts.

Frantz [*after a pause*]. Oh, I'm not angry.

Philippe. You'd have enough guts to talk about it probably and even to prepare it. But not to go through with it.

Frantz. You're probably right.

Philippe. In my job, I often get the chance to follow these things very closely. Killing's a tough business. Sometimes it's a long business, too. You have to have the sort of nerve that'll last to the bitter end.

Frantz. And you think I'm too much of a coward?

Silence.

Philippe. Why worry? . . . Look—why are you asking me all this?

Frantz. No reason. I was joking.

Philippe. You weren't, you know.

Frantz. No, that's true. I *was* toying with the idea, just to see how my nerves and muscles would respond. Now I know. I'm too much of a coward. You're right. There's nothing more to be said. [*He puts his head in his hands.*]

Philippe. Frantz, what is it? What's the matter?

Frantz. I'm too much of a coward. . . . I've managed to see where my happiness lies and blaze a trail to it across all the phony ideas I was brought up on, and I shan't have the guts to hold on to it. Philippe, we're friends. We talk for hours every day and yet I've never told you anything. Philippe, I'm in love with Monime. It's for her that I'm trying to get money. If I give up the idea of money, I must give up the idea of her as well.

Philippe. Is Monime rich?

Frantz. Her father died poor; all the money belongs to her aunt, and you can imagine Madame de Granat wouldn't think twice about me. I needed money to get

Monime away from there so that we could live together.
Bentz refused. I haven't a sou. I've got to sell my business. Monime can't belong to me because Bentz refuses me
money. Can't you see how odious and inadmissible it is!
Can't you understand why I want to shout myself
hoarse? [*Silence.*] You can look at me. You didn't say
what I expected just now. You felt I was too wretched
for you to say what was in your mind. You can say it;
I've been prepared for it for a long time. Go on, say it.
I know it already; it's because of that that I've grown
away from you over these two years. You say you've
noticed it. For two years, we have been having the sort
of conversation that strangers have. Once, remember, we
talked for a whole hour about how they make tar. You
and I. Just the two of us, alone together. During the
whole of that conversation I was feeling wretched and
hopeful. I wanted to tell you about it—about my
wretchedness, and about my hopes.

Philippe. Why didn't you?

Frantz. Because I was afraid of your thoughts, the way
I'm afraid of them now. I knew them already then. I
knew what turn they were going to take. What words
you would clothe them in. I could see a certain twist of
your mouth that I knew so well. One of those looks of
yours—the one I dislike most. I imagined all the futile
explanations I should——[*He has been almost shouting,
but stops suddenly. Silence.*] This scene surprises you, I
suppose? We must have been in short pants when I last
threw one. Living that café life, you've grown up,
Philippe, without noticing it. You've become a man.
You're already incapable of understanding me. Through
the expression of amazement on your face, I can read
in it the signs of your manhood. Signs of indulgence and
irony that have frightened me for two years. Come on,
say it, say it!

Philippe. But Frantz, what on earth's wrong with you?

Frantz. You know what's wrong with me. Say something!
Be amazed! Pity me for being in love with Monime!

Philippe. I'm not amazed, and I don't pity you.

Frantz. Don't pretend! This very minute you're remembering how shy I was with women when we used to go
to Montparnasse, and how they would always go off and
leave me, saying I was crazy. They'll have a good laugh

when you tell them, won't they? A better laugh than you, probably, because you're a bit frightened of me at the moment. . . . "Falling in love with a little girl!" you'll all say . . . "that *would* happen to *him*." . . . Go on, laugh, why don't you? Are you afraid to? You wouldn't have fallen in love, I suppose? You'd have seen the red light and cleared out in time? No nonsense. Little girls when one's thirty-five and ripe to settle down. [*Pause.*] All right, I'll try to pull myself together. Otherwise you'll never say anything. And tonight I've got to talk. Just talk and talk and talk my head off, like a whore. And I'd rather it was to you than anyone else, after all.

Philippe. I don't know what's wrong with you, Frantz.

Frantz. Yes, you do. I'm at rock bottom, tonight, and I'm lonely.

Philippe. In spite of the way we've drifted apart these last two years, I'm still your friend.

Frantz. Yes, but all you can offer me is intelligent advice, and that's what I need least. It's a luxury. Any stranger could give it to me. What I was hoping you could do for me—just for tonight—was what the truest and simplest friends do—take some of my unhappiness on yourself. It's too much for me to bear alone. [*He has seized* PHILIPPE's *hands.*] Philippe, they'll take her away from me. Go on, laugh—you'll be perfectly right. I've lived for two years on the love of this girl, trusting in my success, like a fool. When Bentz refused me the money just now I felt utterly lost and desperate. I realized for the first time how flimsy my hopes really were. If I've no money to take her away, she'll be snapped up by someone else, now that I can't make a decent bid for her.

Philippe. But you say she loves you.

Frantz. Oh, she's fond of me all right. But the first time the Duchess produces some titled feller-me-lad for her to marry, what's to prevent her going off and leaving me in my poverty, even though she is still fond of me?

Philippe. Wouldn't she follow you without money?

Frantz. Oh, I suppose she'd follow me on an impulse. But what should I do with a millionairess, if I hadn't any money? No one in his senses could expect her to be able to put up with the petty irritations of that sort of life, or hope that I could go on loving her, poverty-stricken and humiliated. I know poverty, and I'm not going to introduce her to it. I'd rather marry her off myself to some rich man.

Philippe. You're letting you own pride lead you off at a tangent. If you really love her, you can still marry her.

Frantz. It's useless. I might have known it. Everyone will tell me that. I do "really" love her, Philippe. Why do you always talk, all of you, as though money were something nasty from under a stone, when actually it's the only thing that can protect you from nastiness? I love her too much to do without money.

Philippe. That's blasphemous, Frantz. Real love can do without money.

Frantz. Oh, for God's sake—don't start moralizing. I tell you I'm suffering. You say you're my friend. Can't you try to understand what I'm going through, instead of just churning out ready-made answers? Poverty made my childhood a long train of pettiness and disgust, and now I don't trust myself. My love is too beautiful, I expect too much of it to risk infecting it as well. I want to surround it with a protective wall of money.

Philippe. It's sheer madness, Frantz.

Frantz. Yes, isn't it? I want my love to be spotless. I want us to love each other without calculation or fear or shame. Sheer madness. [*Silence.*] I sometimes think there are probably people about who have too much money. Who are afraid it will spoil their love, just as I am afraid mine will be spoiled by poverty. It's ludicrous.

Philippe. Frantz. I know you'll say I'm talking like an uncle, but . . . be patient. It will probably all come right, one day.

Frantz. There's something else. It's not easy living at close quarters with a young girl. I can't wait any longer. I need her as much as I need air and water.

Philippe. Take her as your mistress at Granat, then. . . .

Frantz. I suppose that's what will happen. I can feel the moment approaching, irresistibly, inevitably, when she will have to belong to me. The only true link between us, our tenderness, is at the mercy of that moment now. I know the value of tenderness, Philippe. I know there is no compromise possible with love, and that any little drab in the streets has only to lift up her arms and show off her breasts for tenderness to be utterly futile.

Philippe [*in a hard voice*]. Frantz, there's another solution. Be a man. Have the pluck to get out.

Frantz. No, Philippe. . . . My love isn't perfect, but I have the feeling that somewhere out of sight, though very near me, there is another love spreading enormous wings, and that this other love will perhaps be mine one day if I prove myself worthy of it. You think it would be courageous to resign myself, don't you?—not to snatch at it and drag it out of the shadows? But it would be cowardly. We all have one chance of love. What we should do is to seize the chance as it passes, and then build up our love humbly, relentlessly, even though it cost a year of our life—or perhaps a crime.

Philippe. But are you sure there is no other solution than the success of your business?

Frantz. Her aunt's death would be one.

They stand looking at each other for a long time.

Philippe. Frantz!

Frantz. What's the matter? You told me yourself I should never have the courage to commit a crime.

Philippe. Were you really thinking—?

Frantz. Just now, yes. I was quite wrong to believe for a moment that it was possible. You saw for yourself.

Philippe. Frantz! You're making me feel guilty! I feel like someone who's pointed out the wrong road to you and gone calmly on his own way.

Frantz [*rising, with a smile*]. Don't be too remorseful. For sensitive people the parting of the ways always comes sooner or later. And we shall have gone a long way together.

Philippe. Why did you want us to separate? I'm sure things would have been different if we had stayed friends. Frantz—drop all these mad ideas . . . let's carry on together, help each other.

Frantz. One could always try, I suppose.

Florentine [*appearing with a coat over her pajamas*]. There you are, you two! I was looking for a man. Country houses give me the creeps. Of course, there's a spider in my room—there always are spiders in country bedrooms.

It's as big as a house. I'm terrified of spiders. Won't anyone come and kill it for me?

Frantz. Go on, Philippe. Florentine knows how bad I am at killing spiders.

Florentine. Oh! If I had to count on you! But I'm sure your friend is much nicer than you are.

Philippe. Yes, I'll come. In a minute. Frantz and I were just talking—something rather important.

Florentine. As important as that?

Philippe. Yes.

Frantz [gently]. No. Not so important. Off you go, Philippe.

Philippe. I can't leave you like this, old man.

Frantz. Of course you can. I swear it's all right. Please.

Philippe. I'll come back in a minute, I promise.

Florentine. My God, there's chivalry for you! I'd better go and find Mr. Bentz. He's older, he won't be such a heel. [*She goes out.*]

Frantz. Go on, old man. Please. You've been very decent. Truly. Now you go with Florentine—*I'm* asking you to. Go on.

Philippe. You're not angry? I'll be back.

Frantz. Yes.

Philippe. I feel terrible about it. But I really do want to know what she's getting at. This little maneuver's been going on ever since you introduced us.

Frantz. Hurry up and catch her.

Philippe. Do cheer up. You're exaggerating, really, you know. . . . We'll talk more about it. You'll see. We'll think of something.

Frantz. Yes.

Philippe [going out and coming back again]. You're not angry with me?

Frantz. Of course not.

PHILIPPE *goes out.* FRANTZ *sits down and holds his head in his hands.* MONIME *enters suddenly.*

Monime. Aren't you in bed, Frantz? You'll be tired tomorrow.

Frantz [sitting up]. What about you? Why aren't you asleep?

Monime. I wanted to talk to you. I was waiting till the other two had gone.

Frantz. Are you pleased with the trip, little one?

Monime. Yes.

Frantz. It's fun, isn't it, to drop in on people one doesn't know of an evening and then have to stay the night? Is your room all right?

Monime. Yes.

Frantz. You don't look happy. If I were a girl boxed up in a castle all the year round with an aged aunt, I should feel highly delighted at having so many things happening in one evening.

Monime. I am happy.

Frantz. Then why the sigh?

Monime. You came to ask them for money, didn't you?

Frantz. Don't you worry about that, Monime. Let me fight it out by myself. You mustn't know anything. I swear I'll manage to get hold of enough for us to be happy.

Monime. As you say that, I can hear that your voice doesn't believe it any more. Why won't you tell me? They refused to give it you, and you're too proud to say so. [*Pause.*] I let you alone at first because I thought that after all it might be better that way, but do you really believe that our happiness depends on that money? Do you, dear silly one?

Frantz. Yes, I do.

Monime. Well, you're wrong. We can be very rich if we want to, and still turn up our noses at money.

Frantz. You're such a little girl, Monime.

Monime. I know, I know—you can be terribly older and wiser just because I'm younger than you, but I know a lot.

Frantz [*smiling*]. What do you know?

Monime. Sit down. S-sh! Don't say anything. And you're not to smile at me or shout at me, and above all—above all, you're not to interrupt me with one of those bitter remarks of yours that you're so proud of and that make you miserable for the rest of the day when you've said them. [*She is standing behind him, her head against his.*] Frantz, I don't want you to be sad any more. Don't say anything. You'll only start lying and telling me you're not sad and that you're earning a lot of money and that you'll come one day in a huge bottle-green car, the sort I like, to carry me off miles and miles away from my

horrible old aunt. . . . I know your little story. . . .
Don't tell me . . . It wouldn't be true. You are sad.
One thing I must say for you, you play your part well.
Breaking the branches off trees as you pass them, just to
infuriate me; sneering at the books I read; pulling down
my hair seven times a day—the same old ritual as when
we were children. And yet, underneath all this byplay
that hasn't changed a bit, I can see perfectly well that
you're unhappy, Frantz. [*She places her hand over his
mouth.*] You were going to lie. Ever since we started out
this evening you've had a face as long as a fiddle. Do you
think I didn't see all those horrid figures you were scribbling in your notebook? You are unhappy, Frantz. Do you
think I don't know why? You jumped, didn't you, and
you tried to move your lips. But I've got my hand tight
there, and you can't say a word. You know very well I'm
as strong as you, my boy! My boy. Frantz, you're not
my boy any longer. You don't look at me the same way. Or
kiss me the same way. You're frightened to take me on
your knee or hold me in your arms. Go on, go on, try
to talk. You'll only tell me that I don't understand. . . .
Just because you were brighter than I was at school
you've got into the habit of thinking you're the cleverer
one still. Idiot! Dear idiot! I know what's wrong. [*Pause.
She has her cheek against his head and is murmuring, far
too tenderly.*] I'll be your mistress, Frantz, whenever you
like. S-sh! Don't talk. Don't move your lips—you tickle
my hand. Just stay like a little boy and let me rock you
to sleep with what I've said, until you're not unhappy
any more. I'll be your mistress whenever you like. You
want to talk, do you? I know what you're going to say.
But it doesn't matter. Nothing matters. I want your arm
to find its way back to my waist and your head to find
its way back to my shoulder—freely and openly. I'm
taking my hand away. You can talk now. Only don't
look at me for a moment. [FRANTZ *remains motionless
for a moment, then turns abruptly and holds her to him.
She feels ashamed.*] Oh, Frantz!

Frantz. I'm looking at you. The same eyes, the same
mouth as when I was a child. You are Monime, with the
wildest of looks and the reddest of lips. Trembling lips,
too. My everyday Monime, is it really you?

Monime. Yes, Frantz, it's me.

Frantz. Stand up straight now. I'm looking at you. You're very beautiful today. Is it for the great occasion that you've got on your new dress and put up your hair? But you've forgotten to make yourself some grown-up fingernails. . . . These are your tree-climbing nails! And your great decision hasn't taught you to make up your face . . . you've put your lipstick on any old how, as usual. . . .

Monime. Oh, Frantz, you're laughing at me. . . .

He has drawn her toward him. She hides her head.

Frantz. My little one, I'm glad it was my wild one that came to tell me this, with her hands all scratched and her lipstick all awry. [*Pause.*] Dear, silly girl. Coming without thinking to stop me from being sad. Without stopping to ask yourself any questions. Do you think I don't know everything? You don't love me as a man, Monime. You came to find your lost comrade, and you offered your body in exchange, the most precious ransom you could give. Our friendship never hurt you. You've never dreamed of a tyranny stronger and gentler than that of childhood friendship. Don't hide your head. What are you ashamed of? I love you for it all, my girl with the quiet voice . . . Monime, who knows everything and nothing.

Monime. I know that I want to be your mistress. I want you to make love to me and hurt me. I want to hear you laughing and singing again.

Silence. He takes her in his arms.

Frantz. Idiot, I love you. You've come to give me a wonderful present; but what could I give you in exchange?

Monime. I'm not a little girl. I don't want you to laugh at me. I want you to take me.

Frantz. But you don't love me, Monime.

Monime. I love you the only way I know how to. I shall soon change, Frantz. I swear I shall learn terribly quickly. Take me, Frantz.

Frantz. You must go to bed.

Monime. You're not well. I can see it in your eyes. Your hands are trembling.

Frantz. Go along, little one. It would be too stupid if anyone found us together here.

Monime. I don't care.

Frantz. Please go.

Monime. Touch me, at least. Kiss me. I don't want to be just your friend any more, your poor little playfellow that hasn't any claim on you. You said once that I should be your wife. . . .

Frantz. When we are rich, and when you love me with a woman's love.

Monime. But I *shall* love you that way, I know I shall. [*She goes up to him and says to him softly, awkwardly.*] Kiss me, please. Kiss me as you would kiss someone you had just met and loved. [*He makes as if to push her away.*] Just once, only once, so that tonight begins another sort of life. You want to, Frantz, you want to. You're trembling and you haven't the courage to tear me away. Why don't you kiss me? Ah! [*He gives her a long kiss.*]

Frantz. Go along now, Monime.

She goes. Curtain.

ACT TWO

SCENE: *The Duchess's antechamber, in semidarkness. It is a huge bare room, with tapestries and armor about. A French window leads to the grounds, where large trees are to be seen.*

TIME: It is evening, near nightfall.

MONIME *and* FRANTZ *come in from the garden and put on the lights.*

MONIME. She didn't ask any questions during dinner, because of Urbain. But she certainly will. Frantz, don't pull that awful face. I was a stupid little goose before, but I'm a very good liar now. You taught me that.

Frantz. Yes.

Monime. Why are you unhappy every time we come back from there?

Frantz. Because you're a very good liar, and because I taught you.

Monime. You're mad! I'm very happy.

Frantz. That's not true.

Monime. It is.

Frantz. No doubt you can lie well enough to your aunt, but not to me. Since we've been lovers, you're not happy, Monime.

Long silence. MONIME *gets up, and speaks with forced cheerfulness.*

Monime. There must be some water in her room. I'm going to take the famous pills before she arrives; with her water—what a joke!

Frantz. Don't take them. It's not worth it now.

Monime. But Frantz, the doctor told you—it's our only chance.

Frantz. There's another, that he didn't think of. Don't take them. It's not worth it.

Silence.

Monime. What's the matter, Frantz?

Frantz. I've had enough of living in this constant state of apprehension. Telling lies. Making furtive trips with Florentine.

Monime. We won't go any more.

Frantz. You know very well we shan't have the courage. We're prisoners now, Monime. We must love each other now, at all costs. Every day. Laboriously. Scrupulously. Taking pills to murder our children and smiling to deceive the old woman.

FLORENTINE *appears at the French window, coming from the garden.*

Florentine. Hullo there! Aren't you coming to Vichy with me? I've got a midnight pass. Good evening, pale and interesting!

Frantz. Good evening.

Florentine. It's marvelous in the evening, you know— there's a whole crowd of us going, the oddest collection you ever saw. But of course you don't like it. God, how difficult conversation is with you! So you really aren't coming?

Monime. You know we can't. Aunt Caroline has forbidden us.

Florentine. What? Isn't the old dear dead yet? She really has no sense of propriety. Tell her to hurry up and not hang about so.

Monime. Florentine. . . .

Florentine. I'm off, dear girl. Frantz is glaring at me quite terrifyingly. Hang it all, Frantz, I was only joking. 'By, darling. Good-by, pale and interesting.

She goes off into the grounds, laughing. Monime *watches her go. Then she fetches a glass of water from the adjoining room and takes the pills.*

Monime. There you are! A little water; two pills at midday, two pills at night, and the babies die off like flies. I have no shame—no shame at all. [*She makes a little curtsy.*] Expert infanticide, at your service.

Frantz. Why do you make fun of it?

Monime. We've got to be happy any way that we can now. Even if it's just by making fun of things.

Frantz. You're better than I am. And not such a coward.

Monime. I won't have you saying such things. Just because a poor idiot of a girl loves you and plays the clown to try and make you laugh. It doesn't happen often.

Frantz. I'm miserable, Monime.

Monime. You see the reward I get.

Frantz. We were wrong to love each other this way. It's all right for Florentine.

Monime. Frantz, there mustn't be any regrets. . . .

Frantz. But it's over now. We're going to get out of this dead end, I promise.

Monime. You're going to have some money? Your business is starting up again?

Frantz. No. Something else.

Monime. Something else? But we've thought so hard—there can't be a solution, however tiny; it could never have slipped through the mesh.

Frantz. Yes, there is. There was another solution I told you about.

Monime. Which one?
Frantz. Get up, there's your aunt coming.

The DUCHESS, *a larger-than-life, almost fabulous personage, comes in followed by* URBAIN, *the major-domo, carrying a fur rug.*

Duchesse. So there you are, both of you! I must say you are most difficult to find these days. You seem to have a way of disappearing as if by magic. [*She installs herself in her enormous wing chair, a slow, meticulous ceremony.*] You may go now, Urbain. And bring me my sleeping draft when I ring.

URBAIN *goes out. Pause.*

Now, I quite understand that you should have a taste for long walks and solitary excursions. The poor Duke was just the same. Except for meals, he was never to be found. Always prowling about the woods with nothing but his cane for company. . . . But is it perhaps possible that you are a little too fond of them? Pray don't interrupt me, Monime. I am not your nurse, of course, to follow you about and spank you when you are naughty. Nor am I at all put out by your close association with this dear boy, please be assured of that. But seeing you flying off to Vichy and here, there, and everywhere by car, as you do, just the two of you, I've been thinking—the people in this part of the country are so stupid—they might begin to imagine there was some sort of relationship between you other than mere friendship. . . . It's ridiculous, I grant you, my dear Frantz, and being as intelligent as you are, you will be the first to laugh at it. . . . Quite so. That is a compliment I really have to pay you! you have always known your place and kept to it. I am sure it is only thoughtlessness on your part, and were it not for the grotesque—you will agree that grotesque is the word— were it not as I say for the grotesque gossip it might occasion, I should certainly not allude to it. However, there *is* this outlandish gossip in the air. And you know how quickly it can take hold of these small provincial places. The curé, who by the way is a perfect fool, is already heaving ecstatic sighs in anticipation of the marriage service.

Monime. Aunt Caroline——

Duchesse. I know. He's been dreaming of that service ever since your first communion, and he would die of chagrin if we were to go to the bishop—which we probably shall, by the way. But from the way he gushed over me last Sunday it would seem that he thinks the ceremony is likely to take place at any moment. And I am sure you will understand, my dear Frantz, that that is quite impossible. I have the friendliest of feelings toward you, but all the same, and in spite of the great respect I had for your poor father, I cannot allow Granat to imagine that I would have my niece marry the son of my late physician. It would be comical, as the poor Duke used to say. It was the only adjective he knew.

Monime. Aunt Caroline——

Duchesse. Now don't interfere, Monime. Frantz is an intelligent boy. He wouldn't dream of taking offense at anything so obviously reasonable. Isn't that so, Frantz?

Frantz. Most certainly, madame.

Duchesse. You are a fine boy, Frantz; I have always appreciated that. I realize that at the moment you are not managing your affairs particularly cleverly—however, let us not go into that now, we can discuss that later—but you are a charming young man in every respect, I must say that. A little weak of course, both morally and physically. . . . When I think of your father, who could pretty well fell a tree with a few blows of his stick, I must say I am baffled. How is it possible that he begot you? . . . It is true your mother was nothing to speak of. . . . He married her against my advice . . . she hadn't a penny to bless herself with and then she had that chronic cough, it seems. I say "it seems," for I could never be bothered with her—never set eyes on her, in fact. If he had taken the wife I had in mind for him, his son would have been quite another proposition, if I may say so, and he would not have died penniless. But we are straying from the point. You are a good boy just the same. I am very fond of you, and have every respect for your excellent qualities. But once having said this, I cannot possibly have people thinking that you are about to become my nephew. Were we in Paris, among sophisticated people, everything would be quite different. It would not enter anyone's head that I could possibly marry you to my niece. But here we are

dealing with people stupid enough to think anything possible—and if I were to announce tomorrow that I had
chosen you for Monime, it would not in the least surprise
them. They are quite absurd. I know them only too well.
That is why, my dear children, I am going to ask you to
space these outings more discreetly, and make yourselves
a little less conspicuous.

Monime. But aunt——

Duchesse. Now do let us leave this ridiculous subject,
Monime my dear. I feel sure you have both understood
perfectly well what I have been trying to say. Let us talk
about you now, Frantz. You have had to sell your business. At a loss, I understand.

Frantz. I have nothing left but debts.

Duchesse. You would have your way, and now of course
you have come a cropper. Were you my own son, I could
forgive you for having neither business sense nor a taste
for study. But you have neither the fortune that makes
idleness possible nor the breeding that makes it impera-
tive. What do you propose to do?

Frantz. I don't know. I don't know what to do.

Duchesse. A bad reply if ever there was one. You must
work, my dear boy. For people of your sort, it is the
only thing to be done. I mean, you can't turn thief or
murderer. [FRANTZ *gives her a long look.*] It would get
you nowhere—and in any case you would be caught in the
end. If only you would bring yourself to marry some fat
moneybags. But you will bring in sentiment. Think it
over, my dear Frantz. I am always happy to have you at
Granat—but I should not like you to take for granted a
leisure and luxury which are not yours by right.

MARIE-ANNE *appears, with red-rimmed eyes and handkerchief in hand. She is torn between distress and timidity.*

Marie-Anne. You must excuse me, your Grace, for disturbing you.

Duchesse. What is it, woman?

Marie-Anne. Oh, your Grace, it's dreadful.

Duchesse. Really. Is this going to be another of your
tedious stories?

Marie-Anne. Oh, no, your Grace . . .

Duchesse. I suppose this time you want me to supply
knickerbockers for some village brat you've taken pity on?

Marie-Anne. Oh, no, your Grace . . .

Duchesse. Take that pitiful look off your face, woman. You know it drives me to distraction. Well, come along, what is it?

Marie-Anne. My cousin, your Grace . . .

Duchesse. Ah, this is a new one. Now what has he been up to? No doubt trying to extort money from you in his usual manner?

Marie-Anne. Oh, no, your Grace . . . I've heard from the hospital at Toulon, where he has been taken; he's very ill; he's going to die.

Duchesse. And you really believe that? How much does he ask for? He must be wanting quite a tidy sum.

Marie-Anne. But he didn't write to me, your Grace— it was the hospital. . . .

Duchesse. An accomplice, of course. Anyone can fool you. Show me the letter. . . . Obviously, they've used the hospital writing paper. . . . My good girl, what do you expect?—we're all going to die.

Marie-Anne. Might I perhaps ask you to allow me a few days' leave, your Grace?

Duchesse. Take it. Take it, my good woman; one can never rely on you anyway.

Marie-Anne. I shouldn't like to displease your Grace.

Duchesse. Oh, my displeasure is of no importance! We all know that here. I shall just have to look after myself; take my medicine by myself, play piquet by myself, and——

Monime. But I'll take Marie-Anne's place for you, Aunt Caroline. . . .

Duchesse. It is true you will have plenty of time, my dear child, now that you are giving up your walks. You may go, then, Marie-Anne. These two children are wearing the most appalling expression, but as they declare themselves willing you had better take advantage of it. It won't last. When are you leaving?

Marie-Anne. There is a train at ten o'clock.

Duchesse. Take it then, and try to be back on Monday. . . .

Marie-Anne. Oh, your Grace, I thought I might stay until——

Duchesse. Of course, of course. But be as quick as you can. . . .

Marie-Anne. Good night, your Grace. . . . I must hurry

and pack my bag. I'm so afraid I might arrive too late, poor boy. . . . [*She goes out.*]

Duchesse. So the creature's going to die. Good riddance to bad rubbish. The old fool's been giving him all her money and he of course has been drinking it away, with the able assistance of any trollop he could find. I never have been able to understand why she stuck to that seafaring Casanova.

Monime. Was he her cousin?

Duchesse. So she said, to cover up her little game. I have never for one instant believed it. Or if he was her cousin, it was certainly not as such that she flew off to see him every time he came into port and gave him all her savings.

Monime. I don't understand, Aunt Caroline.

Duchesse. I know what I'm saying. She was engaged to him once . . . let's hope to God that's all it was . . . and yet at over fifty, she still weeps when he doesn't write. What do you think of that?

Monime. Poor Marie-Anne! Perhaps they were in love once, and couldn't get married!

Duchesse. Pshaw!—is that all? I was to have married the Duc d'Orléans. Ring for Urbain, will you please, dear boy? It never came to anything because his mother unearthed a Spanish princess for him. But did I spend the rest of my life weeping and wailing?

Monime. It isn't the same, Aunt Caroline. . . .

Duchesse. Be quiet, you are a little nincompoop. You really are being most provoking, and I want to get a good night's rest. [Urbain *comes in, carrying a glass on a salver.*] Ah, here is my medicine. Ugh! It's disgusting. You will not forget to inform the kitchen maid, Urbain, that she should choose between that boy and her situation. Send my women in. . . . [Urbain *goes out and comes back later with the maids.*] It would be a fine thing if I were left to the mercy of all my servants' whims. Not to speak of having to put up with their marrying those of my mortal enemy. One of the kitchen maids, if you will believe it, wanted to marry Dr. Fernot's valet-de-chambre! Dr. Fernot—a man who makes me long to pour a little something into his wine. The ninny maintains she's in love with him! Quite magnificent. What is the matter with them all? Let them give their minds to doing their work properly and being honest, and leave the rest to the street girls. Good night, Monime my dear. . . . [*Noise of a merry-go-round in the distance.*] Now of course there's that hubbub. . . . This fair is a positive martyrdom. Scores of times I've asked for it to be postponed until August, when I take my cure at Plombières. But the Mayor says it is impossible, that it's been at this time since the twelfth century. But he is so negligent. . . . Ah well, my sleeping draft has quietened me down. . . . Good night, my dear Frantz. You are quite pale, what is the matter? Perhaps you need a tonic? Good night. . . .

She goes into her room, followed by two Maids. Urbain, *having closed the door, comes back to* Monime.

Urbain. I beg pardon, mademoiselle. But as you are being kind enough to replace Mademoiselle Marie-Anne this evening, I ought to tell you that her Grace has given us all permission to go off to the fair for a while. . . . There will only be old Joseph here. But you know he's deaf, mademoiselle, and always dropping off to sleep. So I should be very grateful if you would be so good as to send for me if her Grace should need anything. I shall not go far.

Monime. Very well, Urbain. [*He bows and goes out. Silence for a while. The two* Maids *leave the* Duchess's *room and curtsy as they go off.*] It will be nice alone together.

Duchesse [*calling*]. Monime. . . .

Monime [*in the doorway, through which can be seen a bed with a canopy*]. Yes, Aunt Caroline?

Duchesse [*who can be heard but not seen*]. If I move during my sleep, please make a note. My doctor claims it is very indicative. As a matter of fact I believe the man's a lunatic. But we have to submit to these people. . . . Make a note, there's a good girl.

Monime. Of course, Aunt Caroline.

Duchesse. Your eyes look haggard, Monime. These walks are tiring you. Where were you this afternoon? At Vichy? Don't overdo this dancing.

Monime. But on the contrary, Aunt Caroline. We went for a very quiet walk in the country with Philippe and Florentine.

Duchesse. Very well, then. Good night.

Monime. Good night, Aunt Caroline. . . . [*She has closed the door, and comes back to* FRANTZ *on tiptoe. She drops a curtsy, laughing.*] Good night, Aunt Caroline. . . .

Frantz. Let's see your real smile again now. Look at me with your real eyes. Be yourself.

Monime. Don't you think I'm a very good liar?

Frantz [*looks at her*]. My Monime with the white dress. . . . Yes, you *are* the same girl. The girl that's such a good liar. The girl that can undress in a flash, take her lover, and dress again in a flash—the girl that's always drinking water.

Monime. I love you, Frantz. . . .

Frantz. Forgive me. That false smile that I reproach you for—I put it there myself.

Monime. What does it matter?

Frantz. I've made you into so many of the things I detest. All because I was too cowardly to give you up and too cowardly to get the money at all costs. It's because I was every sort of coward that we're afraid now. [*Pause.*] Can't you feel them all around us—filthy hands, greasy hands, old wrinkled abortionists' hands . . . ?

Monime. How can they harm us, Frantz, since we love each other?

Frantz. My climber of trees, my girl running in the grass, my little one. I don't want some vile old woman to hurt you and make you feel frightened and ashamed. I don't want it. I don't want it. [*He puts his head in his hands.*]

Monime [*goes to him*]. Let's go away, Frantz. We'll go and live in a big town and get some work. I don't mind a bit about being poor.

Frantz [*without moving*]. We shouldn't be able to love each other if we were poor.

Monime. Why do you say that? I should love you even if you were ugly and poor and sick.

Frantz. Oh, my God, what a monster I am. Other people believe in an eternity of love, in a humble cottage, with clear cold water. Why am I blessed with this love, but not the credulity to feed it on?

Monime. You don't love me, Frantz.

Frantz [*taking her by the arm and shouting*]. I forbid you—do you understand—I forbid you to say that!

Monime. You're hurting me!

Frantz. I know there'll come a time when other people will say those things. I can hear them sneering already . . . and I don't care. But you mustn't doubt me, not you, not even for a second. [*On his knees.*] I love you, Monime.

Monime [*stroking his head gently*]. Why are you afraid then?

Frantz. Because I love you. Because I know what petty things can kill the greatest love.

Monime. Ours can't die.

Frantz. Yes it can. Even ours. Try to understand, my little one. People don't love each other like lovers in stories, naked and forever. People who love each other are constantly battling against hordes of hidden forces that attack them from within or from the world outside. Against other men and other women.

Monime. We are strong enough to fight them.

Frantz. Not with poverty to fight as well. Poverty will line up with our enemies, with all the fatal germs that love has to resist from the very first moment. Oh, you're talking like a spoiled darling. . . . You don't know the way that poverty goes to work; how ingenious it is— how persistent. For twenty years now I have had it at my heels like a snarling dog—I know that nothing can resist it, even youth, although youth is as vital and as strong as love. I'm afraid of it. I'm afraid of the beautiful women we shall pretend not to notice when you are poor and ill dressed. . . . I'm afraid of seeing you diminish every day —taking orders from a boss or doing sordid chores about the house. I know that that shouldn't matter and that I shall feel all the more tenderness for you because of it. But I'm afraid of that very tenderness, too, because little by little it will take the place of love.

Monime. Perhaps if we're happy you'll stop being afraid. . . .

Frantz. You're not listening. You're following your own sweet dream. No one will listen to me. No one will believe me. . . . But what if I know that we have no right to take this thousand-to-one risk of spoiling our love? Supposing I know that one morning we shall wake up in our room and look at each other with hatred; and that you will ask yourself if it wouldn't have been better to go on leading the peaceful, happy life of the rich?

Monime. Oh, Frantz!

Frantz. You will ask yourself that, whether you want to or not. . . . You'll look at me quite differently when my back is turned. And I shall watch the almost imperceptible marks of poverty at the corners of your mouth and on your hands, and it will be enough for our eyes to meet for our love to be killed.

Monime. Oh, how can you know all that in advance?

Frantz [*crouched on the ground, clasping her legs, stays wrapped in thought for a while*]. Monime, I should like to believe in fairy tales too. . . .

Monime. Frantz! You're crying.

Frantz. You won't be able to understand it all perhaps, but promise me that if one day you see me hauled up for judgment and you find that I fill you with disgust—promise me you'll remember these tears.

Monime. What's wrong with you?

Frantz. They'll tell you I was a weakling; that I hadn't the courage to work and endure poverty; they may even tell you I didn't love you, as though they had the right to judge me. . . . But you won't listen to them. You will think of these tears and of how much I longed for perfection.

Monime. I don't understand you.

Frantz. I don't need you to. I need you to believe in my love, even without understanding it.

Monime. I do believe in it, Frantz, and we'll do whatever you like. You must never cry any more. [*A long silence. They remain motionless close to each other, looking very small in the great hall, surrounded by armor.* MONIME *looks thoughtful.*] Oh, why haven't I any money of my own? Everything would be so simple. . . .

Frantz [*raises his head and looks at her*]. When your aunt dies you will be rich.

Monime. Why do you say that? We shouldn't wish she were dead.

Frantz. We can wish we were happy. And it's the same thing. Monime, if you want us to love each other, you will wish for her death. Every morning, like a prayer.

Monime. Oh, Frantz, no!

Frantz [*taking her face in his hands*]. Look at me. There is only this one chance left for us. Will you dare not to wish her dead so that we can be happy?

Monime [*turns her head away*]. I love you.

Frantz. Look at me. Please.

Monime. I'm ashamed.

Frantz. What are you thinking?

Monime [*hiding her head on* FRANTZ's *breast*]. The same as you, but it makes me unhappy.

Frantz. There's no need, silly one. It's never been known for wishes to interfere with destiny, even for a second. . . . Besides, I may be wrong. We may be able to love each other for a long while the way we are. . . . [*He takes a few steps away from her.*]

Monime. Frantz, you say "we," but you still mean yourself! Is it true that you could stop loving me because of it being this way? [*He shrugs his shoulders.*] Oh! Then let her die . . . let her die quickly! I don't want you to stop loving me.

FRANTZ *goes slowly to the door of the Duchess's room, opens it a fraction, and looks in. After a moment of silence—*

Frantz [*softly*]. There she is lying in state. . . . You're asleep. . . . Your old heart is beating feebly, but doggedly of course. You can't even be dreaming . . . except perhaps of social caste. You take every possible precaution, don't you? You're on your guard; you're holding on like glue. . . . You'll squeeze out another twenty years yet, day by day, as cleverly as you squeeze bargains out of shopkeepers with your highfalutin talk. You're alive, you old thief. . . .

Monime. You'll wake her up. Come back.

Frantz. She'll stick it out. She'll stick it right out to the end if someone doesn't see to it. She's spent all her life preparing this glorious old age; not devoting herself to anything—love, charity, not even wickedness. Every act of pleasure or devotion or enthusiasm cuts us short. She knew that all right; she was on the look-out all the time so as to last a little longer. [*He laughs.*] The old miser. . . .

Monime. Frantz, please! Come back.

Frantz. She's never had a cough, has she? Lungs in perfect order. Never taken cold in a garden at night, or in a church. . . . Her liver functions splendidly. She could have been a glutton, but she denied herself that as well. What about her heart? She's never complained of any trouble there, has she, Monime? Answer me, Monime—she's never suffered with her heart, has she?

Monime. I don't know. This is horrible. Stop it.

Frantz. What intense joy or suffering do you think could arouse that old carcass? She can have hardly any blood in her at all.

Monime. Frantz!

Frantz [*suddenly coming back to her*]. Have the courage to admit to yourself what her life is worth compared with our love. She's never been kind to you. Never a smile or an affectionate word. Never a hand stretched out to protect you from some childish heartache. . . .

Monime. No, never.

Frantz. It was not thanks to her that you learned to live and love; you were brought up by servants, below stairs.

Monime. Yes.

Frantz. You can't remember a single thing she did to make you happy. All you associate with her is harshness and meanness.

Monime. Yes, Frantz.

Frantz. Well, then you must have the courage to wish she would die. Die, and let go of all that money that she's been hanging on to ever since she was young, for no reason at all, all that money that represents our happiness. Look at me, Monime. . . .

Monime. I'm ashamed, Frantz.

Frantz. Surely you don't love her?

Monime. No.

Frantz. Then why don't you answer me?

Monime. I'm frightened.

Frantz. You must take a tight grip of your fear. It's like a dog that tries to jump at your throat. You must strangle it and kill it. Take hold of it—turn it to face you, press yourself against it, mouth to mouth, until your hair stands on end and your teeth chatter. It isn't fear any longer then. You'll see. It's something else. Silence and darkness become one's accomplices. Then it's possible to go to bed, and sleep, even though there's a corpse nearby.

Monime [*stares at him and cries*]. Frantz! We must go

upstairs and put on all the lights! Something is happening that I don't understand. Why did you say that just now? Give me your hands, I'm frightened. They're all cold. . . . Let's get away from here. Please!

He remains motionless. Silence for a while. The noise of the fair can be heard.

Frantz. Why are you afraid? You used not to be so timid. We used to play hide and seek at night in the antechambers. Shall we play it now? Remember, how we used to hide behind the armor?

Monime [pressing herself against him]. Don't leave me.

Frantz. I shan't leave you. I don't ever want to leave you. Only for one minute. One long, terrible minute. Then I shall never leave you again as long as I live.

Monime. What are you saying?

Frantz. Nothing. Just talking. I'm listening to my voice. It's the same as ever. It's astonishing.

Monime [crying out suddenly like a mad thing]. What does all this mean? What are you talking about?

MARIE-ANNE *appears, dressed for the journey and carrying an old-fashioned suitcase.*

Marie-Anne. Good-by, mademoiselle, monsieur. . . . Is her Grace asleep? I do hope she will not be upset about my leaving. But I had to go at once. Poor boy, it will be the last time perhaps, the last time. . . .

Monime. Will you be at Toulon tomorrow?

Marie-Anne. Yes, sometime tomorrow. . . . I'm afraid it may be too late. My poor dear, my poor dear. . . .

Frantz [suddenly]. Did you love him, Marie-Anne?

Marie-Anne [stops short, nonplused]. Why do you ask me that, Monsieur Frantz?

Frantz. Madame de Granat told me he had been your fiancé.

Marie-Anne. Yes.

Frantz. Why did you never marry? Were you lovers? Tell me. What are you afraid of? Is it your one-time fiancé you're going to see, or the man who made you into a woman? Taught you to love, made you suffer? Why won't you answer me?

Monime. Frantz, leave her alone.

Frantz. Answer me, Marie-Anne.

Marie-Anne. That is my grief, not yours. . . . You have no right to ask me.

Frantz. He's going to die, and when you're dead as well, no one will know that you were happy once. Tell me. Wasn't he your lover? [*Pause.*] Marie-Anne, you can tell me.

Marie-Anne. He wouldn't have wanted me to be his mistress. . . .

Frantz. Why not?

Marie-Anne. Because he was proud . . . and I couldn't be his wife.

Frantz. Why?

Marie-Anne. We had no money to set ourselves up, or even to go away together. He earned barely enough to live on, and that kept him at sea all the year round. I was already serving the Duchess, who would not have kept me on had I married. We simply had to resign ourselves. There was no other way of getting money. We could hardly have murdered someone for it, could we?

Frantz [*taking her forcibly by the arm*]. Are you sure?

Marie-Anne. What are you saying? What is the matter? Let me go.

Monime. Frantz, let her go. What's the matter with you?

Frantz. Are you sure he loved you?

Marie-Anne. Oh! yes, he loved me. . . . You have no right to doubt it; he would have taken his own life for my sake.

Frantz [*softly*]. That wouldn't be any good. If he had loved you he would have taken someone else's life for you.

Marie-Anne. You are mad! Do you know what it means to kill someone, that you talk so glibly about it? He knew. He had been in the war. . . .

Frantz [*suddenly*]. I know, too. To kill is to take a knife or a club and deal blow after blow until there's not another sound, not another twitch.

Monime. Frantz! Stop it! You're out of your mind! [*She clings to him but he tears her away.*]

Frantz [*shouting at the top of his voice*]. You think I'm raving, don't you? Do you think I'd dare call him a coward if I hadn't thought and thought and thought about it? Yes. I know what it means to kill someone. I know every way there is of doing it. I can tell you the best and the worst.

Monime. Frantz, what are you saying?

Frantz. I know what you're going to say! But don't try and fool yourselves with ready-made moralizing. It's because we're cowards, that's all. What else stops us killing? You simply don't have to look at your hands when it's done; you just wash them very thoroughly, and then you've earned the right to be happy.

He is positively yelling. MONIME *suddenly cries out loud and runs to shut the door of the Duchess's room. She flattens herself against it as though to prevent* FRANTZ *from passing.*

Marie-Anne [stammering, panic-stricken]. I don't know what's the matter with him. . . . I don't know what's the matter with him. . . .

Frantz [continues hollowly]. Do you think I don't know what killing means? Do you think I don't feel the cringing of every muscle at the very thought of it? Do you think I don't know how the blood would stick to your fingers, and how the screaming would echo in your ears for days? I know it all. I know all about it, but it isn't going to make any difference.

Marie-Anne. It grieves me to have upset him like this. I don't understand it.

Monime. You must forgive him, Marie-Anne; he is ill.

Marie-Anne. Yes.

Monime. It's not true what he's been saying. You mustn't take any notice. It doesn't mean anything, does it, Marie-Anne?

Marie-Anne. No, mademoiselle.

MONIME *crosses to* MARIE-ANNE.

Monime. I'll come to the gate with you. You must hurry, or you'll miss your train.

Marie-Anne. Yes, mademoiselle. Au revoir, monsieur.

Monime. Leave him. Leave him. He's ill.

They go out. He remains where he is, completely spent. MONIME *comes running back.* FRANTZ *has not moved. There is silence for a while.*

Monime. Frantz!

Frantz. It's true, Monime. I didn't tell you because I knew the secret would be too much of a burden. I've quite made up my mind; in a few minutes from now, I'm going to kill her.

She has not allowed him to pronounce the word "kill": she has sprung at him and taken him in her arms—her hand over his mouth.

Monime. Be quiet. You mustn't say that word. They would take you away afterward and kill you. We'll go away; we won't see each other any more. We'll do anything, but not that. . . . They would kill you. [*Pause.*] Come upstairs to my room. We'll put on the light and then we'll think. But not until we're up there. Come.

Frantz. I want to stay here.

Monime [*falls on her knees*]. Frantz, please, I beg you to.

Frantz. Get up. Don't cry. It's no use. Don't raise your voice. I'm staying here. [*He lifts her up and lays her on a couch. She is in a half-fainting condition.*] S-sh! I'm here. Close beside you. Don't try to talk. No, I shan't go away. I'm here, holding your hand. [*Long silence. He strokes her forehead now and again; she makes a few nervous movements. He tries to soothe her.*] You must keep very calm and listen to me. . . . You mustn't make me lose heart. I've thought of everything. S-sh! Don't move. . . . I've had something ready for a long time—something wrapped in cloth so that there won't be any blood or any noise.

Monime. Frantz, you're talking like a murderer.

Frantz. I'm talking like a murderer because I'm going to be a murderer.

Monime [*struggling with him*]. I don't want you to! I don't want you to! I don't want you to!

Frantz [*holding her*]. Be quiet. Don't move, I must, Monime. . . . Tears and shouting will only take away my courage and my nerve. My hands mustn't tremble while I'm doing it; I'm calm now, very calm. Don't say any more. It must be tonight. . . .

Monime. Let's get away from here, Frantz. It's not true. . . .

Frantz. Yes. It will be true. We shall love each other

and have nothing to be afraid of. This little one of ours, this hidden life that is struggling and growing inside you—we'll let it live if you'll let me do as I want. An old woman will die, but our child will live; that will be our justification, Monime.

Monime. No. I don't want it! I'm frightened.

Frantz [watches her struggling]. I know you. You're my own kind. Those wild eyes; those trembling lips— they're my own cowardice.

Monime. You're afraid, too!

Frantz. Yes. I'm afraid. I'm a coward. But I've been trembling for months now. I'm used to my fear.

Monime. Go away! I don't want any more to do with you!

Frantz. I want you all to myself, every day. I can't do without you any more. Life would be pointless and empty without you. You're going to go up to your room and go to bed as usual. I'm going to mine to disarrange my bed. Then I shall come down here, and come straight back to you afterward.

Monime. No! I won't do it.

Frantz. I order you to.

Monime. I won't go.

Frantz [getting up]. Very well. Stay.

Monime [also getting up]. Frantz! You shan't go in there. You're mad.

Frantz. Let me pass.

Monime. You shan't go in there. I'll call for help!

Frantz. There's no one there. And if she wakes up, I shall knock her senseless.

Monime. You can't do it, Frantz!

Frantz. Come away from there.

Monime. No, I shan't come away.

Frantz. You're shouting. Stop it!

Monime. Yes. I'm shouting. I'm shouting!

Frantz. Have I got to hurt you?

He has taken her violently by the wrist and gives it a violent twist. She falls at his feet.

Monime [crying out wildly]. I don't love you, Frantz!

Frantz. It's too late to say that now. Let me go. [He opens the door.]

Monime [she is clinging to his leg. She talks rapidly,

and in a low voice]. You shall listen to me, or you'll have
to drag me right up to her bed and kill me first. I realize
now. We don't love each other. You said so yourself.
We don't love each other enough. . . . Our love is a
lost cause. I'm not beautiful; you're already looking at
other women and wanting them. . . . You only half-
desire me, and I can't love you. We come back tired and
miserable from that beastly room. If we really loved each
other, do you think we should be unhappy and ashamed
every time we made love? Do you think we should have
been together so long without becoming lovers and
that we should have been afraid of being poor? We
didn't really love each other, Frantz. . . . We only felt
tenderness for each other, and one doesn't kill for that.

Frantz [*pulls her violently toward him*]. You're lying.
. . . You're lying. . . . You know there's something else
that's eluding us, passing us by . . . something we've
wanted madly ever since we've been lovers. You know
that there is a part of us that belongs together now and
that it's only for the two of us that love means anything.
We are bad lovers, bad friends, but all the same you
know you'll never have any other lover or any other
friend as long as you live. So why are you lying? [*He
kisses her passionately. She submits.*] You see, tenderness
can be forgotten for a while. We'll escape that too. . . .

*She has fainted in his arms; he carries her off. The stage
remains empty for a moment. Then one of the lower
servants, old and half-witted, dodders up to the door and
knocks.*

Servant. Monsieur . . .

Frantz [*coming back alone*]. What do you want?

Servant. It's me, Monsieur—Joseph. I've been left in
charge. It's a telegram for you; a lad from the post office
has just brought it by bicycle. To be delivered even in
the night, he said.

Frantz. Thank you.

The servant leaves. FRANTZ *opens the telegram, reads it,
and crumples it up without any expression having passed
over his face.*

Duchesse [*calling from her room*]. Monime . . . Monime, are you there?

FRANTZ has started violently at these words. He goes to the door and answers the DUCHESS, *who can be heard, but not seen.*

Frantz. Monime has gone up to her room. She wasn't feeling well, but she'll be coming down again.

Duchesse. Is that you, Frantz? I woke up with a start. I thought I was alone. I was frightened.

Frantz [*suddenly*]. Are you frightened of being alone?

Duchesse. It seems to be stormy outside.

Frantz. Are you afraid of death?

Duchesse. Why do you ask me that? We mustn't talk about death. [*Pause.*] Get along now, Frantz. I want to go to sleep.

Frantz [*stares at her without moving, then murmurs*]: I don't hate you.

Duchesse. I don't know what you mean.

Frantz. Thank God. I don't hate her any more now. . . .

Duchesse. Now go along, my dear Frantz, I don't know what you're talking about. . . . What are you doing standing there staring at me like that?

Frantz [*with a sort of appalling tenderness*]. Poor old woman! We're trembling with fright, both of us. But it'll soon be over, you'll see. . . . [*He approaches like a sleep-walker; suddenly he falls on his knees.*] Oh, please! I beg of you! You're old now, you can't be deprived of love or of strength. There's only hatred left for you to give up. I love Monime; she loves me. Give us a little of your money and let us be happy! It's of no use to you.

Duchesse. Aha! At last I understand. That's what you were leading up to. . . . Ha! ha! ha! You are joking, my young friend!

Frantz. Don't laugh. I assure you you shouldn't laugh. Look how my hands are trembling. Look at my eyes. I'm afraid. I'm afraid now. I implore you to let us be happy, quite simply, with your blessing. We are two poor sweethearts like any others and we'd prefer it that way, after all. Listen—let me marry Monime. It would be better that way, I assure you. It would be better.

Duchesse. This scene is ridiculous. You're asking the impossible. I'd rather see her dead than married to a little good-for-nothing like you, do you hear? [FRANTZ *has got up. There is silence for a while.*] There now, you've quite made me lose my temper, I shall have to take another sleeping draft if I'm to get any rest now. . . . Call Urbain.

Frantz. He's at the fair.

Duchesse. So he is. Go and fetch Monime and tell her to come and give it me.

Frantz. I'll give it to you myself.

Duchesse. Why you?

Frantz. Why not me?

Duchesse. But you're not going to come into my bedroom. I'm in bed! I forbid you to!

He goes in, and closes the door. Nothing more is heard. The stage remains empty for a moment. MONIME *appears in a distraught state.*

Monime. Frantz, where are you? [*She goes to the door, but dares not open it. She goes out calling.*] Frantz! Frantz! Frantz!

She can be heard slamming doors and calling further off. FRANTZ *has come out of the Duchess's room, very pale. He remains in the middle of the room, motionless, staring straight ahead of him. He draws the crumpled telegram from his pocket and looks at it.* Monime comes back.

Monime. Ah! There you are! What is it, Frantz? [*She takes the telegram from him, reads it, and throws her arms round his neck with a cry of joy.*] Oh, Frantz! I knew it wasn't possible, and that something would turn up first. We're saved, Frantz. We're saved! Oh, I'm laughing and crying at the same time! So Bentz is offering you forty thousand francs a month to help run your old business; isn't that wonderful? You see, he's not so bad after all. Now we shall be able to go away and be happy, thanks to him. . . .

Frantz. Not on forty thousand francs a month.

Monime. But you're mad. We shan't have to be poor any more.

Frantz. You've had that much every month to buy your dresses. Just try and see whether you can live on it. . . .

Monime [drawing back]. I detest you. I never want to see you again!

Frantz. It's too late, now.

Monime. What are you saying?

Frantz. I'm saying it's too late.

Monime [falls back crying]. You killed her just the same. . . . You killed her just the same.

Frantz. Don't shout. . . . Come along, we must get back to our rooms. I say we must get back to our rooms. . . .

He tries to drag her away, but she lies on the ground, sobbing.

Monime. You killed her just the same. . . . You killed her just the same. . . . You killed her just the same. . . .

Curtain.

ACT THREE

SCENE: *One of the central rooms of the château. It is circular and scantily furnished. Three exactly similar doors lead off it. The small hours. The lights are still on.*

FRANTZ *is sitting on a chair, deathly pale and exhausted, with his clothes in a state of disarray. Opposite him, at a table, a* Police Officer *is going through a batch of papers. Another is seated beside the table, legs crossed, manner detached. A third is pacing up and down the room.*

SECOND POLICE OFFICER *[in a low voice to the* First Police Officer*].* He's a tough nut. He did it, I'll bet you anything. But God knows whether we'll ever pin it on him.

Frantz. What's the time?

Third Police Officer. Six o'clock.

Frantz. How is Mademoiselle de Granat?

Third Police Officer. There's a doctor with her.

First Police Officer. Well, now. We'll proceed with the evidence. I've been acquainting myself with the answers you gave my colleague in my absence.

Frantz. You're rested and fresh. I want a drink. Let me call a servant. I'm dead beat.

First Police Officer. Later. Let's first of all get a few things straight. You say it was at half past ten that you went to bed.

Frantz. I've already told you it was half past ten.

First Police Officer. You went to sleep immediately?

Frantz. You've already asked me all these questions at the beginning of the inquiry.

First Police Officer. And I'm asking you again. Let's assume I'm afraid I shall forget what you said.

Third Police Officer [*stops walking and stands behind* FRANTZ]. You said the first time that you couldn't get to sleep right away.

Frantz. I beg your pardon, I said, and I say again, that I went to sleep very quickly. Whereas usually, as a matter of fact, I don't go to sleep immediately.

Second Police Officer. Did you read?

Frantz. I told you—I usually do read in bed. But yesterday I was tired, and didn't.

First Police Officer. A light was seen in your window at half past eleven. According to the first investigations, this is just about when the crime was committed.

Frantz. I didn't put the light on; I've already told you that. The witness who says he saw a light in my window must have been confusing it with the next one, which is the window of the entrance hall. There's a lamp burning there all night.

First Police Officer. The witness insists that he is not mistaken.

Frantz. That surprises me. All the more because, as you can check for yourself, my window is not visible from the town side. So we can only conclude, can't we, that the witness in question was in the castle grounds at the time of the murder?

Third Police Officer [*between his teeth*]. The bitter-end type. [*Coming up to* FRANTZ.] The old man saw you in the antechamber at a quarter past eleven. . . .

Frantz. That's unusually precise for Joseph. He's a doddering old half-wit whose sole claim to distinction is that he can't tell the time and never knows what day of the week it is. Ask the other servants. They'll confirm it.

First Police Officer. You never carry a hunting knife?

Frantz. No. I abhor hunting.

First Police Officer. It has been established as a result of this inquiry that the Duchess was killed with a knife.

Frantz. With a knife?

Second Police Officer. That surprises you, doesn't it?

Frantz [*recovering himself*]. No. it only confirms my first impression that it must have been one of the gipsies camping out in the market place.

Third Police Officer. But of course you know that it was a hammer that finished the old woman off?

Frantz [*not batting an eyelid*]. A hammer? But you've just said it was a knife.

The Police Officer *resumes his pacing.*

First Police Officer. You are very stubborn. But it is quite useless for us to go on playing cat and mouse. You say you went up to your room at half past ten.

Frantz. I didn't look at the time. I must make that clear. But I imagine it was about half past ten.

First Police Officer. In your previous statement, you said exactly half past ten.

Frantz. That surprises me. But I may have said it inadvertently.

First Police Officer. Why are you going back on it now?

Frantz. I'm not going back on anything. I'm simply telling you that I couldn't possibly have known the exact time. I never wear a watch and there are no clocks, either in the Duchess's antechamber or in any of the other rooms between there and my bedroom.

Second Police Officer. So you admit being in the antechamber after half past ten.

Frantz. You're twisting my words again. I admit nothing. I have never denied being in the Duchess's antechamber before going up to my room. And I suppose it was "about" half past ten when I went up.

First Police Officer. I'll just take this one point; you were in the antechamber, alone, at about half past ten?

Frantz. Yes.

First Police Officer. Can you tell us what you were doing?

Frantz. I had spent the evening with Mademoiselle de Granat. She had gone up to her room a few minutes before, not feeling well.

Second Police Officer. At twenty past ten. This time we actually have precise information, thanks to the statement of a maid who came back for a few minutes to do her hair and met Mademoiselle de Granat on the stairs.

Frantz. That's possible.

First Police Officer. How long do you think you stayed in the antechamber after Mademoiselle de Granat had gone?

Frantz. I repeat, I can't say exactly. Perhaps ten minutes, perhaps less.

Second Police Officer. What did you do in those ten minutes?

Frantz. I was getting ready to go to bed.

Second Police Officer. Do you mean to say you really need ten minutes to make up your mind to go to bed?

Third Police Officer. Come now, admit it. The old lady saw you. What have you done with the hammer?

Frantz [*coolly*]. You're asking me several questions at once. To which do you wish me to reply? [*Third Police Officer withdraws*.] I can well understand that you are surprised at my taking ten minutes to make up my mind to go to bed. But your surprise is due to the fact that— by force of professional habit, no doubt—you *will* look at the situation from an angle that has no relation to real life. Obviously it didn't take me ten minutes actually to make up my mind to go to bed! But you know yourself that between intending to do something quite without urgency or importance and actually doing it, there is often quite a time lag. It's the same with everyone. I must have been sitting in the armchair dreaming, or even just simply finishing my cigarette. I don't remember anything else.

First Police Officer. You don't remember anything else?

Silence.

Third Police Officer [*between his teeth*]. Bastard.
First Police Officer [*calls him over*]. Gérard?

The other comes up and the First Police Officer *says
something in his ear. He goes out saying.*

Third Police Officer. Right, sir.

First Police Officer. Let's go over your statements again.
Mademoiselle de Granat went up to her room feeling
unwell at twenty past ten. You stayed in the Duchess's
antechamber alone for about ten minutes, and you can
think of nothing—not one single thing—that you did
during those ten minutes. Agreed?

Frantz. Agreed.

First Police Officer. You then went up to your room,
and at about the time of the crime, that is at about eleven
o'clock, you were asleep?

Frantz. Yes.

First Police Officer. Good. Now can you tell me how it
is that a telegram arrived for you at the Granat Post Office
at ten-thirty? I repeat, ten-thirty. And—fortunately for the
purposes of our investigation—the Post Office, which by
the way keeps exact national time, can supply precise details. The messenger took ten minutes to reach the
château. It was therefore at ten-forty that he handed the
telegram to the servant in charge. Is the telegram in your
possession?

Frantz. Yes. I forgot it. Here it is.

First Police Officer. Funny thing to forget.

Second Police Officer. May I see it, please?

First Police Officer. How can the telegram be in your
possession, if at ten-forty you had already gone up to your
room, where, according to your statement, no one came to
find you?

Frantz. But I've already told you I couldn't say precisely at what time I went up to my room. I left the antechamber as soon as Joseph had handed me the telegram.
So it was at ten-forty that I went upstairs.

Second Police Officer. So your "time lag," as you call
it, was twenty minutes? Rather a long time to be just
hanging about. Plenty of things could be done in twenty
minutes.

Frantz. It's quite possible that I stayed there smoking
and thinking for twenty minutes, and that it seemed like
only ten. I'm quite sure such things must have happened to you.

Silence.

First Police Officer. Let us leave that point for the moment. I see the name Bentz on the telegram. You had to sell your business as a result of the refusal of this man Bentz to advance you some money?

Frantz. That's correct.

First Police Officer. And you sold it at a loss, if one is to believe the witnesses. You were in a desperate situation.

Frantz. Not in the least. The telegram offered me forty thousand francs a month. Moreover, I would point out, gentlemen—in order to assist the calculations this will no doubt give rise to—that the telegram, which puts an end to a financial situation that, if not exactly desperate, was obviously straitened, was handed to me at ten-forty; we have, thank God, your own word for it that that has been exactly specified. So I had been reassured for quite a while at the time of the murder, and there was every reason for me to sleep soundly, as I assure you I did.

Second Police Officer. Your reasoning is very persuasive. But this crime could have been committed much earlier than you seem to think. We have not yet heard the conclusions of the medical expert; we can only be sure that by eleven o'clock everything was over.

First Police Officer. We are also justified in asking whether forty thousand francs a month is adequate for the needs of a young man like yourself.

Frantz. But a young man like myself, who is poor and has always been poor, and who would probably not become any richer on the death of Madame de Granat, could be very happy with forty thousand francs a month. Judge for yourself. Without wishing to be indiscreet, may I ask how much you earn in your profession?

Second Police Officer. That's not the question.

First Police Officer. How much longer are we going to carry on this battle of wits?

Frantz. I don't know what you mean.

A Policeman [enters abruptly]. Excuse me, sir. Drop this one for a moment. We'll take him up again if need be. I've just come from the boss. He's had a complete confession from the old man. It's him that did it. He says he threw the hammer in the lake. They're checking up on it now. The boss wants both of you to come. [*He goes out.*]

First Police Officer. That'll be all for today, then, sir. Sorry to have kept you so long.

Frantz. That's all right.

Second Police Officer. I'll keep your telegram as evidence. The alleged murderer handed it to you here at tenforty, you told us. It's a point that might prove interesting.

First Police Officer. I would ask you, sir, not to leave this room, please, and to remain at our disposal until the first inquiry is over; it won't be long now.

Frantz. Of course. And *I* would ask *you* please to have the first servant you see bring me something to drink.

First Police Officer. Certainly. You must be very tired.

Frantz. Yes. Very tired. [*When he is alone, he passes a hand over his eyes.*]

A *Policeman* [*coming in*]. Shall I send in the journalists? They're asking to see you.

Frantz. No. I don't want them here.

The Policeman *goes out and comes in again.*

Policeman. There's one that insists on seeing you. He says he knows you.

Philippe [*who is in front of a crowd of journalists*]. Frantz—it's me.

Frantz. Oh, you. Come in then. . . .

Exclamations of disappointment. The door closes.

Philippe. You're going to give me a jolly good scoop. It's good of you to remember a friend. What's up, Frantz? . . . Do you want me to call someone?

Frantz [*has fallen, half fainting, into an armchair*]. No. It'll pass. They've reduced me to pulp. They've been questioning me since midnight.

Philippe. The old man confessed this morning.

Frantz. Yes.

Philippe. Strange, isn't it—about the old man? I'm glad he spat it out, though.

Frantz. Yes. Me too. They won't need to question Monime.

Silence.

Philippe. His confession had everyone floored. He had
an absolutely watertight defense. They were going to let
him go. Suddenly—a burst of dramatics and there he is
accusing himself with a wealth of the most extraordinary
detail. I think he's dotty.

Frantz. You think so?

Philippe. What's the matter? You've gone so pale?

Frantz. You sound like the walking-on part in a melodrama. That's exactly what he always says, remember? But
the other character doesn't reply. He leans back in his
chair, very pale, as you astutely observed. And the walking-on part becomes very suspicious. . . . [*He walks toward* PHILIPPE.] But *you* happen to know that it was me.

Philippe [*recoils*]. Frantz!

Frantz. What have you come here for with your newspaper and your questions? Just to see me suffer, to stage a
free show for yourself? Look at me. Pretty good, aren't
I? They didn't get me, you see. . . .

Philippe. Frantz, it's impossible.

Frantz. On the contrary, it's perfectly possible. Come
on, sit down. Pull yourself together. Have a drink. Give
me a cigarette, I haven't got any. I shan't even be getting
the one they give the condemned man.

Philippe. You're loathsome.

Frantz. Yes, aren't I? I can still manage to be loathsome. Of course the thing that's lacking is remorse. I'm
not conscious of any of these hidden eyes. Did you see
how I answered their questions? For six whole hours.
. . . [*Pause.*] You said I shouldn't have the courage.

Philippe [*taking him by the arm*]. Frantz, what's this
game you're playing with me? It's all over now. The old
man has confessed. You're free. You'll be able to go to
bed now, and tomorrow, when you get up, all this will
have been just a nightmare.

Frantz [*in a low voice*]. I did it, Philippe.

Philippe. You're ill. This business has cracked you up.
Either that or you saw the doubt in my eyes when I came
in and you want to frighten me. Frantz, this is a horrible
trick to play. You're lying. It wasn't you. . . . The old
man has confessed. . . . It can't have been you.

Frantz. The truth must scare you pretty badly if you can't face it. Do you find it easier to believe that it was that old scarecrow that can hardly stand up and who had nothing to gain by the old girl's death? It's fantastic. You have to want your happiness badly to become a murderer . . . and what's more you have to have a fist on you, let me tell you. . . .

Philippe. My God, it's frightful. . . .

Frantz. Oh, yes, frightful. More frightful than you can imagine. [*He looks at* PHILIPPE *for a while, then in a hard voice*] Put down that stick. And your hat. And that infernal notebook. Something tells me you won't want to take any notes now and that what I'm going to say wouldn't be of interest to your newspaper. I killed her, Philippe. There's nothing to it, you know. You have no idea. I had a hammer wrapped in cloth. I lifted it. . . . She watched me all the time. It's a long time, you know, a second. The first blow didn't kill her. I clubbed her and clubbed her because she was still moving. I was kneeling over the old witch. Lying on her in her bed. We fought like animals; like two monstrous lovers straining after some unthinkable union. When she was finally quite motionless, I got up. I had to walk, open the door, shut it again, go up to my room, pretend to sleep, pretend to wake, give the alarm myself, and then spend the entire night answering their questions—all without making a single slip.

Philippe. Stop it.

Frantz. Am I frightening you? I was frightened, too. [*Silence.*] And now it's all over. But I wanted you to know what it was like to kill someone—to have killed someone. Have you got some idea of it now, with your poor little smug imagination? The screams, the blood, the convulsive movements, the spine-chilling looks they give you—can you feel it all? [*He takes him by the lapel and stares hard into his face.*] Now listen. I let you in, rather than the others, because I needed to say this to someone! I'm glad I killed her. I don't regret anything. If they get me, I shan't defend myself. I have nothing to say that a judge would understand. And yet I must shout it out while her body's still warm in there. . . . I hate crime . . . I hate death. I believe it's a vile collusion with nature even to be glad when someone dies, however much one hates them.

. . . In other circumstances I might have thrown myself in the river to save the life of this old hag, much as
I hated her. But I killed her—not for her money, but
because her money, in the mysterious balance of things,
had become the exact price of our perfection. Philippe,
don't think people kill for money because they haven't the
courage to work. Look at my hands—how they're trembling still. Better ten years' hard labor than one second of
crime. Only I wanted my love to live, to be beautiful, to
be perfect; and to enable it to live, I would have done
even more terrible things.

Long silence. PHILIPPE *goes slowly toward* FRANTZ.

Philippe. Frantz . . .
Frantz [*turns, as though surprised to see him there*].
What do you want? Go away.
Philippe. I'm your friend.
Frantz [*looking steadily at him*]. Yes, I suppose that's
true, you are my friend. Or should I say you've taken the
place of a friend. You've occupied that difficult position
without lifting a finger, where someone else more conscientious or more simple might have offered me a helping
hand. You shouldn't have reminded me of that!
Philippe. I don't understand. I don't know what all
this is about.
Frantz. Oh, don't worry! I'm not blaming you. I've
killed her and I'm glad.
Philippe [*still stammering*]. But it wasn't you, it was the
old man.
Frantz. However, since you've come here uttering pious
clichés and brandishing friendship at arm's length to get
the truth out of me, you can have it. Who knows? Maybe
you'll be the one to regret it. Maybe *you'll* suffer from the
famous remorse that all the moralists say follows inevitably
on any crime—because *I* don't. Are you a true friend,
Philippe? Real friends share joy and sorrow, you know.
Fine—you take the remorse and leave me the rest. [*He
laughs.*]
Philippe. You're terrifying. Why are you laughing?
Frantz. Because it's funny. Drama is a mixture of the
tragic and the comic. We learned that together, remember? [*Pause.*] It's a mistake to remember you as you were

then—a kid in short pants, sitting next to me in the gods. I shan't be able to indulge in the magnificent tirade I promised myself.

Philippe. What's going on, Frantz?

Frantz. The old Philippe was making me sentimental. It's true, we were friends then. Real friends. [*He becomes thoughtful.*]

Philippe. What were you going to tell me?

Frantz [shrugs]. What's the good? Go on now, Philippe. I'm going to try and get some rest in case they start questioning me again.

Philippe. What were you going to say? I'm asking you to talk now.

Frantz [looking at him]. It was partly because you were my friend that I killed her.

Philippe. But you're mad! You don't realize what you're saying!

Frantz. Ah. Whites of the eyes showing, beads of sweat at the nostrils, hair standing on end. . . . I promised myself I would provide this spectacle as a proof of our friendship. Yes, it was because I had a friend like you that I was able to kill her.

Philippe. You're mad! It's not true! You're lying! It isn't true! It couldn't have been because of me! [*He is breathless and shouting.*] I always gave you good advice! . . .

Frantz. True. You always gave me good advice, but it's immoral that those who give good advice should be eternally sheltered from blame. I just wanted to tell you that this morning, so that for once at least it's been said to what is known as a good man. Go on, now, get out.

Philippe. What's going to happen to you? I'm frightened for you!

Frantz. I said get out.

PHILIPPE *goes toward the door, looking embarrassed. From the doorway, he murmurs.*

Philippe. All right, then, Frantz. See you later.

Frantz. You'll go back to your women, your friends, your cafés. You must pluck up courage one day, Philippe. You'll see how easy it is. You'll see how easily the answers come when the police start questioning. How one feels like the lord of creation afterward. . . . [*He goes and opens the curtains; the morning sun floods the room.*] Ah! it's morning. That horrible night—it's over. I've done it. It's finished. It's finished.

He has forgotten PHILIPPE, *who again stammers.*

Philippe. Au revoir, Frantz.
Frantz. Good-by, my boy. Make it a good story.

PHILIPPE *leaves. Enter* URBAIN. *He, too, is looking disheveled and haggard. He is carrying a drink.*

Urbain. I'm very glad it is all over for Monsieur. It must have been most fatiguing to be questioned all night like that; I tried several times to make them let me bring Monsieur something to eat, but they wouldn't let me in. They didn't keep me long because I was seen at the fair at the time of the—— But who would ever have thought it could be Joseph, monsieur? He had been serving her Grace longer than I.
Frantz. Yes. What is Mademoiselle Monime doing? Is she up?
Urbain. Poor young lady. They haven't questioned her at all. Fortunately so; in the state she was in last night it would have killed her. . . . The doctor came and gave her an injection. She is up now.
Frantz. Tell her that I have to stay here in case they want to question me further, but that I should like to see her immediately. Ask her to come down.
Urbain. Very well, monsieur.

FRANTZ *goes to the glass, studies his reflection and smooths out the lines on his face. He arranges his hair and collar, then goes and sits down. Suddenly he looks at his hands, and continues to gaze at them silently, with a strange smile. Enter* MONIME *in a dark dress, looking drawn and unkempt.*

Monime. Here I am.
Frantz. Oh! I'm glad. They haven't asked you any questions?
Monime. No. . . .

Frantz. My little one. . . . You've been ill. Come and sit down. There. I'm so happy, so happy.

Monime. Have they left you?

Frantz. Yes. Joseph has confessed, I don't know why. They asked him too many questions, I suppose. They must have turned his brain.

Monime. What are they going to do to him?

Frantz. I don't know. I don't dare. Neither of us must care. What is certain is that they won't kill him. He's too old. They'll see he's crazy and put him in an asylum. We'll go away, Monime. They won't ask us any more questions. We'll get out of this house—out of the country . . . among people who won't make us feel afraid any more. . . . I'm happy, my little one. . . .

He is sitting at her feet, clasping her knees, his eyes closed. She is very pale, and remains silent.

It's all over, Monime. Yesterday was the last time we had to hide; now we have the right to live. You can belong to me without fear and without deceit. Oh, my little one, my little one. . . . [*He strokes her legs.*] Monime, how easy it is to kill for your sake. If I managed not to tremble last night, not to slip up with my answers to their questions, if I've escaped all their traps, it was because of you. I love you, Monime. I am your lover. I've won you. What chance do they stand with their questions against that? I was stronger than they were; I shall always be stronger now. Stronger than anyone else, stronger than poverty even. . . . I've purified myself in the blood of that old woman. . . . Today, I'm a man. How could you love him, Monime, that poor little wretch that was ashamed to be poor, that lover who hadn't the heart to make love, that tender youth who was so afraid of falling a prey to his tenderness? Oh, it wasn't only her that I killed; it was that unspeakable little creature that hadn't the guts to take you. One blow of the hammer for the tender youth. One for the man that was afraid of abortionists. One for the man that wanted to be rich! Ah! The charming little greenhorn's quite dead. And with him all the sordidness—all the impurity. . . . I love you, Monime. I want you. [*Gently.*] All the time I was battering her there on her bed, I wanted you.

*Silence. He buries his head in her lap. She opens her eyes
and looks at him sadly. But she is hard, too.*

Monime. Frantz. Get up. You must get up. All night
long I've been in agony, turning things over in my mind.
You must listen to me. Frantz, get up. . . . Just now,
you were talking and talking. . . . I was listening to your
voice and not understanding a word you were saying. I
don't know what you said, but I must tell you something
now, something I discovered during the night—I felt it
with the whole of my being. Ever since you killed her, it's
as if something had been torn to pieces. We shall go away
and live together because we must, now. . . . We shall
try to be as happy as we can. Helping each other as much
as possible. But I've thought it all over—I shan't be your
wife.

Frantz. What are you saying?

Monime. It will be as it was before. I shall be your
cousin, your friend. We shall live together and try to
forget. Try to forget everything—our love, and the crime
we committed.

Frantz. But what are you saying? You're mad. I don't
want to forget anything. I want to love you. It was for
that I risked my neck.

Monime. No, Frantz, it's not possible any more.

Frantz. Monime!

Monime. Don't start shouting. You'll make both of us
unhappy.

Frantz. Monime, you look like something out of a grave-
yard. Stop it. What's the matter with you? What's happened? What have they said to you?

Monime. Nothing. Please stop it, Frantz, please. It's
no use talking. It's too terrible. We've got to forget.

Frantz [*shaking her*]. But it's not possible! You're
dreaming . . . wake up. . . . It's me. It's me, Frantz;
it's your lover come to take you away to live and be happy.

Monime. Let me go! . . .

Frantz. My little one . . .

Monime. Let me go. . . . [*She pulls herself up like a
Fury.*] I don't want you to touch me with those hands—
those filthy hands. . . .

FRANTZ *looks at them and stammers in distress.*

Frantz. They're not filthy. They killed her, but it was for the sake of our love.

Monime. Leave me alone! You disgust me! You killed her for my money.

Silence. She is breathless and panting. Suddenly she falls sobbing into the armchair. FRANTZ *remains rooted to the spot. He looks at his hands, bewildered, then at* MONIME, *who is weeping.*

Frantz. Monime. . . . Monime. . . . It isn't true! You don't think that—— [*Silence. She continues to cry.*] But answer me. You can't just ignore me. . . . Other people can think that. . . . I knew they would and I don't care a damn, but you . . . it isn't possible . . . you . . . Monime?

Monime. Think of the telegram. Bentz offered you forty thousand francs a month.

Frantz. It meant poverty, Monime, and I thought it was impossible. You know it was so that I could love you properly that I wanted the money, so that nothing sordid could come between us and our love.

Monime. It's not true. If you had loved me, you wouldn't have been afraid of being poor and having to hide. It was for my money you did it.

Frantz [*taking her head in his hands*]. Look at me.

Monime. Don't touch me.

Frantz. I shall hold your eyelids back by force, and then I shall have to read what is in your eyes. Don't you believe it was for you, and only for you, because I loved you? [*Silence. She does not reply. He looks at her and then suddenly recoils, frightened at what he sees in her face.*] It was horrible, but it was only for your sake, Monime . . . to protect you from poverty.

Monime [*repeating with a faraway look*]. It's not true. It was for my money.

Frantz. Oh! This is all too stupid!

Monime. It was for my money! It was for my money!

Frantz. Why do you keep on repeating those idiotic words? I don't even believe in your money any longer. I'm a man this morning. A lover, poor and resolute. Come, let's go away without it, if it frightens you. Let's love each other, poor as we are. And when poverty and wretched-

ness, which of course are ennobling to people like us, have
worn you out, I shall take another wife and leave you to
get old by yourself. . . . What a coward I was to look
for a solution, to try to protect you. I didn't love you
cruelly enough. Tenderness made me want to wrap you
up in money. Come then. So much the worse for you. I
love you without it. Come!

Monime. Leave me alone. I don't love you.

Frantz. Why are you lying? You do love me. We love
each other.

Monime. No.

Frantz. Yes. You can say no, because you're afraid of
the corpse that's lying in there. But your mouth says yes,
your body says yes.

Monime. No.

Frantz. Yes. You loved me last night. You do love me,
I tell you.

Monime. Let me go! I hate touching you. I gave myself
to you to make you happy.

Frantz. You're lying . . . you're lying. . . .

Monime. You've chained me to you, you've dragged me
down into the mud, into all these lies and all this blood,
but I hated you last night. It was monstrous of you to
want to come straight from her bed to mine, where there
was nothing left of me for you. I feel as though the whole
of me were shut up tight—dried up forever. . . . I don't
want any more of your sort of love. Soaked in blood and
sweat. I want to live, to be happy like other people, and
forget everything else.

Silence.

Frantz. I mean nothing to you any more?
Monime. No.

Silence again.

Frantz. And yet you never said a word. You let me believe myself a man. You let me think I was master, let me
talk like a master, and I was nothing any more. You must
have had a good laugh.

Monime. We mustn't go on hurting each other, Frantz.
I assure you we can live together without doing each other
any harm. We'll share my money.

Frantz. Why do you say "your" money? I gave it to you, at the price of my own neck. What do you think I want with your sordid bargaining? Do you think I killed her to get half the money? Keep the lot of it. I'll make you a present of it. . . . So you don't love me any more? [*He laughs insanely.*]

Monime. What's the matter with you?

Frantz. Yes. You're the strongest, the richest, the most beautiful of them all. I can tell you now that having you was my only treasure. And today you don't love me any more. Look at me, with your new woman's eyes. I'm nothing to you any more, nor to anyone else. Last night I stood up to them for six hours because I thought I was a man and that you loved me. They can come now; they shall have me. Oh! What a fool I was! God knows how long it is already since I possessed her. Perhaps I never possessed her at all. . . . The little greenhorn was still alive. I hadn't killed him after all! Look at him. Look at me. I'll help you if you can't see it all. This pout of the lips— that's my cowardice; this network of lines on my forehead —that's my laziness and indolence; the fixed expression in my eyes—that's my egotism. . . . Did you think I was tall and you were small? Look, I don't stand straight and I only look tall because I'm thin. You thought I was strong, courageous, and calm, didn't you? Look at my hand—it's been trembling since yesterday. Look at me. . . . Your lover was ugly, unkind, stupid, poor, and cowardly, and yet, before, you thought yourself unworthy of him and followed him into the trap that meant the end of your happiness. [*She has buried her head in her arms.*] Go on, cry! Cry! It was for your money I killed her! I wanted to go to bed with your money! It was your money I wanted to make love to! [*Both of them are panting and exhausted; there is a long silence.*] Go and be happy. You are a charming girl. You know how to take things. How not to give love more than it deserves. You'd better marry someone else who'll help you to become what you want to be. With the millions that will be coming to you, you'll find a husband to your taste all right. Later on if you think that perhaps love was worth the name after all, you'll be able to take a lover and go to bed with him between meals.

Monime. You're loathsome.

Frantz. I shall believe that in the end. That's twice today I've been told so. You're the salt of the earth, no doubt, both of you. . . . I really wonder what I'm doing, loathsome as I am, demanding friendship or love from either of you, as though such things existed. It's ridiculous. I'm utterly ridiculous. Forgive me.

He is crying. She watches him for a moment and then goes gently toward him.

Monime. Frantz.
Frantz. Oh, no! Not pity. Get away from me!
Monime. Frantz, you've been proud, and I've been foolish. Now both of us are suffering for it. You said to me once that God doesn't give passion to everyone. We ought to have been content with what we had and gone on living that way. Without that pride of yours, we might even have been happy. It was your pride that wanted this mad, impossible love. It was because of that that you killed her and that we've been destroyed. I would have loved you poor; I would still have been your mistress on the sly, bad lover though I was. Remember, I threw myself at your feet. I clung to you and you dragged me across the floor. I told you I should never marry and that I would always stay with you. I even told you to go away, that I detested you. But you would do it just the same, out of pride.
Frantz [*shattered, humble*]. I was all alone. Alone against the world.
Monime. You're proud, proud. . . . I loved you as a little girl loves her childhood's playfellow when she meets him again. That's all. And now I hate you for abusing that poor love, I hate you for pinning your wild, insane dreams on me.

A long silence. They remain motionless. Two Policemen pass through on their way out, slipping on their overcoats as they go.

Third Police Officer. I know the old boy confessed. But you'll never be able to convince me it wasn't the youngster that did it.
Other Police Officer. All right. All right. Don't get

worked up about it. The boss is quite satisfied with things as they are. So am I.

He goes off; the other stays behind a moment looking silently at FRANTZ. *He is a man with a huge red moustache and a not-too-intelligent appearance. Suddenly he puts on his hat, comes up behind* FRANTZ, *and takes him by the arm.*

The Police Officer. What did you do it with?

FRANTZ *replies immediately, without even turning round.*

Frantz. With a hammer wrapped in cloth.

The Police Officer *is surprised in spite of himself. He hurls himself at Frantz, who has not budged, and handcuffs him, yelling at the top of his lungs.*

Police Officer. Hey! Chief! Boys! Chief! I knew it was him . . . I knew it was him!

The Police *come in at all the doors.* MONIME *has looked up at first without understanding, then throws herself at* FRANTZ's *feet.*

Monime. I love you, Frantz!

Curtain.

THE REHEARSAL

Translated by

LUCIENNE HILL

CHARACTERS

THE COUNT
THE COUNTESS
DAMIENS
VILLEBOSSE
HERO
LUCILE
HORTENSIA

THE REHEARSAL

ACT ONE

SCENE I

A drawing room. The Countess and Monsieur Damiens come in. They are in Louis XV costume.

COUNTESS. Dear Monsieur Damiens, I do want to thank you for lending us your ward.

Damiens. Obliging you, milady, is the first and sweetest of my duties. You needed her; she came.

Countess. I don't know what we should have done without her. Our poor aunt the marquise—God rest her —was the most fantastic creature! This idea of leaving us Ferbroques on condition that we spend a month here every spring was, I must say, rather touching. The place is a desert where she could never bear to live for longer than a week. She spent all winter sighing for Ferbroques and with the first snowdrop she fled to Aix-les-Bains. She was a tireless invalid, you know. When she had bathed her way through every spa in Europe, back she dashed to Paris for the season, swearing, by all she held most dear—us, probably—that the very next April would see her at Ferbroques. When death called her to the final Watering Place, she left it to us to keep her broken pledges.

Damiens. Very delicate thought, if I may say so.

Countess. Wasn't it? A month in the country, with a ball or two to break the tedium, is quickly over. Besides, who could say no to Ferbroques? It's a gem. But as for the clause obliging us to rear a dozen orphans in the east wing—my word—she must have laughed when she wrote that!

Damiens. The stirrings of Christian charity perhaps. . . .

Countess. My aunt was weaned on rationalism. If she felt the belated urge to do a little something for the Lord, it can only have been out of politeness. She loathed children. She had a footman—poor old Jules, he died two months after she did, corroded by tranquillity—

whose duty it was to precede her in public places and clear the streets of them. She developed a child phobia through being hit on the head by a diavolo in the Botanical Gardens.

Damiens. A twinge of remorse perhaps?

Countess. You didn't know my aunt. No, I see only one way to explain this orphanage: the desire to play a posthumous practical joke on Tiger and myself. I must say Tiger took it very well. He adored squabbling with his aunt. I see, said he, when the lawyer had finished reading the will. She wants those twelve screaming urchins to drive us mad for four weeks every year, does she? Very well. We'll take twelve little deaf-mutes. I'm sure when my aunt heard that she turned in her tomb in the family vault. Particularly as in her lifelong fight with Tiger, he had scored the final point. Short of haunting the ballroom in a shroud—and the poor sweet was too much of a lady ever to stoop to that—she was powerless against him from then on.

Damiens. Yet you abandoned the scheme, I see. I thought I heard the prattle of tiny voices as I passed the shrubbery just now. . . .

Countess. Yes. Unfortunately the will stipulated "orphans." And the world may be brimming over with distress, but a dozen deaf-mute orphans is rather a tall order. So we selected twelve orphans with sturdy vocal cords and took refuge in the west wing. Ferbroques is enormous, thank heaven. The next thing was to organize the Grand Charity Ball for the inauguration of the orphanage. A regiment of decorators arrived posthaste from Paris. We spent nine delicious days in a blizzard of tin tacks and swaying ladders. Tiger was amazing. He had a brain wave a minute. He all but killed two plasterers, who had to be treated for nervous collapse in the gardener's cottage. In short, things were going with a swing when, the other morning—catastrophe!—the orphans descend on us! We'd forgotten all about them. That's when I sent you my telegram, and you very kindly lent us your goddaughter. Does she like it here?

Damiens. She adores children.

Countess. That is her profession, I believe?

Damiens. Yes. She had to earn her living when her mother died. She opted for child welfare.

Countess. It's as good a hobby as any other, I suppose. Personally, I prefer my rose trees. They don't grizzle. Have you seen the greenhouses yet? I never saw such a display of marvels!

Damiens. I've seen nothing. Since I arrived last night, it's taken me all my time to fit myself into my costume and try to learn my lines.

Countess. It was sweet of you to join the cast at such short notice. Gontaut-Biron's dropping out so unexpectedly—he was playing Trivelin, you know—threw Tiger into an abyss of despair. I feared the worst.

Damiens. Really?

Countess. Yes, really. Tiger has a way of caring about the most unlikely things. It seems he distinguished himself quite marvelously in 1940. He held out alone on the Loire, when everybody else was already in Marseille, with a small patched-up machine gun, against a horde of Prussian fusiliers. He was still firing five hours after the cease-fire. The enemy yelled themselves hoarse with their megaphones and their white flags, but Tiger didn't turn a hair. The fall of France was emphatically not his concern. But, his last bullet fired, he asked the Germans for a bath, shaved and had a manicure—his batman, the only other survivor, was a beauty specialist—and never once referred to the defeat again. But an unsuccessful ball is another matter! He would be quite capable of killing himself, like Vatel.

Damiens. I am happy to spare him that painful obligation by undertaking this small role. I had a tidy talent as an amateur in my young days.

Countess. You still have, I'm sure. Lawyers have an inborn sense of drama. You're sure to steal the play.

Enter the COUNT, *also in costume.*

Count. Where is everybody? I want to read through the play before dinner. Monsieur Damiens, where is your goddaughter? It really is scandalous the way those twelve orphans are monopolizing her. We need her too, you know.

Damiens. She was putting them to bed. She said she would be here directly.

Count. Go and fetch her, there's a good fellow. We can't begin without her.

DAMIENS *goes out.*

My dear, all promises well. The performance during dinner is an exquisite idea. Character number one stands up and addresses number two. The others listen, intrigued. The turn of phrase sounds a bit odd at first, but you and I will have taken care to give a mild eighteenth-century flavor to the table talk—to make the transition fairly painless. Then, just as the speakers seem to be holding forth a bit too long, enter character number three, the footman. He joins in the discussion. General stupor. Our servants are thought very badly trained. And then—they recognize the play! Too late: it's begun. So we avoid the icy shudder that sweeps through a society audience when you sit them on chairs in front of amateur theatricals.

Countess. There's just one snag. They'll never recognize the play. They haven't read a line of Marivaux since they left school.

Count. Splendid. They'll think I wrote it.

Countess. Snag number two. If they listen to the play, the food will get cold.

Count. Never mind. We always feed them far too well. Anyway, the menu will be planned to suit the requirements of the drama. I shall have lobster and champagne brought in just when the plot wears thin, and I'll serve toothpicks at the poetic patches. Nothing makes a man more pensive than rooting out a little scrap of meat wedged in between two molars. If they make the gesture, there's at least a chance the thought may follow. I think that girl will make a charming Sylvia.

Countess. I think she's colorless. I can't imagine why you moved heaven and earth so she should play the part.

Count. Exactly. She'll stand out against your highly colored friends. She burns with inner fires. She'll make a change from all those incandescent beauties who'll use any kindling to make a blaze. They shoot gorgeous flames an entire evening, and when you get them home alone the fire's gone out.

Countess. You wouldn't be in love with her, by any chance?

Count. I? Not in the slightest.

Countess. Good. She's no girl for you.

Count. The real headache is the Louis XV costume—
and those wigs! Pure candy floss. But Ferbroques is an
eighteenth-century mansion and there's no way around
that. In a Renaissance house, now, like your place at
Grandlieu, we could have achieved something quite
sensational.

Countess. Either way, it's too late now.

Count. True. But I shan't sleep until I've hit on
something to liven up the fifteenth Louis. I did think
of making the men wear beards, but that was too obvious
a way of being different. Or else Louis XV in the
naughty nineties—Watteau in the idiom of Lautrec—
but they'd never have caught on. We mustn't ask too
much of them.

Countess. How old is she?

Count. Just twenty. I wish you'd give a little thought
to it.

Countess. To what?

Count. The costume. It's quite enough to turn the
whole affair into a quagmire of banality. The strain of
it is killing me. [*He removes his wig and fans himself
with it.*]

Countess. Why not ask them all to come without
wigs?

Count [*looking at himself in the glass*]. That would
help, certainly. Especially as that child's hair is an ex-
ceptionally striking color. It would be a crime to powder
it.

Countess. I think she's plain.

Count. So do I. I was referring to the color of her
hair.

Countess. You're free to do as you please, Tiger, you
know that. Have the grace to admit that I've never in-
terfered in your private life. But don't flutter around
her too much. Damiens has been the family solicitor
for over thirty years. I should be most distressed if he
had cause to complain about us.

Count. My dear, what do you take me for? My failings
are considerable, but no one has yet questioned the fact
that I'm a gentleman. With my title and my family crest,
that's about all I have left, if I except Ferbroques and
the twelve orphans.

Countess. That doesn't alter anything.

Count. Pardon me, that alters a great deal. My father, who was the perfect gentleman, took the trouble to prime me on that score before he died. I was very young, but I never forgot his advice.

It was an hour or two before his death. The bishop was waiting in the anteroom for the last sacrament. He asked for me to be shown in first. My boy, he said, I realize, a trifle late, that I have never paid you over-much attention. I haven't much time. I'm pushing off. The question of honor I can safely leave to you. But there's just one thing. You're young, you'll be wanting to enjoy yourself. Do whatever gives you pleasure, but always with girls of your own set. With the others it always ends in tears. You finish up by marrying your cook—or else you get a shopgirl with bastards and they grow up bitter and stir up revolutions. Be as licentious as you will, lad—we aren't saints. But keep it in the family. Now show in the bishop. I've a few things to declare before he checks me out. It's high time I was off. [*A pause.*] My father was an admirable man. I hardly ever saw him, but I knew then that I loved him with all my heart.

Countess [*after a slight pause*]. I have a feeling—and this isn't a reproach—that you really did give him your heart, and that you never had a scrap over to give since.

Count [*shaking himself*]. You're in a murky mood today, my dear. Come now, let's not dramatize. Anyway, you know I'm very fond of you. I never genuinely cared for anyone but you. Don't tell Hortensia, I'd never hear the end of it.

Countess. Do you tell your mistresses that you're in love with them?

Count. I have to. Women are such sticklers for form. I do believe you are the only woman to whom I never said it.

Countess. Because it wasn't true. How very generous of you. Am I expected to say thank you?

Count. Because there was something else between us, something exquisite and rare, which absolved me of the need to lie to you. Eliane, enough of this. We'll get maudlin in a minute. Love is the poor man's meat. Let us not start this late in the day sniveling among our heirlooms because we've never known it. I have no other

ambition than to live life as one successful holiday. And
that's a good deal harder, let me tell you, than beating
one's breast and suffering agonies. Besides, I don't wish
to be indiscreet, but you have Villebosse, my dear, if
you want to play that little game. Villebosse—or another,
if you will. The world is full of roaring men.

Countess. Villebosse bores me.

Count. Oh, does he? I think he's charming. He's
young, he's handsome. He's always willing to dive off
the top board or jump through flaming hoops on request.
Come now, you aren't going to force me to sing that
character's praises for you, surely?

Countess. Remember your manners. That character
happens to be my lover, Tiger dear.

Count [*briefly*]. Let's leave it at that, shall we? You
are free. I am free. We love each other dearly and we
have to give our friends a ball, which is a positive gamble
in this wilderness. People have never spent a tedious
minute under our roof. With this piece of folly we can
sink in one evening a fifteen-year-old reputation. [*Looking
in the glass.*] Do you really think it's better without a
wig? Yes, you're right. There's something unfinished
about it that makes the eighteenth century rather en-
dearing. I'll wire the new instructions to everybody.
[*Kissing her hand.*] You are right, as always. Eliane, I
am very fond of you.

He goes. HORTENSIA *comes in from the other side, also
in costume.*

Hortensia. Excuse me. I thought Tiger was with you.

Countess. He's just left.

Hortensia. Can't he think of anything but this ball?
He's never to be seen!

Countess. My dear Hortensia, I spent my time, in the
days when I was in love with Tiger, being jealous of
his parties.

Hortensia. Oh, I'm not unduly wretched! Are we going
to rehearse? I don't feel too confident.

Countess. That's the very first time I ever heard you
say so. We're waiting for that child who's playing Sylvia.

Hortensia. Why did Tiger insist on giving her the part?

Countess. She's charming.

Hortensia. I think she's colorless.

Countess. Don't you believe it. She burns with inner fires. She isn't like those incandescent beauties who'll use any kindling to make a blaze. They shoot gorgeous flames for a whole evening, and when one is alone with them, apparently, the fire is out.

Hortensia. What is this new whim of Tiger's? True, he's given his valet a part too. Let's hope when the play's over he'll send them both back to the servants' hall.

Countess. I shouldn't be too sure of that either. If I know Tiger, he'll dance with her all night.

Hortensia. How very disagreeable. This was one of the few houses where one could still be certain of meeting one's own kind.

Countess. My dear, Tiger has taken the trouble, in fifteen years of constant care and effort, to make himself the uncontested arbiter of taste in Paris. If he'd devoted the half of all that energy to business, he would be the richest man in France. He can do as he pleases now. If he decrees that Damiens' ward is admissible in high society, then admissible she'll be.

Hortensia. It's grotesque! Why, she's a sort of nursemaid, isn't she?

Countess. Had the children been our own, I daresay Tiger would never have dared. She's in charge of my aunt's orphans. And there are twelve of them. Tiger has a genius for splitting hairs. Besides, you may as well know it—I think he's wild for her.

Hortensia. Do I sense a note of malice, Eliane?

Countess. Not the slightest hint of it, darling! I'm delighted to be able to say that you are just the girl for Tiger. He's very much in love with you, you know.

Hortensia. Is he really?

Countess. So he says. Of course it's a moot point whether everything that Tiger says is true. It's many a year since I gave up trying to find out.

Hortensia. Anyway, he won't dance with her all night, I can promise you that!

Countess. No scenes. That's the surest way of driving him to do it.

Hortensia. Thank you for the tip, Eliane, but I think I know Tiger quite well too.

Countess. Your dress is absolutely ravishing!

Hortensia. Yours is a perfect dream!

Countess. I can't tell you how grateful I am that you're beautiful. I should have been hideously mortified if Tiger had flaunted himself with just anybody. Turn round. Heavens, how cunningly those little panniers are worked in! Jacquot really is a genius!

Hortensia. Does Leonora still dress you? It's breathtaking the way she's contrived a pure Pompadour line with the little side drape they brought out this season. Will she be there?

Countess. Who?

Hortensia. Leonora. Oh yes, of course she will. That woman is seen everywhere, even at Tiger's.

Countess. Especially at Tiger's.

Hortensia. Why especially at Tiger's? It's an established fact that Leonora—who started as a button hand, by the way—is *persona grata* in society now. He's only following the trend.

Countess. Tiger never follows a trend he didn't start himself. One must be fair. He'll share a jug of beer with cabmen in a roadside café, but Tiger is only at home to people of his own class.

Hortensia. And what could possibly win the woman this passport extraordinary into society? The fact that she has genius?

Countess. Tiger doesn't believe in genius as a social asset. My dear, it's the royal touch, no less. He receives her because he wanted her and she said no, some four years ago.

Hortensia. How gracious of you to let me know!

Countess. I'm telling you because it's ancient history. But the fact of resisting Tiger would seem to be a rare enough distinction, darling, if it allows one to move in the best circles!

Hortensia. Eliane, you're wasting your arrows. Tiger or the next man, I'm determined never to be hurt.

Countess. I'm sure that's why he's so attached to you. And so am I. [*She kisses her.*] Darling little Hortensia! When one thinks of it, one does have so few friends!

HERO *comes in, holding his wig.*

Countess. Oh, there's Hero! Hero, I adore you.

Hero. Eliane, you take the words out of my mouth. Are we going to rehearse? What a tyrant Tiger is, making us wear costumes three whole days beforehand. I can hardly breathe.

Countess. That's why. He wants us to get used to it. He says the chill of the first hour of every costume ball is due to everyone's wondering if his breeches will stay up.

Hero. My breeches are quite secure, thank you. It's my waistcoat. It's too tight. He says we needn't wear a wig, that's something.

Countess. Yes. The tyrant's latest whim.

Hero. Pity. It's what I liked the best. I'm beginning to lose my hair.

Countess. You're thirty-seven, Hero.

Hero. I'll be bald at forty. My doctor told me I make love to much. We haven't spoken since.

Hortensia. Why? Because he dared to tell you that?

Hero. No. The whole of Paris knows that I'm the ladies' pack horse. It was he who fell out with me. He's bearded like the pard and as hairy as Esau. When he told me that venery makes a man bald, I couldn't help it—I burst out laughing in his face. Doctor, I said, something tells me you don't have fun every day of the week! He took it very badly. He said he was a family man and had better things to do in life, and he threatened me with God knows how many unmentionable mishaps. And if they didn't carry me off, I'd go down with cirrhosis of the liver. The whole thing cost me 2,000 francs. A man can't enjoy himself in peace any more. You have to pay folk like that to tell you that you'll die of it.

Countess. You should get married, Hero.

Hero. Unless you find me Aphrodite, I shall merely have one more woman to keep happy. My strength will never rise to it. And even if you made me fall in love, do you know a breed of woman that quenches thirst?

Countess. Hero, you act the cynic and you're the softest-hearted creature in the world. One has only to look at you.

Hero. Your taste for paradox is muddling you, Eliane. These melting blue eyes are the eyes of a drunk. And I'm soft-hearted, true. But I like hurting.

Countess. I never heard anyone really vicious say so.

Hero. I'm not vicious. I like breaking things. It's a taste little boys lose when they grow up. I kept it.

Hortensia. When will you hurt me, Hero? I can hardly wait.

Hero. Whenever you like, my sweet. But it wouldn't amuse us much. We're too alike.

VILLEBOSSE *comes in.*

Villebosse. Have you heard the news?

Hero. Of course. We always know everything before you do.

Villebosse. We're to perform without wigs! We're going to look ridiculous!

Hero. I don't think the wig would have sufficed to save you, Villebosse. [*Going to the drinks table.*] May I?

Countess. Hero! We're going to rehearse!

Hero. My talent lies at the bottom of a glass. Unfortunately, I can't remember which. That's why I have to drain so many.

Villebosse [*to the* COUNTESS]. That man infuriates me! I will not have him hanging around you like this!

Countess. Villebosse, don't be so tiresome. I didn't take a lover to be criticized for things my husband doesn't see fit to mention.

Villebosse. Tiger is a cad and he doesn't love you. I do love you. I don't want to start a brawl under your roof, but if that dreary little tippler dares to lay a finger on you, I'll seize on the first excuse to slap his face!

Countess. Hero is quite likely to slap yours back and then refuse to fight you.

Villebosse. I'll have him thrown out of every club in town! He'll die of shame!

Countess. I don't think it's shame Hero will die of. That was swallowed long ago—along with everything else.

Villebosse. At least say you despise him!

Countess. I don't know that I do.

Villebosse. Good God, Eliane, I insist on knowing this instant that you despise him! Otherwise I'll pack my bags and I shan't appear in this show!

Countess. If you play that dirty trick on Tiger, I'll never speak to you again.

Villebosse. Tiger's futilities are the last of my worries! Eliane, I love you, and I *am* your lover! Good God, that counts for something, doesn't it?

Countess. I'm beginning to find it counts for a horrible lot. My dear Villebosse, you've achieved the extraordinary feat of making sin more tedious than virtue.

Villebosse. Very well. I'll pretend not to know my lines. I'll ruin the show! I'm tired of being the only one to suffer around here!

Hero [coming back with his glass]. What has Villebosse got to say for himself?

Countess. He's suffering.

Hero. Isn't that interesting? Hortensia, my granite girl, come and look at this fascinating natural phenomenon—a man with an aching heart.

Villebosse [turning his back on him]. Sir, I am not speaking to you!

Count comes in, leading LUCILE *by the hand, and followed by* MONSIEUR DAMIENS *and the* Valet, *also in costume.*

Count. I have, with conspicuous valor, snatched Sylvia from those twelve monsters. *[Sucking his thumb.]* Look, blood. One of them tried to maul me. Now, are we all here? Good. Let's begin. The *Twofold Inconstancy* is a grim play, I beg you to remember that. Sylvia and Harlequin are truly in love. The Prince wants Sylvia—who knows?—maybe he loves her too. Why always deny princes the right to love as deeply and innocently as Harlequin? All the members of his court conspire to further his designs. They aim to make Harlequin forget his Sylvia and tempt Sylvia to lose her virtue to the Prince. It is, in fact, the elegant and graceful story of a crime. Villebosse—Harlequin—is good-natured and affectionate, but weak and greedy and a little simple too. Flaminia and her sister are so lovely, and they smell so sweet! Remember that even as he spurns them he is sniffing them. Flaminia and Lisette are brittle, shallow, frivolous, and pleasure-loving. The little country lad must smell good to those fine, languid ladies too. Then again, it's in the service of the Prince, the supreme law of their little world. So why deny oneself the pleasure of a day? Eliane, Hortensia, it would be innocent of me to attempt to coach you. You'll be magnificent, the pair of you. *[Turning to* DAMIENS.*]* Trivelin is ponderous, servile and as frisky as a bloodhound at the thought of joining in the hunt on his lord's behalf. He is a liveried servant and it's sweet to bully this little country bumpkin. He's been through it all himself and worse. Let the youngsters have a taste of it. That's the way of the world. As for Sylvia—[*Turning to* LUCILE.] What can we say of Sylvia? She is not romantic, she is tender; not guileless, but sweet; not heartless but clear-cut. Neither the fine court ladies nor the Prince can dazzle her. In this little universe, corrupt and cynical and tittering under its silks and plumes and winking gems, she stands alone, bright and clean in her little cotton dress, and she watches them, upright and silent, as they moil and toil and plot around her. And all that made the Prince's power and his delight is in her hands now—valueless. Sylvia is a withdrawn little soul who looks at him from a thousand leagues away and casts a ripple in his heart. There was something else to life then, besides pleasure— and he never knew it? [*His voice has altered slightly as he speaks.* HORTENSIA, *the* COUNTESS, *and* HERO, *behind his glass, look at him in mild surprise. He concludes tonelessly as if embarrassed.*] But there's no need to explain the part, mademoiselle. Just be yourself.

They all stand quite still, looking at them both as the curtain falls.

SCENE II

Same set. The COUNT *and* LUCILE, *in costume, are on-stage.*

COUNT. It's wrong of me to talk to you like this, I know, but I am halfway through my life and I never yet had the will power to say no to pleasure. [*He looks at her and stops.*] I'm sorry. I said the forbidden word. Be patient. I'll learn the vocabulary too. [*He shakes himself.*] I wonder incidentally what freemasonry of prudes and bigots has managed, in two centuries, to discredit the word "pleasure." It's one of the sweetest and noblest words in the language. Why should love not be, first and foremost, what gives pleasure to the heart? Time enough for the heartache that comes after. [*He looks at her.*] Anyway, it's exhilarating to be in love with a young lady who is dumb. It trains a man to introspection and soliloquy. One never talks to oneself half enough. I hadn't spoken to myself in years. I underestimated myself. What hasty judgments we do make, don't we? Now that I've got to know myself a little better, I find I'm very affectionate and really quite profound.

Lucile. We're supposed to be rehearsing. . . . And they're sure to be listening outside the door.

Count. The dumb girl speaks. How fascinating! And wonder of wonders, she doesn't tell me to be quiet, but only to be quieter!

Lucile. If I had really wanted to silence you, I could have. I've had a week to do it in. I'm merely afraid they'll hear us, it's true.

Count. Why won't you see me elsewhere but in this room during rehearsals? What game are you playing, if it's true that I don't bore you?

Lucile. No game at all, I promise you. When I find my true love I'll do all I can to please him and I'll be his at once, without playing a game.

Count. I wonder what credentials that important personage will be expected to produce?

Lucile. None. I'll be his if he's poor, or shy of me, or has no place to sleep at night; if he has a wife and children and only one short hour a week to give me in a café.

Count [*with a touch of asperity*]. You swathe yourselves in mystery and you're all alike! Especially if he's poor, oh certainly!—especially if he's shy of you! When we don't take you by force, you always need a little pathos before you'll give yourselves.

Lucile [*gently*]. Even if he's rich and happy. I shall feel the same.

Count. Well then! I'm rich and happy and I should like you to love me.

Lucile. Little children cry for the moon too. It's my job to explain that it can't be had so easily. Do you think I shouldn't like to love you? You or someone else. . . . It must be so good to give one's all.

Count. Yes, mustn't it? And we're in luck. It so happens I'm a willing taker. Between the two of us, we might come to some arrangement.

Lucile. My poor sir, one only gives to the rich.

Count. Explain yourself: I was always bottom of the class in Scripture. The parables were never my strong point.

Lucile. The boy who loves me as I want him to love won't need to ask.

Count. But how will you know he loves you? Because he'll tell you so, little sparrow!

Lucile. No. He won't dream of telling me so, probably —and certainly not in an entertaining way like you.

Count. And what will he do, the tedious fellow? Bay at the moon? Thump his chest at the place where he vaguely thinks his heart is?

Lucile. He'll be bashful, he'll say nothing, I imagine. He'll avoid my eyes, maybe. He'll ask another girl to dance—but I'll know that I'm the one he loves.

A slight pause.

Count. The rules are a bit tricky. But I'll learn. I'm very quick at picking up games.

Lucile. I'm afraid that there may be no learning this one. But please, let's rehearse. We'll never be ready. It would be dreadful if we didn't know our lines.

Count. As you wish. Thank you for putting me in my place so sweetly. I am an idiot. Fate has been a little too indulgent with me and I have rather bad habits, I know. You are quite right. Let's forget it all and rehearse. [*He begins.*] "How now, fair Sylvia, will you not look at me?" [*He stops.*] One word more. I'm a miserable devil, I agree, and it must be wonderful to give one's all in all simplicity. That's a divine grace I never had, that's all. You are an enchanting girl under your light veil of mist, for those with eyes to see. For the last week—I don't know why—I can think of nobody but you. I told you so, in my fashion—that is, by trying to be amusing. You gave me to understand that my way of saying so or the fact itself displeased you. Very well. I have been well brought up, I shan't try to kiss you in the corridors. I shan't throw myself in the lake either. There's a middle way between the two, which is regret for a charming affair that never was, that's all. Mademoiselle, let us rehearse. You are right, they might hear us. I have been quite absurd enough this evening. There's no need for all the world to know it. [*He begins again.*] "How now, fair Sylvia, will you not look at me? Your brow darkens each time I come near you. It grieves me to think you find my presence irksome."

Lucile [*looking at him with a smile*]. You're very sweet. . . .

Count. What do you mean, I'm sweet?

Lucile. You're quite the dapper little man with his white gloves and his cane and his first bowler hat, who sauntered through the Bois de Boulogne every morning.

Count. Who told you that? When I had my first bowler, you were bawling in your cot, my child!

Lucile. That makes no difference. I can see you very clearly. It's hard, isn't it, growing up? But I'm sorry, let's go on.

Count. This is extremely disconcerting! This is the first time you view me at all kindly, and it's to inundate me with compassion! Yes, I sported a bowler—I was a shade young perhaps, but they were fashionable then. Yes, I took my constitutional every day at noon. But I wasn't all that ludicrous, as I remember. At least, the girls of your age—at the time—didn't appear to think so. And I fail to see how my behavior entitles you to treat me as a fop!

Lucile. Don't be angry. It's very nice to have stayed a little boy.

Count. I am not a little boy! I was in the war, I had a gun, a real live gun! They gave me a medal—like to a child, I know, but I don't wear it. I drive a car. I've even raced one. I was a diplomat for a while, and had I persevered I might be answering for my country somewhere at this very moment. Dammit, I'm as good as the next man—rather more brilliant if anything, or so they tell me. I'm tired of swaying to your little tune like a great browbeaten snake!—Act II. Scene I! "How now, fair Sylvia, will you not look at me?"

Lucile [*obediently getting into position for the scene*]. You know, what I say doesn't matter very much. You mustn't take too much notice of my chatter. Please don't be offended.

Count. I'm not offended! I astonish myself, that's all. Come, let's do our scene. I'm a good loser—that's another aspect of my first-class education. But don't brag of it, that's all I ask.

Lucile. Brag? To whom?

Count. I don't know. To your godfather, to a girl friend. . . .

Lucile. I never talk to my godfather. You must have noticed that there isn't much love lost between us. And I haven't any friends.

Count. Well, to your twelve orphans, then?

Lucile. Oh, yes, I shall tell them. I have to tell them so many fantastic stories to send them to sleep at night. And I've run out of my stock of fairy tales. But I'll adapt it a little. I'll set it in the Middle Ages.

Count. Good. Now then. "How now, fair Sylvia, will you not look at me? Your brow darkens each time I come near you. It grieves me to think you find my presence irksome."

Lucile. "You are mistaken, Sire. Why, I was speaking of you not long since."

Count. "You spoke of me? And what said you, fair Sylvia?"

Lucile. "Oh, many things! I said that you did not yet know what I was thinking."

Count. "I know you are resolved to deny me your heart, and that is to know the essence of your thoughts."

Lucile. "You know less than you think, then. But tell me, you are a man of honor and I am sure you'll tell me true. You know that Harlequin and I are promised. Now, take it that I have a mind to love you. Were I to gratify my whim, would I do right?—would I do wrong? There, counsel me, in all good faith."

Count. "As one is not master of one's heart, had you a mind to love me you would do right to gratify your whim."

Lucile. "Do you speak as a friend?"

Count. "A faithful friend."

Lucile. "I think so too. So I shall love you, if I fancy, and no man shall say me nay."

Count. "What do I gain, nymph, since you do not fancy me?"

Lucile. "Pray do not try to guess——"

Count [*interrupting*]. That's it, by heaven! It's clear as daylight! You were lying! You're in love with someone else! Some young man in child welfare to whom you write ten-page letters every evening in your room.

Lucile. I don't think you are speaking script.

Count. I'm asking you a question. Answer me, quickly
Here they come.

Lucile [*gravely*]. No. There isn't anyone. I haven't
ever been in love.

The Countess, Hortensia, Hero, Villebosse *and*
Damiens *come in.*

Countess. How is the scene shaping?

Count. Beautifully. We both find we have a lot of
talent.

Countess. As we have rather less, it might be as well
if we rehearsed.

Count. Shall we take it through from the beginning?
Monsieur Damiens says he isn't very sure.

Countess. Monsieur Damiens is used to an audience.
From the days when he held the floor at the assizes, he
has always known how to draw tears at will. He'll acquit
himself better than any of us.

Damiens. I'm not so sure, dear lady! I was very young
at the time. Besides, the script was of my own inventing.

Countess. Monsieur Damiens, what a shameless barn-
stormer you are! All this false modesty, just so we can
see you shine again! No, I've no fears about *you*. Besides,
there isn't time to do the whole play before dinner.

Count. In that case, let's do the beginning of Act II.
We'll cut Sylvia's long speeches. Hortensia, my sweet,
this rehearsal is for you. You're a touch too waspish in
your scene with Sylvia. Be your own charming self. You
have to fool this girl, remember.

Hortensia. If you think I'm incapable of playing the
part, Tiger dear——

Count. Hortensia, it fits you like a glove! It needs
a shade more subtlety, that's all. Really, actors are impossible! They go into a trance of bliss at the sound
of their own voices and they're convinced that we share
in their ecstasy! Naturalness in the theatre is the most
unnatural thing on earth, my pet. Don't imagine that
all you have to do is copy the accents of real life. To
begin with, in real life the script is always terrible. We
live in a world that has completely lost the instinct for
the semicolon. And as for the naturalism of speech that
actors take such pride in—the stammering and the errums
and the pauses and the fluffing—it's hardly worth en-

ticing five or six hundred people into a building and charging them good money to present them with that. Life is very nice, but it lacks form. It's the aim of art to give it some. But I'm boring you. I'm beginning to take myself seriously now. Act II. Sylvia, begin.

Lucile [*to Hortensia*]. "Yes, I believe you. You seem to wish me well. You are the only one I can abide in this place. I know the others are my enemies. Where is Harlequin?"

Hortensia. "He will be here directly. He is still at dinner."

Hero [*eying* VILLEBOSSE *through his glass*]. Wrong! He is not at dinner, he is at bay. He appears to be eating but he is munching the cud of his rancor.

Villebosse. Sir, I am not speaking to you! I'm warning you, don't try my patience too far!

Count. Hero, do be serious, for once.

Hero. Impossible, my dear fellow. I'm still sober.

Lucile. "This kingdom is the most alarming place. I never saw men so civil, nor women so fair-spoken! One would think them the kindliest creatures in the world. There's an error for you!" [*To the* COUNT.] Shall I cut to the end of the speech?

Count. Yes. You do it very well.

Lucile. "To scoff at virtue, to break one's word, to lie and cheat and be a scoundrel, that is the aim of the great ones in this accursed place! Tell me, what kind of folk are these? What are they made of?"

Hortensia. "The same stuff as other men, sweet Sylvia! They think the Prince's favor would set a seal upon your happiness."

Lucile. "Can one forgo one's virtue and be happy? Besides, is not my faithful heart my charm?" Shall I skip?

Count. No. It's lovely. Go on.

Lucile. "And no one has the courage to say to me: Do this evil thing. Bring naught but harm upon yourself. Betray the one who trusts you and lose your life's delight. They woo me with sweet phrases, and because I'll not be won they think me surfeited."

Hortensia. "The poor things know no better! They wish to please his Highness and would wish the Prince pleased you."

Lucile. "But why will the Prince not pick a girl who'll yield with a good grace? What whim is this, to want one who'll have none of him?" [LUCILE *has looked at the Prince as she speaks.*]

Countess. Tell her the Prince isn't on-stage yet, Tiger. It's Hortensia she must look at.

Lucile. "In all my born days I never saw man so lavish to so little purpose! All those grand balls, those entertainments, those banquets magnificent as weddings—those jewels he sends me! Sweet heaven knows the money it must cost him! And what does he gain by it? If he gave me the whole stock of a draper's shop, it would not please me half so well as the little ball of wool Harlequin gave me."

Hortensia. "That is true love. I have known love like this. . . . A little ball of wool once meant as much to me." [*To the* COUNT.] Is she being sincere? It doesn't feel right. Did she ever prefer a ball of wool to all the Prince's jewels?

Count. And what about you, Hortensia?

Hortensia. Tiger, we aren't discussing me! You just said we weren't playing ourselves——

Count. Excuse me, when I cast the play I knew perfectly well what I was doing. You said that line quite beautifully.

Hortensia. I played it straight. . . .

Count. And as you never preferred the tiniest ball of wool to your own pleasure, by playing it straight you sounded abominably false. Perfect. It's just what I wanted. Go on.

Hortensia. You're manipulating us like puppets! I warn you, we won't stand for it much longer!

Count. Count yourselves lucky that I don't bawl your heads off. There's no inspired production without tears. A play produced by a polite man rarely smacks of genius. Go on, Sylvia. "Let him forget me."

Lucile. "Let him forget me, then. There are some here I could mention who have their swains as I have, but they'll love anyone for all that. Let him choose one of them and let me be."

Hortensia. "Ah but, dear child, where will he find loveliness to rival yours? There is none here can hold a candle to you!"

Count. Good! The gall behind the smile. You must have worked all night to get that right, Hortensia!

Lucile. "Indeed there are—and prettier than I. And were they only half so comely, 'twould serve them better than flawless loveliness would me. I have seen ugly ones work their features so well that one is fooled."

Countess. Look at Flaminia, child. I'm not on-stage yet. I don't come on till later.

Hortensia. "But yours needs no artifice. That makes its charm."

Lucile. "But I look nothing. I cannot glitter to advantage, whilst they are always spirited and gay. They have eyes that dance and linger, and invitation in their smile, and beauty that is challenging and free and without shame. That is more pleasing than such a bashful one as I, who dare not look at people and am confused they think me fair."

Countess. She ought to say that more modestly, don't you think so, Tiger? She sounds as though she's on the attack now.

Count. But she *is!* She *is* on the attack! Everybody is dying for her to attack!

Countess. Mademoiselle is charming, we all think so— and you did very well to give her the part. But really—I know I can say this in front of her, she's an intelligent girl—her appearance is hardly striking enough to warrant the confidence in her beauty indicated in the text. She ought to say the lines more simply.

Count. I don't agree with you. I think she says them very well. Go on, Hortensia.

Hortensia. "But that is what stirs the Prince, 'tis that he values! This innocent air, this natural beauty, this artless grace! And do not praise the women of this court so highly, for, believe me, they have little praise for you."

Lucile. "Why, what do they say of me?"

Hortensia. "They mock you, and chaff the Prince, and ask him how his rustic beauty does. 'Did you ever see countenance so common?' said those jealous cats the other day; 'or form so lumpish?—or complexion so dull?' And even among the men there was not one but thought you middling plain. La, I was in a rage!"

Lucile. "Why, what wicked men to betray their real opinion so! And all to please a pack of silly geese!"

Count. I adore that! Isn't she funny the way she says that?

Hortensia. "Alas, how true!" Don't keep cutting in, Tiger, it's very irritating. "Alas, how true."

Lucile. "How I hate those women! But why, then, if I am so unpleasing, does the Prince love me and pay so little mind to them?"

Hortensia. "Oh, they are certain he'll not love you long. 'Tis a whim, they say—and he'll soon tire of you!"

Count. Lord, you do that well, Hortensia! You've got it, my sweet, you've got it absolutely! Now we'll cut to my entrance with Lisette. [*Taking the* COUNTESS's *arm.*] Come along, Eliane.

Lucile. "Why sir, 'tis you! You knew that I was here?"

Count. "Yes, lovely maid, I knew. But you told me I was not to see you and I never would have dared appear alone. Milady wished to make your acquaintance and requested the honor of curtsying to you."

Lucile. "I thank her Ladyship kindly. I do not deserve it, but let her make her curtsy if she has a mind to. I'll curtsy back as best I can. She must excuse me if I do it badly."

Countess. "Yes, my love, I'll excuse you gladly. I'll not ask the impossible of you."

Lucile [*aside to* HORTENSIA]. "I'll not ask the impossible! What a way to talk!"

Countess. "How old are you, my child?"

Lucile. "I forget, my dam!"

Countess. "She is angry, methinks!"

Count. "Why, madam, what means this? You come to greet Sylvia and you insult her?"

Countess. "Why, not at all! I was curious to meet the little girl who inspires such passion and I am trying to see what is so lovable in her. They tell me she is artless. That's a rustic charm which is sure to be diverting. Pray ask her to give us a few samples of artlessness. Let us see her wit."

Lucile. "No, madam, 'tis not worth it. It has less art than yours."

Countess [*with a pearly laugh*]. "La, there's village drollery for you!"

Count. "Leave us, madam."

Countess. "My patience, sir, is wearing thin. If this pert wench does not go, I shall—and for good!"

Count. "You will answer to me for your behavior."

Countess. "Farewell! Such a creature is revenge enough on him who made her his choice!"

Count. Excellent. Scene III.

Countess [*almost in the same tone*]. That's enough. I'm tired. Tiger, I should like a word with you. Will you come up to my room?

Hortensia. Yes, let's have a rest. It's all great fun for Tiger, but rather less so for us. We must get our breath back, my dear!

Count. Very well. We'll break for ten minutes.

HORTENSIA *goes out.*

Count [*to* HERO]. Women don't know the first thing about the theatre. Once they stop playing themselves they lose all interest.

Hero. They ought to drink. That makes all pastimes pleasant. Villebosse, so should you.

Villebosse [*darkly*]. One day I'll suggest a less pleasant pastime, I promise you.

Countess [*at the door*]. Well, Tiger, are you coming?

Villebosse [*suspiciously*]. When do I see you, Eliane?

Countess. I don't know. Villebosse, you bore me.

The COUNT *and* COUNTESS *go out and* VILLEBOSSE *follows, brooding.*

Hero [*going to* LUCILE]. Mademoiselle, you play your part to perfection. I speak as a drunkard—I drank your every word. I even forgot to drink anything else. I'll write my doctor to that effect and he'll send you a small note of thanks. I shall now slip into something loose. This waistcoat is killing me. It appears I have gallons of water in my stomach—which is odd, seeing I never touch the stuff. Life is full of such weird contradictions. Have you found that out yet, pretty one? [*He comes a little too near and she shrinks slightly.*] You draw away. I smell, perhaps? I smell of spirits, what else? It's not bad, as smells go. Why, they pickle the livers of great alcoholics in spirits to scare off clean-living young men. Do I scare you?

Lucile. No.

Hero. That's because you can't see my liver. They tell me it's in full flower. A jungle of multicolored blooms. You don't care for flowers, I see. That's good. I disgust you, do I? [*He is very near her. He gives her a malicious smile.*] That's good too. I need to spread disgust a bit. It's part of my role. Not the one in our little play, the other —the one I really play in. Your goddaughter is charming, Monsieur Damiens. Now if, instead of Hero de—I'll spare you my name, it's far too long—I were called Monsieur Damiens, I swear I'd take her away. [*He turns in the doorway.*] A drunkard's promise. [*He goes out.* LUCILE *shudders slightly and turns to go.* DAMIENS *restrains her.*]

Damiens. Lucile, I want to talk to you.

Lucile [*stonily*]. I'm listening.

Damiens. You're young. You know very little about the world. When your poor mother died, you insisted on earning your own living, and a very worthy sentiment that was, too. Although, as you know, there was no need.

Lucile. No need? Mamma lived on a widow's pension. When she died I was left with a Renaissance table, two Regency chairs we always thought were genuine and which were fakes, my gramophone, and an old cat. What else was there for me to do?

Damiens. You had me.

Lucile. You're my godfather, I know. And it was very kind of you to take an interest in me. But I didn't want to be beholden to you.

Damiens [*gently*]. Why not, Lucile?

Lucile. You know why.

Damiens. My offer seemed monstrous to you at the time. Heaven knows the dreams a little girl of eighteen cherishes! . . . That's why I let you go your own way. I wanted life and hard work to teach you a little sober wisdom. I know that this has been a very difficult two years for you.

Lucile. Did I complain?

Damiens. No, never. But do you think I enjoyed seeing you struggle on your meager salary, with your made-over dresses, your threadbare gloves, your ageless shoes? You're attractive, and at your age a girl yearns for pretty clothes.

I should have liked to give you a little modest luxury.

Lucile. I should have liked to have it too. I'm no heroine! But not from you.

Damiens. You are alone in the world. I had a right to spoil you a little, it seems to me—even a certain obligation.

Lucile. You know that's a painful subject. Let's not reopen it, do you mind? You gave me dolls and workbaskets when I was little—and you found me this place. You've done your duty by me. I shall manage quite well on my own now.

Damiens. Why will you not let me give you the security you need?

Lucile. At my age it isn't security one needs.

Damiens. I'm not speaking only of financial security. I mean sincere affection, thoughtfulness, protection too.

Lucile [*looking him squarely in the eye*]. From whom were you thinking of protecting me, had I accepted your proposition? From other men who might make me the same offer?

Damiens. From less scrupulous men, who haven't the love and the respect I bear you. Other men who might think only of taking their one night's pleasure with you.

Lucile. Didn't you gather that I knew how to defend myself?

Damiens. Against me, perhaps, who had the honesty to tell you what I had to offer. But against some younger, more attractive man, who'd lie to you . . . ?

Lucile. If he's younger and more attractive, at least the whole thing will be less depressing, even if it lasts less long. Especially if it lasts less long. Better, after all, if shame isn't a blueprint for the future. . . . Besides, that one night's pleasure might be shared.

Damiens. I cannot bear to hear you talk like this! I wish I had never brought you into this house!

Lucile. Why? Because they've dressed me up and made me act for the same wages? In my position I know that there are certain things one has to swallow. The matron at my first children's home soon taught me that cardinal rule, don't worry. And a good deal more sordidly. I had my little lot of slights in exchange for my plate of mutton stew. I know all about it now. And if that was what you hoped that life would teach me, it's been done.

Damiens. My little girl, that man wants you—and he

won't rest until he has his way! And everybody has seen through his little game. Did you notice them all just now, during rehearsal? The Countess is a shrewd woman. She lets him have his mistresses—just as he, on his side, turns a blind eye to her lovers—so long as the game is played in their own set, with cards she is familiar with. She'll never allow him to dance attendance on you. She'll heap insults on you—she'll throw you out of the house!

Lucile. Is that what you're so frightened of? That I'll lose my job? I'll go to another orphanage, that's all. You wouldn't believe how rich one is when one has nothing to lose.

Damiens. You cannot be this man's mistress!

Lucile. I shan't be, never fear. But for other reasons, which are my concern.

Damiens. He's trifling with you! The man's a libertine, a——

The COUNT *comes in quickly, looking a little pale.*

Count. Forgive me, Monsieur Damiens. I must seize your goddaughter again. There's a scene I want to touch up with her before tonight's rehearsal. Will you excuse us?

Damiens [*stiffly*]. I leave her in your care, your Grace. I was just warning her against the pitfalls of a style of living that is not her own. It was a sweet thought to have her in the play and I want to thank you, and her Lady-ship, for being so kind as to treat her as your equal. But I don't want her to forget that she is here, when all's said and done, to earn her living, and to look after those children.

Count. My dear Damiens, I hoped to do my best to make her forget it. And I mean to see to it that nobody takes it upon himself to remind her. Mademoiselle Lucile is my guest and if, as well as the favor she is doing us in acting in this play, she has the goodness and courage to devote herself to my aunt's twelve little fiends, instead of lying in bed till noon and prinking in front of the glass, that's one more reason why we should respect her. I shall make a point of informing everyone to that effect.

Damiens. If you would be so kind as to see to that personally, your Grace, I shall leave you, perfectly calm in mind. [*He bows and goes out.*]

Count. No, don't say anything. First let me beg your pardon. I have spent so much of my life in the company of shallow rogues that I may have grown into one myself. Before this show there's nothing to be done. A ball is a ball and this one must be given. They'll make life unbearable for you, but you're brave, I know. I have just had a talk with my wife. I thought I knew it all, but I have just discovered to what depths a woman of intelligence and taste can sink when she senses something dangerous and unfamiliar in the air. They've guessed, all of them, that I'm in love with you and that this is no passing fancy. So here is what I suggest. Let me finish before you say anything. You must see that I'll never consent to lead my merry little round of pleasure while you are busy wiping dirty noses for brats who aren't even your own, somewhere in this wide world. No, wait. I have very little money—let that set your mind at rest. It's many a year since I wasted my substance. But by selling the odd trinkets I have left I can raise enough to send you abroad. You can complete your education. You will be free. And in a year or two—a month or two—I hope with all my heart that you will find the young man you deserve and that you'll build a life together. I shall never see you again. [*A slight pause.*] Money embarrasses you, I think, but money is nothing to the truly free—necessary counters, no more. And I am asking you, very humbly, to share what little I have left of it with me. You will leave the day after the ball. [*Another short pause.*] It's an egoist's offer. An egoist who never once held you in his arms and who is very unhappy. [*He asks humbly*] Do you accept?

Lucile [*looks at him a moment*]. No, of course not. . . . [*He looks at her, dumbly, and she adds, softly*] I prefer to stay . . . now. [*He hesitates a second, then takes her swiftly in his arms and kisses her.*]

Count. My little one. . . .

Lucile [*in a murmur*]. It's too good. Is this what they call tenderness? I thought it only came much later.

Count. I thought so too. We must have traveled fast.

Lucile. We've traveled well. This is the best of love. [*Still in his arms, she murmurs suddenly*] I'm afraid.

Count. Of what?

Lucile. That I shan't amuse you long. I'm not beautiful.

Count. You are.

Lucile. Not like Hortensia.

Count. No, thank heaven.

Lucile. I'm not intelligent.

Count. Are you stupid enough to want me to say yes, you are?

Lucile. Anyway, I can't think of something clever to say at the right moment.

Count. I hope not.

Lucile. I'm poor. I dress badly—and if I had money I might dress even worse. You can't but tell from my hands that I've washed a great many clothes and done quite a few dishes too. Anyway, that these hands have been used. . . . What else is there to love in me, once the appeal of novelty is over?

Count [*gently*]. The fact that you aren't beautiful like all the rest. That you are awkward, and poor, and that, instead of blood-red claws weighed down with diamonds, you have two little naked hands with close-trimmed nails—that have been used. [*He kisses them.*] The hands of a real woman.

Lucile [*murmuring*]. If it's a taste for dairymaids that makes you want me, I think I should be so ashamed I'd die.

Count. It would be very foolish of you not to understand, you who know it all. Do you think it's a coincidence that in the length of legend captive princes searched so avidly for beggar maids to set them free? And do you imagine it was easy? The world is full of little servant girls who long to love Prince Charming.

Lucile. Everyone will think that's why I love you.

Count. You can be sure they'll seize on that as well to part us. Will you think it, too?

Lucile. No.

Count. Nor I. Well then, little silly, if neither you nor I believe it, who is "everyone"?

Lucile. They're coming.

Count. The walk-ons. The supernumeraries in the play we'll act together, you and I. [*The others come in.*] "Yes, Sylvia, I concealed my rank from you till now, so I might owe your love entirely to my own. Now that you know who I am, you are free to accept my hand and heart or to decline them both," etc., etc. [*To the others.*]

Punctual, I see. Thank you. I hope you had a good rest. Now, if you will, we'll see to a very important matter that real actors never fail to settle at the dress rehearsal. The curtain calls. We'll take them in this order. I take Lucile's hand, Eliane on my right, then Hero, then Hortensia. Damiens on the other side, and Villebosse —— [*Looking round.*] Villebosse! Where is he?

Enter VILLEBOSSE, *in a rage as usual.*

Villebosse. I was told we were rehearsing on the terrace! It's four o'clock. Are we rehearsing or are we not?

Count. Just one moment, Villebosse. We are doing something even more important in the theatre. We're taking a bow.

The company bows as the curtain falls.

ACT TWO

Same set. HORTENSIA *is seated. The* COUNTESS *is pacing nervously up and down. Enter* VILLEBOSSE.

VILLEBOSSE. Are we rehearsing or are we not?

Countess. Villebosse, you bore us.

Hortensia. Tiger wanted us dressed and ready by four. We're waiting.

Villebosse. What exactly is going on, will someone tell me? Last night's rehearsal was a farce! Today we're an hour late! Dammit, we open in three days!

Countess. Villebosse, please go away. I want to talk to Hortensia.

Villebosse. Eliane, what's the matter? Your attitude is absolutely baffling. What have I done?

Countess. Nothing. Absolutely nothing. That's the trouble. Go away.

Villebosse. But Eliane, I'm miserable!

Countess. Go and enjoy a moment's misery in the garden. We'll call you.

Villebosse. I really don't see how I could have offended you since yesterday!

Countess. My dear man, it's nothing to do with you. I'm asking you to leave us alone a second, that's all.

Villebosse. I'll go, but I've had as much as I can stand! I'll wait outside on the terrace till you call me. You owe me an explanation.

Countess. You shall have it. So shall we all. [VILLEBOSSE *goes.*] My dear, I don't understand you. Why, he's infatuated with the girl! He's acting like a moonstruck calf! And you aren't lifting a finger. You disappoint me, Hortensia.

Hortensia. You know as well as I do, making a fuss won't solve anything.

Countess. You surely aren't expecting me to make the fuss? I didn't make a fuss over you. I've no reason whatever to do so over this girl.

Hortensia. Let him be. He'll win his way up to her room tonight and by tomorrow he'll have forgotten all about her.

Countess. You must be blind. Tiger is a changed man. I was watching him at dinner yesterday. He looked like a snapshot of himself a friend took during the war, the morning of the German offensive. That little boy, solemn and perfectly happy, standing beside his gun. I never thought that anything but death could bring that face out from the depths of him. I tell you he's in love with her!

Hortensia. Tiger can't love anybody.

Countess. He's starting to learn! Please yourself, but I shall never stand for it. Were things not quite right between you, physically?

Hortensia. Eliane, you embarrass me.

Countess. My dear Hortensia, this is hardly the moment to be coy. We must fight for our own. Was he always very ardent?

Hortensia. Tiger is a wonderful lover.

Countess. That's what they all said. Still, there are degrees of accomplishment. . . . Put your cards on the table, Hortensia. I must know if I can rely on you. Was it a success between you, on that plane?

Hortensia. Dear Eliane, shall I go into details?

Countess. Thank you. That activity of Tiger's interests me in much the same degree as his passion for polo. But at least when he comes off the field, I can ask him point blank if his horse came up to scratch. When it came to love, I had up till now confined myself to guesswork. Today I want facts.

Hortensia. I think his horse comes up to scratch.

Countess. Good. That's important. He hasn't touched the girl yet. She's a virgin, you can tell that a mile away—probably clumsy, and not especially gifted in that direction. If he makes a little trip to the east wing—you're right—he may easily come back to us with his tail between his legs. He has a morbid hatred of the second-rate.

Hortensia. Eliane, I think you're being the tiniest bit glib. Love-making, you know, is a far more complicated game than polo. I speak from hearsay, of course, but I should imagine that a feeling of tenderness for an awkward, unspoiled little creature may teach Tiger new delights—beyond sheer pleasure perhaps, or subtly allied to it.

Countess. I don't like a woman to have to clear a picture of what her lover may feel with another. I thought you more healthy-minded, Hortensia. On my own ground, the sphere of intelligence and our mutual zest for living, I feel he may escape me. That's enough for me. I shall act, with or without your help.

Hortensia. Why, with it, of course! Believe me, my one concern just now is to get Tiger back, even if I leave him the next day.

Countess. Do both, there's a darling. In the intervals between mistresses, Tiger is an enchanting husband. He usually feels the urge to take me on a holiday and pay a discreet court to me—quite platonic, of course, but then I was never one to crave for it. I'll make it the occasion to leave Villebosse. He's beginning to bore me. It will be sheer heaven!

Hortensia. Delighted to make some contribution, however humble, to your honeymoon trip, Eliane. Where will you go—Italy?

Countess. No, that's so hackneyed. Tiger is dying to go to Kashmir. He says it's the only country he feels the faintest urge to visit.

Hortensia. How entrancing! We'll make Kashmir our objective then. How shall we do it?

Countess. Darling Hortensia! Let me kiss you again!

[*She does so.*] But tell me, if he really means so little to you, you wouldn't turn the tables on me and allow him to get serious about this girl? I feel I may have shown my hand a shade too openly.

Hortensia [*kissing her too*]. Dearest Eliane! I should be delighted, of course, to do you that small disservice! I'll never forgive you for remaining Tiger's friend while he was my lover. But my pride wins the day, don't worry. I cannot allow him to leave me for that little frump. I am the one who does the leaving. I'll keep you up my sleeve for another occasion.

Countess [*kissing her again*]. Aren't we a darling! And don't we smell delicious! Is it still "Plaisir d'une Nuit"? I used to think it smelled of aniseed, but I'm working round to it. Pity. When I'm completely used to it, Tiger won't reek of it any more. Come up to my room, darling. I have an idea. That little cuckoo is sure to be crammed full of complexes and wounded dignity. I'll say one of my rings is missing, and insist on having all the staff's rooms searched. We'll find the ring later in a flower pot or under a cushion—that's a detail. But it may do the trick and drive her away. You'd never believe, my dear, how sensitive the poor can be!

They go out. HERO *and the* COUNT *come in from the opposite side.*

Hero. Are we rehearsing or are we not—to quote Villebosse. I can just about exist in my waistcoat for the space of three acts, but that's the limit. A minute more and I'll explode, scattering my liver like a shower of poisonous blossoms on the assembled company. Exit one alcoholic, to applause.

Count [*sitting*]. Hero, I've lost interest.

Hero. What in, the show? Don't tell me you're thinking of doing another play? I was delighted with my part. A lord. What are you playing, Hero dear? A lord. It's discreet and mysterious and not too many lines to learn.

Count. It no longer amuses me to amuse myself.

Hero. You've taken your time finding it out. Try drinking, then.

Count. Being drunk wouldn't amuse me either.

Hero. You don't think one gets drunk for fun, do you?

It's no sinecure being a soak. If you knew the energy it takes, my boy! Forever filling glasses and emptying them and filling them up again. Which gives me an idea. Why don't you work?

Count. That's a bad habit one must indulge in very young. I doubt if that would amuse me much either.

Hero. Do as I do, make love. Not that that's so wildly amusing, but it keeps hope on the bubble.

Count. I have. Less often than you, but often enough. I'll tell you something. It's no life for a man.

Hero. You're getting doleful. How old are you?

Count. A year older than you, as if you didn't know it. We met in the third form, when I failed to get my remove. We owe our friendship to a prolonged bout of scarlet fever.

Hero. Don't tell me you're harboring the dark design of doing something useful?

Count. Heavens, no.

Hero. Or making money? With Eliane's fortune that would be downright immoral.

Count. I hate money.

Hero. Now, now, no big words. Just despise it, that's quite sufficient. You've only one choice left. Be a neurotic. That will fill your days up nicely. They'll coax you to talk about yourself every day for a whole hour, stretched out on a sofa. It's always absorbing to talk about oneself. It will cost you a fortune and you'll learn, at the end of a year, that you took an abnormal pleasure in the breast because your wet nurse was boss-eyed.

Count. Hero, imagine, if you can, that one day everything fell into place around you. That it all became serene and simple suddenly but, at the same time, out of reach.

Hero. I'm finding it difficult. Wait till I adapt it slightly. Whisky is suddenly recommended as the elixir of life, but all the bars I know are closed.

Count. That's it. No. There's one bar open, just one. A modest little provincial saloon that it would never have crossed your mind to enter.

Hero. There are no saloons that it would never cross my mind to enter.

Count. But you do go in, and when you've crossed the threshold you discover that living was really much simpler, and more serious, and much, much better than you ever thought it could be.

Hero. These bucolic analogies are too obscure for me. Besides, they'll make me thirsty. Enough of parables. Are you in love?

Count. Yes.

Hero. Good. Then there's nothing to worry about. You've told me so a dozen times.

Count. That's true. Then I'm not in love.

Hero. Ah, then it's "true love," is it? You told me that at least three times, twice with a lump in your throat.

Count. Then this time it can't be "true love" either. Because it's like nothing I ever knew before.

HERO *gets up and looks at him as he pours himself another drink.*

Hero [*abruptly*]. You make me sick.

Count. Why?

Hero [*softly*]. I don't like your face.

Count. Why—am I ugly?

Hero. No. Handsome. You've the look you had at school, before that day when we jumped the wall at fifteen to go to a bawdy house together. The look you had when we walked back from the games field in the winter, red and muddy and sweaty and happy, and we catcalled at the girls together. The look you had in the dormitory that night when we swore eternal friendship and slashed our wrists with a rusty penknife for our blood to mingle. [*He says heavily*] Don't do this to me, Tiger, or I'll never forgive you.

Count. It took us a whole hour, do you remember? How scared we both were, for all our bravado! Do you remember the oath?

Hero [*roughly*]. No.

Count. I'll find it for you. I came across it last night in some old papers.

Hero. No! I don't want to know! Don't do this to me, Tiger. Look, my hands are shaking. I'm a wreck. In a year, two at the outside, I'll be in a wheel chair or underground. I won't let you become the old you, now. That's too easy.

Count. Become who?

Hero. You heard me. [*The glass he was holding breaks in his grip. They both look at the broken glass and* HERO *says softly*] I'm sorry, old man. I like breaking things.

Count. You're mad! You've cut yourself! Take my handkerchief. You're lugubrious in your cups today.

Hero [*bandaging his hand*]. Liquor is always lugubrious. [*Holding out a piece of glass.*] Here, cut yourself too and swear.

Count. Swear what?

Hero. Swear that we're pleased with ourselves, you and I, and that we'll go on enjoying ourselves bravely till the end. If Hortensia bores you, change your woman. If you're short of cash, take some of mine. If you want to forget, I'll teach you how to drink. But play your time away like me, for sweet Jesus' sake. And don't wear that face again.

Count. It's part of me now.

Hero. One has to choose, Tiger. And we've made our choice. It's too late now. [*He takes another drink, and says in a different tone of voice*] In the first place, old man, it would grieve me to see you make an idiot of yourself. And it would grieve me even more to see you happy in that way.

A *pause.*

Count. You haven't forgiven me for Evangeline, have you?

Hero. No.

Count. She was no wife for you. You were nineteen—you would have buried yourself alive—you . . . [*He stops.*] Forgive me. Today for the first time I see that I may have been wrong to stop you marrying that girl.

Hero. What's done is done. And you weren't wrong. We've had a lot of fun together since. No regrets! With my wife, my six children and my livestock, on my small country estate, I should probably have come to the same end, and cut less of a dash doing it. We are drunks from father to son in our family—like blacksmiths. But one piece of advice deserves another. Steer clear of this thing they call love. It's not for us.

Count. If you care for me, you ought to wish me joy.

Hero. Not any more. Not that sort of joy. Anyway,

let's not fool ourselves. It's a good twenty years since we
stopped caring for each other—since our first long pants
in fact. That doesn't stop us being friends. [*Pouring*
TIGER *a drink.*] Your health. Good luck. And enjoy
yourself in your own way, you're a free agent. But no
confidences. And not too much hope either. Life has a
way of setting things in order and leaving them be. Very
tidy, is life.

Count. We'll see.

Hero. We'll see. One always does. That's the wonder
of man's condition. You cry Eureka five minutes before
dying and the curtain falls. [*Enter* HORTENSIA *and the*
COUNTESS.] Good morning, Eliane.

Countess. Hullo, Hero. Tiger, I am very worried. I
must talk to you. My emerald is missing.

Count. Tell your maid to look for it, my dear; don't
ask me. I can't bear it. You get your nails full of dust
poking down the sides of armchairs and you pull out an
old letter usually best left unread—always provided it
isn't a bill.

Countess. The servants have been looking all morning.
I had it yesterday. I remember distinctly. I took it off in
the cloakroom where we leave our costumes. The green
didn't match my dress. It's very worrying. I'm afraid
someone may have done something silly.

Count. No dramas. Have them look again.

Countess. Of course. But I must let the insurance
people know if I don't find it. They'll send someone to
investigate. It will be most unpleasant.

Count. After the ball, my dear, after the ball. Don't
oblige me to dress up your detectives in ruffled shirts
and knee breeches in the hope they'll pass unnoticed.
Wait till after the ball.

Countess. I'm sorry, Tiger, but the insurance company
must be informed within twenty-four hours. I'll have
another look. Hero dear, come and help me.

Hero. Overjoyed to be of service, at last. I've waited
thirty-seven years for a chance like this.

Count [*calling after them*]. But no dramas, please!
[*They go. To* HORTENSIA.] We poison our lives with
fear of burglary and shipwreck and, ask anyone, the house
is never burgled and the ship never goes down. Have you
noticed that life, real honest-to-goodness life, with

murders and catastrophes and fabulous inheritances, happens almost exclusively in the newspapers?

Hortensia. This ring business is very worrying.

Count. Eliane can afford to lose a piece of jewelry from time to time. She has plenty.

Hortensia. I don't think Eliane will take it quite so blithely. It was a lovely stone. She means to have the rooms of the entire staff searched.

Count. These people have been in the family service for over twenty years. You must admit they've taken their time before turning dishonest.

Hortensia. Eliane is determined to have the whole house searched. I do think it's an elementary precaution. Let me see, who is there here besides the servants . . . ? There's Villebosse, Hero, Damiens, myself——

Count [*interrupting*]. Hortensia, I loathe detective stories. Whenever I open one, in my low moments, I always drop off before the discovery of the first murder.

Hortensia. If I know Eliane, she'll be as good as her word. She'll search all the rooms in the east wing.

Count. If Eliane searches the east wing, I shall insist that the west wing be searched too. I'll lose my watch, my sweet, and I'll hide it in your room. [*Looking at her sternly.*] Did you think up this little fairly tale together? Congratulations.

Hortensia [*wide-eyed*]. What fairy tale, Tiger?

Count [*holding her by the elbows*]. My little Hortensia, I loved you once. It's a big word, but there are so few words that we have to lump several sentiments under one label. My hands, at least, have loved you. And each time we met, I felt a sort of joy, very pure—yes, it's funny, very pure and very near to happiness—when I touched you.

Hortensia. Thank you, Tiger.

Count. Don't thank me. It was none of your doing. I'll pay you a compliment, Hortensia—my first and my last, I daresay. You are very beautiful. I don't mean your face, delightful though it is. I don't believe in faces much. But your body is very beautiful. Noble and lovely as an animal's. And beauty, real beauty, is something very grave. If there is a God, He must be partly that, I think.

Hortensia. My God!

Count. Yes, it's an odd word on my lips. But the memory of the day when I held you in my arms for the first time is as clear and bright in me as my first sight of a palazzo in Florence, with my father, when I was eight years old. The same wound and the same joy. Eliane is a clever woman, but I don't rate cleverness very high. Let the brain elbow its own grubby little way through life. You, hold your head high. Be worthy of your beauty. She's a great lady.

Hortensia. I suppose this is your latest game, Tiger, but you left me unprepared for so much earnestness. You frighten me.

Count [*letting her go and lighting a cigar*]. I frighten myself too, a little. Do you think I relish diving to such depths? I haven't the training for it. I expect to be out of breath at any moment.

Hortensia. Tiger, that girl isn't even pretty! She'll shame you, in her neat little black frock, the first time you go anywhere with her. And if you dress her up she'll shame you even more. I know you.

Count. I'm fool enough to be ashamed of her, it's true. But that won't matter.

Hortensia. Tiger, you belong to a different breed. The head and the heart commit a hundred idiocies, but the hands rarely go wrong. I am sure that you still desire me.

Count [*looks at her with a smile and says softly*]. Of course. I'll stoop to anything. But you see, I love her.

Hortensia [*moving away with a peal of laughter*]. Oh, it's too absurd! I'm so sorry, but it really is too ludicrous!

Count. Isn't it? You're right, the whole affair is making me downright foolish. But, Hortensia, I love it!

DAMIENS *comes in.*

Damiens. Your Grace, your lady wife has lost a ring and she has ordered the butler and the bailiff to search all the rooms in the east wing. You gave me your assurance that my goddaughter should meet with every consideration in this house. Are you going to stand by and let them search her room?

Count. Certainly not. Follow me. We'll soon put a stop to this charade.

They go. Enter VILLEBOSSE.

Villebosse. Are we rehearsing or are we not? We've been hanging about for two whole hours!

Hortensia. But we're performing, Villebosse! The play is in full swing! Do you mean to say you hadn't noticed? [*She goes.*]

Villebosse. By God, they're making mock of me in this house! [HERO *comes in.*] Sir!

Hero. Sir?

Villebosse. I am being made a mock of in this house!

Hero. Very likely.

Villebosse. And it wouldn't surprise me if you were at the bottom of it!

Hero. It wouldn't surprise me, either.

Villebosse. How would you like it if I demanded reparation?

Hero. My dear sir, I like to break things, but I never repair them. [*He goes.*]

Villebosse [*pursuing him*]. Sir, you have refused my challenge! The Jockey Club will hear about this!

Enter the COUNTESS, *furious.*

Countess. Villebosse!

Villebosse. Eliane, beloved, you look angry.

Countess. I am angry! Tiger has just behaved quite atrociously to me! My emerald ring has been stolen. I ordered Fourcault and Jasmin to search the east wing, and Tiger has forbidden them to set foot in that girl's room. He insists that they search my room first. He says I've hidden the ring myself. I was never so insulted in my life!

Villebosse. Eliane, I will not stand for this! Allow me to go and provoke him!

Countess. Will you never understand the first thing about anything? I'm not asking you to take up the cudgels because Tiger has been rude to me! After all, he has a perfect right to be—I *am* his wife! It's a question of getting him to see that he is making me look ridiculous by running about with that tuppeny halfpenny little nursemaid! He can have his mistresses! Hortensia is a friend of mine! And she's a well-bred girl! But what will people say if my husband loses his head over a flea? If he brings her back to Paris, I shan't go out all winter. I swear I shan't dare show my face in public!

Villebosse. It's outrageous! I shall deal with this! Leave it to me, Eliane!

He marches out. Enter LUCILE.

Lucile. Here is the key to my room, madame. I would like it to be searched along with the others. It's possible the ring may be found there. Then everybody will feel easier.

Countess. My dear child, I don't know what you mean. My husband and my maid are still looking in my room. I may quite possibly have put the ring away somewhere and forgotten.

Lucile. I hope you find it.

Countess. Yes. Suspicion is always unpleasant, isn't it? I'm most sincerely sorry if I've hurt your feelings. I daresay you've come to tell me that you would rather not be in the play now? Perhaps you don't want to look after the children any more, either? Poor little mites, they were getting so attached to you, too! Still, if you've definitely made up your mind, it would be best, don't you think, to make the break as ruthlessly as possible, for their sakes. There is a train in an hour's time. The car can take you to the station as soon as you've packed your things. Naturally, although the decision comes entirely from you—I know how hard up you are—I shall give you six months' salary. [*The* COUNT *comes in. She turns to him, perfectly self-possessed.*] Mademoiselle tells me she is leaving. I'm most distressed for you, Tiger, about the play. But we still have three days to find someone else. I was telling her that it would be better, for the children's sake, to go without saying good-by. They were very fond of her—as indeed we all are—but they might be even more upset.

Count. Here is your emerald, Eliane.

Countess [*slipping it on her finger*]. Oh, I'm so glad! Where did you find it?

Count. In your room. Inside the chandelier.

Countess. Really? Whatever possessed me to go and put it there?

Count. Now, will you please apologize to Mademoiselle.

Countess. Apologize, good heavens, what for? But, of course . . . Mademoiselle, I am so sorry if I was hasty. I do hope you won't take away too unpleasant a memory of this house. I think you will be agreeable, Tiger, if Fourcault gives the child six months' salary? It's a silly impulse of hers, I know, but still, if I hadn't mislaid my ring, she wouldn't have thought of leaving us.

Count. My dear Eliane, I am not in the habit, as you know, of letting anything interfere with a ball I have decided to give. We cannot find a replacement in three days. I must ask you to be so good as to see to it that Mademoiselle changes her mind.

Countess. I assure you I said all I could, Tiger. She is quite determined to go. And I must confess I do see her point.

Count. I am sure you did not say all you could say. I insist on this little diplomatic victory from you, Eliane. I'll leave you together. We start rehearsing in half an hour.

He goes. LUCILE *still says nothing. The* COUNTESS, *greatly at ease, sits down.*

Countess. Oh dear! Now I have to persuade you to stay, or Tiger won't speak to me for days! You must admit it's laughable! But I'm weak as water underneath, and Tiger's whims are law to me. When the time comes for you to choose—my dear, *don't* fall in love with a frivolous man!

Lucile [*quietly*]. Do you love him?

Countess. Why, what a question! He's my husband!

Lucile. Do you think it makes him happy to play all the time?

Countess. My little girl, don't count on me to let our talk—since talk we must—follow *that* pattern! I have a horror of familiarity. I had an English nanny who taught me never to make personal remarks. Tiger asked me to ask you to stay. So I am asking you. He will go into a decline if he has to give up his play. Besides, why go at all? The children are devoted to you. And we shan't be staying at Ferbroques very long. We'll go back to Paris the moment the festivities are over. Then everything will be all right, won't it? Let's part good friends and, once again, please forgive me for our little misunderstanding. We don't know each other very well. But I have a very high regard for your godfather. Damiens and I were talking about you only this morning. He's very, very fond of you, you know.

Lucile. Yes. He told me.

Countess. He hasn't had a very happy life, either. Under his rather forbidding exterior, he's a surprisingly sensitive man. He talked at great length about you.

Lucile. Did he?

Countess. Yes. My dear, I was a little hasty with you, I know. I like you very much, really. You are so young, so helpless, under that funny little air of wisdom you have. I'm sure, beneath your Quaker girl solemnity, you're longing to burn your wings like a little mayfly on the first candle flame you meet. One thinks, how wonderful, life will be the way I always dreamed it! And a week later you've nothing but your eyes to weep with. [*A pause.*] Damiens and I were most concerned about you this morning. [*A pause. She rises and says casually.*] He's still a very handsome man, you know. I remember, fifteen or twenty years ago, when he used to come and see my mother. . . . Shall I tell you something?—of course I was only a youngster, but, do you know, I was in love with him for a whole winter! Anyway, think about it. When one is alone in the world, as you are, one must plan for one's future. Dear God, I know it isn't very glamorous. But that's the way of the world, my dear, and you and I won't change it. [*A pause. She says impulsively*] Here. Damiens has served us so long and so faithfully—and I need hardly say I should look upon you as his wife. This emerald will be my wedding present. [*She hands it to her.* LUCILE *looks at the ring a second and then hands it back.*]

Lucile. Thank you, madame. But it's too fine a gift for the kind of ceremony it would be.

Countess [*taking it back*]. You're wrong. I meant it kindly.

Lucile. Anyway, I'll never marry, that way or any other way. I swore it.

Countess. How can you possibly know that at your age? How long ago did you make that rash promise?

Lucile [*softly*]. Last night.

Countess [*rising abruptly*]. Very well. At least tell Tiger, when you see him, that I did all I could.

Lucile. I shall. Thank you, madame.

She goes. The COUNTESS *paces restlessly up and down, fanning herself. Then she goes to the window and calls.*

Countess. Hero! No, Villebosse, not you. Hero, come up. I want to talk to you. [*A few moments of silence, a few more restless strokes of the fan, and* HERO *appears.*] Hero. We must stop Tiger before he completely loses his head. He's in love with that girl. She has been his mistress since last night. It's utterly absurd! I don't know if you've noticed him during this last week.

Hero [*inscrutably*]. I have.

Countess. It's repulsive.

Hero. Quite repulsive. I told him so.

Countess. Hero, if you're on my side, do something. You're the only one who can.

Hero. With him? Tiger is persuasionproof.

Countess. With her perhaps?

Hero. And what have you in mind? A little gentle seduction?

Countess. You could, Hero, if you set your mind to it. All Paris knows you're irresistible. Give her the famous Hero charm. It smacks of melodrama, but never mind.

Hero. There's just one snag. The girl is not a member of that exclusive club you call "all Paris." She doesn't know I'm irresistible. That cuts my chances of success by fifty per cent.

Countess. Nonsense! In two days, whether it's Tiger or you, her mind will be in a whirl. She'll burst with vanity, as any girl would, to have the two most sought-after men in town dancing attendance on her. I needn't tell you how to set about it, Hero darling. Get her drunk one evening. Tell her you're madly in love with her. With a little moonlight and soft music the young goose will believe you. Enough at least to yield to you that night. After that Tiger will drop her, or if he agrees to sharing her. there really won't be any further danger.

Hero. How do you know she won't resist me? You do me too much honor. I'd say yes over any woman, even not belonging to "all Paris"—after all, I'm a professional! But for a virgin, no. They're strange animals, and I never ventured too near any one of them.

Countess. But I tell you she isn't a virgin! She's his mistress!

Hero. Since last night. She'll keep her state of grace for a while longer yet.

Countess. I see. So you're going to let him become totally besotted with her? It's all the same to you, is it, if Tiger adores her like a lovesick schoolboy?

Hero. You're wrong. It is not all the same to me.

Countess. You're afraid of hurting him, of breaking both their hearts, is that it?

Hero. No. I told you. I like breaking things.

A pause.

Countess. She sleeps alone at the far end of the east wing. It may not be so easy to seduce her, assuming that she really loves him. But we all know what a brute you are. You want the girl madly. You've been drinking. You break into her room. The lock won't work that night—the local locksmith's boy will see to that. She'll scream, of course—but it's miles away from anywhere out there. And what can one little girl do with her weak fists and her tears against a man's desire? If she loves him, she'll run away from shame the following morning.

Hero [*softly*]. Evangeline. . . .

Countess. What did you say?

Hero. The name of a girl. Madame Blumenstein. You must have met her. She married a banker. She was very beautiful. She wasn't very happy as a wife and hostess and she died, several years ago.

Countess. A slight, fair girl, with huge dark eyes? The look of a stricken doe? I remember her very well. I met her at the Rothschilds'. What's the connection?

Hero. A very vague, very distant connection. I'm glad you remembered her. Come, let's go and rehearse. They're waiting for us. Her husband was a rat. They say he used to beat her. . . .

Countess [*as she goes*]. I've an idea. I'll have someone

send Tiger a telegram calling him out this evening. Gontaud-Biron will do that for me. He owes me a good turn.

They go. Curtain.

ACT THREE

SCENE I

A *small attic room.* LUCILE *is curled up by the fire, dreaming. The door opens quietly. She looks up in surprise. It is* HERO, *still in costume, his ruffled shirt open at the neck, and carrying a bottle and two glasses.* LUCILE *rises.*

HERO. Don't be alarmed. Tiger has just telephoned. He won't be back till very late. He sent me to keep you company. May I sit down?

Lucile [*indicating the only chair*]. Yes.

Hero. A little drink?

Lucile. No.

Hero. May I? [*He pours himself a drink.*] Do you mind if I stay and chat a while? When others sleep, I begin my long, one-man battle until dawn. In the daytime I can just about get by. I drink, I talk—nonsense usually, but it stops me thinking. Would you help me to stop thinking for a moment? It's Tiger's orders, you know. He said, "Go and tell her I shan't be back and keep her company a while." [*A pause.*] He must have hoped that you would say a word or two yourself from time to time.

Lucile. What do you want me to say?

Hero. I don't know, something nice. That you made a mistake, that it isn't Tiger whom you love, it's me. . . . [LUCILE *smiles and does not answer.*] Tell me you love Tiger, then. It won't please me quite so much, but it's better than nothing at all.

Lucile. I can't believe he wanted us to discuss that. I'm sure he didn't talk to you about me.

Hero. Ah, child, child, you don't know men. We're as thick as thieves, his Grace and I.

Lucile. Are you fond of him?

Hero. We were throwing stinkbombs at the girls before you were even born, dear infant! We even mingled our blood in the dormitory one night. Faithful even unto death! The chance of dying for each other didn't turn up right away, that's all. So we've lived, as they say, Castor and Pollux, you know. Anyway, we were devoted to each other and no woman ever managed to come between us.

Lucile [*like a little girl*]. Has he had many women?

Hero. Dear baby! He adores you, we know, but you'll agree it would have been rash of him to wait for you. Does it upset you very much to know he's . . . lived a little?

Lucile. That's my secret.

Hero. Keep it, my dove, and put your nice clean hanky over it. I don't care for confidences much. You are disembarking in the land of love: you feel like an explorer at the gateway to new worlds. Don't protest, that's very sweet. You'll learn soon enough that the play only consists of two or three roles, two or three situations, and that what gushes from the heart in the high moments of elation is never anything but an old and hackneyed text chewed over, since the dawn of time, by mouths now toothless and decayed. Even the vices are dismally cut and dried. A proper catalogue, with current prices in the right-hand column. Sodomy: solitude and the universal ailment. Drink: remorse and ruined liver. Lust: exhaustion. True love: dear little broken heart. You pay cash down!

Lucile [*quietly*]. But I love Tiger and I'm twenty. So you see, your little speech is a waste of time.

Hero. Touché. There was only one answer to my alcoholic disenchantment, and you thought of it at once. Lucky devil, Tiger. He's made a success of that too, damn him! He wins all the prizes, from show jumping to love.

Lucile. Made a success of what?

Hero. Finding you. Touching you. I underestimated you. Serves me right. That'll teach me to look at girls more carefully in future. You know, it was inspired of you to give everyone the impression you were a tongue-tied little bore.

Lucile. I am a tongue-tied little bore. I wonder how

he set about discovering me under my shell and getting me to talk.

Hero. Tiger has all the gifts! And I'll bet you were as virginal as all get out, eh? [LUCILE *does not answer.*] Lord, now I've hurt her feelings! Come, have a little whisky. We'll never talk if I do all the drinking.

Lucile. No, thank you.

Hero. "No, thank you!" Nice manners too. All trim and prim and proper. A bright little, smooth little pebble his Grace found on the beach—without even looking for it, too! Just sauntering along with his hands in his pockets and his nose in the air, as usual! He's too lucky, it's becoming a bore. [LUCILE *looks up, surprised at his tone.*] I mean, if I didn't love him dearly, it would bore me. But I do love him—not like you, of course; like a brother. So I forgive him everything. Well now, let's talk about him, shall we? Sure you won't take a little something? [*She shakes her head.*] Tell me, what made you give yourself so soon? After all, before yesterday you'd hardly spoken to him. [*A pause.*] I'm not a thief of secrets, but it *is* such a pretty story! Who knows, it might manage to convert me. No? You won't say? Shall I never know, even at second hand, how the floodgates of love open?

A *pause.*

Lucile [*very softly, as if to herself*]. I could never bear anyone to touch me. And when he took me in his arms, I suddenly felt I had come home. I was no longer that frightened girl buffeted this way and that with her cheap suitcase. I've a place of my own now, too. What more could I ask?

Hero. Suppose he had merely wanted to have fun with you?

Lucile. That's a risk a girl must take. She should be able to tell. One mustn't shed too many tears for fools, you know.

Hero. Still, I know the old scamp when he wants to make a good impression. Be honest, he almost overdid it, didn't he?

Lucile [*smiling almost mischievously*]. A little, yes. But I made allowances.

Hero. What could you possibly hope for, tell me, from this dandy, this distinguished pantaloon?

Lucile. Nothing save to be happy in his arms a minute, as I was.

Hero. And after that?

Lucile. After that, if you have to live the other life, the real one, the living you merely have to earn, why, there's no scarcity of orphans in the world. That doesn't matter. I'll have had my share.

Hero. Not even a clinging vine! God blast him, he's by-passed all that's even faintly vulgar on this earth! Halfway through a life of wine and women: fatigue, futility, a vague disquiet. His Lordship lifts a finger. Enter an angel, who gives herself to him at once and for always. Because, of course, it is for always, isn't it?

Lucile. Of course.

Hero. And if he breaks his neck on the drive home tonight you'll die tomorrow morning. Daphnis and Chloe. Tristan and Isolde—without King Mark and that tiresome sword between you. His Grace has a sudden fancy for an idyl? One idyl coming up! One young girl, elusive, rare, carefully kept on ice for you? Here she is, sir, on a silver salver. She was waiting for you.

Lucile. It's true. I was waiting for him.

Hero. All he had to do was come and take you! And it's stainless, color-fast and guaranteed to last for ever! Let others make do with women who lend themselves to every Jack during the day before they give themselves to you at night; women who sit smiling in the showcase like enameled figurines. For I'm sure you'll never learn, will you? You'll always be as dour and unforthcoming, even when he buys you clothes and everyone admires you and pays you compliments.

Lucile. He'll never buy me any clothes, don't think it.

Hero. Why not?

Lucile. Because I don't want them. I've formed the habit of buying myself a dress from time to time. I want to keep it.

Hero. Everything! He'll have everything! Intelligence and wisdom, with unselfishness thrown in! I bet you'll insist on taking care of his aunt's twelve orphans too, and leaving the door of your attic ajar for him at night?

Lucile. Oh, no! But I'll find another children's home

not far from Paris, and he'll come and see me when he wants.

Hero. Won't that be sweet? He'll ask for you very politely in the parlor, red to the ears like a schoolboy, and you'll both sit there quaking, in case Matron disapproves. But there's a fly in the ointment. You don't know his Lordship. He's a chip off the good old French nobility. He'd starve sooner than let you work.

Lucile [*lightly*]. He'll have to. Man must live by the sweat of his brow. Did they never teach you that when you were little?

Hero. We went to very smart schools. That wasn't part of the curriculum. I tell you he'll die of shame.

Lucile. One doesn't die of shame that easily. Besides, working isn't so tiresome, not much more so than doing nothing. And it takes much less imagination; think of the lengths both of you go to, to kill time!

Hero. You're right! We've sweated blood all our lives. There's guts and drive for you! Look at what the poor do with their Sundays. They drag along the streets, yawning, worn out with waiting for it to be Monday. And we've had seven Sundays every week for years! It's been no picnic. But we stuck it. The worst is over now. Tiger can play for fifteen hours a day without feeling the strain. Leave it to him. He'll teach you.

Lucile. No.

Hero. But if you spend your life in the nursery and he on the racecourse, you'll be like the daily woman wed to the night watchman. You'll never meet at all! Dammit, you must be sensible!

Lucile. I don't want to be sensible. That's the first thing one says when one plans to do something bad.

Hero. Something bad, she says! Whatever that may mean. Anyway, you could do worse, my little one. It's better than doing something silly.

Lucile. I want to be silly. That's my way of loving. Can you see me waiting in a lovely rented flat, and him coming to call with a little parcel done up in pink ribbon? I'd loathe him in a week.

Hero. She knows it all! You won't let him put a foot wrong, will you? And he'll be only too delighted, the old humbug. He'll buy himself a neat little pin-striped suit and come and wait for you after work with a penny bunch of violets. He'll be nineteen again, with all his dewy-eyed felicity before him! To treat oneself to that at forty! [*He rises abruptly.*] No, it's too much!

Lucile. What's the matter?

Hero [*recovers, sits down again, and says with a wicked smile*]. I mean it's much too lovely. A real fairy tale.

A *pause.*

Lucile [*rising*]. I think you ought to let me go to bed now. I have to get up early in the morning.

Hero [*still seated*]. We haven't been talking five minutes. Sit down, my dear. Give me a little longer. I assure you I'll have less sleep than you will. Can't you see I'm terrified of being alone? Of your charity, fair damsel.

LUCILE *sits down again. He pours himself a drink.*

Besides, you're quite safe. A young lady can entertain me quite late into the night without risk to her good name. Not very appetizing, am I? I know. A ruin. And I'm a year younger than Tiger. That's what's known as a life of pleasure.

Lucile [*gently*]. Why don't you try drinking less?

Hero. Why should I? I should have to meet an angel like his Lordship to lend me a helping wing. And angels are so rare.

Lucile [*murmuring*]. You'll meet one someday. . . .

Hero [*with a mirthless laugh*]. Glass in hand? With my bloodshot eyes and my whisky breath? Tell me frankly—as an angel—if it had been I who courted you, would you have smiled on me? [*He looks at her and smiles.*] Another tactless question! I'm a little heavy-handed tonight. And yet . . . When you landed in this place some days ago, that first night at dinner—apart from Villebosse, who doesn't count—none of the men could take their eyes off you.

Lucile [*surprised*]. None of the men?

Hero. Bless the child, she never even noticed! Yes, my dear, three of us to be exact. The butler is too old, but the footman was so bemused he kept mixing up the serving spoons. He was burning to be converted too.

Lucile. I think you've said enough.

Hero. Why? Have I offended you? Could you be a snob, my heart? The lad sleeps in the east wing too. I'd bolt your door at night if I were you. He's the grandson of Tiger's grandfather's head gardener, I know, but he was a paratrooper in the war and that's an episode that smartened up a lot of lads. What would you have done had it been he—or I—instead of Tiger, who had said, "Be mine"?

Lucile. But I love Tiger, you see.

A *pause.*

Hero. You have disarming answers. What can I say to that?

Lucile [*kindly*]. Nothing.

Hero. A man can't have any fun with you. Let's pretend a second, just for fun—just to help kill the night a little. Tiger never even glanced at you. You aren't in love with Tiger. I have been making sheep's eyes at you for a week and tonight I've come to your room to tell you that I would like very much to make love to you.

He has risen heavily as he speaks. LUCILE *rises too.*

Lucile. I can't play that game. Why won't you understand? You are his friend. What would he say if he knew you were amusing yourself like that this evening?

Hero. Bless you, it wouldn't be the first time we'd slipped each other the odd girl friend. Besides, it would be tit for tat, you know. I was lying; there was an angel in my life, mademoiselle. A long time ago now. I was nineteen and I'd done very little drinking.

Lucile [*stammering*]. You mean, he——

Hero. No. He didn't steal her. But he made me leave her—for reasons I thought were valid at the time. She married someone else who made her wretched and she's dead now. It is to that trivial episode that I owe my present delectable condition.

Lucile. That's horrible. . . .

Hero [*briefly*]. Yes. It is. But Tiger owes me a girl now. That's why I've come to your room tonight.

Lucile [*backing away*]. If you don't go I'll call someone.

Hero. There's no one on this floor. But don't worry, I shan't touch you. I want to talk to you, that's all.

They stand and look at each other.

Lucile [*crying out in sudden fear*]. I love him! I shan't listen to you!

Hero [*softly*]. Yes, you will, my heart.

Lucile. I'm not interested in your neurotic ravings. I'm young, I'm normal, and I love him! You're wasting your time. Go back to your room. You'll be ashamed tomorrow.

Hero [*softly*]. I don't know what shame is, my dove.

Lucile. Are you friends with his wife to that extent? You know she doesn't love him! I'm not asking him to marry me. He needn't even be responsible for me. I'll be invisible, I'll work, he can go on leading his own life in his own world if that's what you're all so scared of!

Hero. His life, his world? Be damned to that! I'm not old man Duval, my little Lady of the Camellias.

Lucile. Then why have you been trying so hard ever since you came in? Why are you going to such trouble to spoil something that's real and good, and asks only to live? Is it because you hate him?

Hero. No.

Lucile. Why, then?

Hero [*in a murmur*]. I like breaking things.

She looks at him, standing very straight. He tries to hold her gaze for a while, then nervously pours himself another drink and drains it off.

Lucile [*quietly*]. Poor Hero. Poor little monster. You don't frighten me now. How unhappy you must be with all that load to bear.

Hero [*hoarsely*]. That's my affair! Mind your own business!

Lucile. It is my business. You're trying to hurt me. And all I feel for you is pity.

Hero. Don't you dare! You trashy little nursery maid! Poor little high-minded maggot with its watery blood and its nicely scrubbed hands and feet and its cheap little off-the-peg dress! I loathe you more than anything else on earth. Give me a whore who'll lift her skirt for the price of a drink—give me a tramp who takes your money and sleeps with all your friends—give me a drab gulping her red biddy under a railway arch—but I hate you! And I'll thank you not to look at me like that! [*He tosses down another drink. Then he sidles over to her, scarcely concealing his malicious glee.*] Do you know where Tiger is tonight? You remember he had a telegram, don't you? Do you know what message he told me to give you?

Lucile. I don't believe you!

Hero. What don't you believe, little cuckoo? I haven't told you yet. [*He leers at her.*] No pluck even? I can just see you at the dentist's, screaming before he's even touched his forceps. Looks down her nose at you, plays Antigone and Joan of Arc and all the heroines she read about at school, and when it comes to the point, out come the sniffles and the squeals like any other feeble little crybaby! And she has the nerve to sit in judgment! To have pity on you!

Lucile [*quietly*]. You are a fiend.

Hero. What did I tell you? Do it the nice way. Break it gently. Fall over backward to give them confidence. Tell them till you're blue in the face that they're attractive, that you'll be only too glad to dry their tears—you or the first footman. . . . That's all the thanks you get! [*Shouting.*] Come on—hysterics, a good cry, quickly now! I shan't talk until it's over.

Lucile [*stiffening*]. I won't cry.

Hero. Contempt. That's better. I can't stand tears. They turn my stomach. [*Coming closer.*] You're very beautiful just now, all hard and taut, like a little cornered animal. One must be as blind as those two peahens not to see it. The little household pest, the interloper we have to throw out, the little killjoy.

Lucile [*crying out*]. Talk, can't you!

Hero. Impatient now, are we? There's no hurry. We're alone up here. The butler is getting drunk belowstairs with the cook and I sent the paratrooper to do likewise in the village. And the others are safe in their rooms in the west wing, wondering what the upshot of it all will be. I can see them now, tossing and turning in their beds: Damiens, black and hairy like a big fat crow that's lost his cheese; Hortensia and the Countess in their filmy laces, with their thrillers and their sleeping tablets on their bedside tables. But sleep won't come! There's that little sly-boots scheming her dark schemes against the *status quo*, up there in her attic room at the far end of the east wing. Are we going to be rid of her at last? [*A pause.*] Tiger, my dear, realized too late that he had made a bloomer. If he'd asked my advice first, I'd have told him to spare you that heartbreak. You were a virgin. That was your little nest egg. He shouldn't have touched it. But you mustn't be too hard on him. He's incurably emotional. And it's such a sweet thing, an innocent little creature who nestles in your arms and swears to love you for ever and a day! A man would really need to be a saint to loose those arms and to say no! The bother of it is, the next day the child still cares. For ever and a day, for her, begins at breakfast the next morning. And she starts to tell you about her sweet old mother who's so lonely these days, and about the little dishes she can cook so well, and the name she'll give to her first baby. Gone the rare delight, the sacrificed gazelle of the night before. You see yourself pushing a perambulator before the season's out. A manner of speaking, of course. You're discreet and sensible, I know. "I'll work, he'll never have to buy me things, we'll be free, our love will be enough. . . ." Shall I tell you the whole truth, my dear? Yes, I think you're strong enough to take it now. That was what frightened Tiger. He would have preferred it if you'd asked for a mink coat and a nicely furnished flat. An accommodating little lady friend—that he can afford. A great, selfless love is a bit too pricey. So he decided—put yourself in his place—that it was kinder to be ruthless and make the break at once, before it became too painful.

Lucile. Why didn't he tell me himself?

Hero. Why expect that amiable playboy to be a hero? He believes, like Napoleon, that in love the only victory is flight. So he fled. He couldn't trust himself not to get hopelessly entangled. You lent that facile charmer a great many imaginary qualities, you know, my little one.

Lucile. But . . . why did he say he loved me, then?

Hero. Excitement, the fever of the moment, propinquity—love is as catching as flu. You'll meet others like him. Beware of sentimentalists, my pet, they are the worst.

A pause.

Lucile. Is that all he told you to say to me?

Hero. No, of course not. He's a gentleman. First of all,
a check—[*He puts his hand in his pocket, but stops
as* LUCILE *instinctively steps back.*]—which you'll refuse,
naturally. That, I must say, was a bit uncouth of him.
I wouldn't have mentioned it, only he did make me his
messenger. . . . Then, as I told you, he said, "Talk to
her; try to comfort her, if you can. . . ." [LUCILE
*struggles with herself for a second, then crumples onto
the bed, sobbing.* HERO *goes to her.*] There, my little
cardboard heroine, there. That's better. Let the tears come.
[*He sits on the edge of the bed and speaks gently, almost
maternally.*] We steel ourselves, we act the noble,
grown-up lady, and only yesterday we were playing with
our dolls and running to Mother at the first upset.
Only Mother isn't there any more. We're a big girl and
all alone. How alone one can be in life, can't one, my
little kitten? [*He reaches for his glass.*] Now we'll drink
our glass of whisky, won't we, like a good little girl. [*He
holds her head and gives her a drink.*] And then she'll
have another. And another. She'll have learned her
lesson too. [*His arm is round her shoulders. The tears
run down his face as he murmurs.*] Evangeline. . . . [*A
pause. He holds her closer and caresses her gently as he
murmurs, gazing into space.*] My little one, my poor little
one. How ugly it is, living! We danced with impatience,
we yearned for the moon and there we are, suddenly, left
all alone, with life yawning ahead like a great black
chasm. We tell no one, we cry modestly into our pillow
for a while, and then we marry a swine of a banker chosen
by the family, who have waited long enough. A brute in
her bed at night, and the thankless round all day,
festooned with diamonds, parading for him. So we weep
for two or three years more, very quietly, and then one
day, too sick at heart, we die, with no fuss, leaving as
little trace on earth as a bird's flight across the sky. [*The
tears are running down his face. He strokes her.*] My
child, my tender child, my poor little lost waif. [*His arms
are round her now. She sinks back, unresisting. The
curtain falls.*]

SCENE II

VILLEBOSSE *is alone, in costume, furious and determined,*
one does not yet know on what. Enter the COUNT.

COUNT. Ah, Villebosse, down already? I'm late. I got
back in the early hours. Forgive me, my dear fellow, for
foisting a morning rehearsal on you all. But we open in
forty-eight hours and I have the orchestra on my hands
all afternoon.

Villebosse. Sir, I have been waiting for you for over an
hour. I was unable to speak to you in private yesterday.
I have something very serious to say to you. You seem
very cheerful, sir.

Count. I am, Villebosse, very. I'm happier than I have
ever been in my life.

Villebosse. You're very lucky. Others are less fortunate,
sir. Others do not have your reasons for self-congratula-
tion.

Count. I fondly hope not. My reasons are extremely
personal, for once. Up till now, I was spineless enough
to enjoy myself collectively. I begin to notice that happiness is a solitary exercise.

Villebosse. Might there be some implication to your
words, sir?

Count. Words have always had *some* sort of implication, Villebosse. In fact, that's the reason why they were
invented.

Villebosse. Because if there were, it would be in poor
taste, sir. Our situation is a delicate one, never forget
that.

Count. My dear fellow, I can't say I ever lost any sleep
over it. But since this morning, you're out of luck; I have
decided to forget it altogether.

Villebosse. What exactly do you mean by that?

Count. I am delighted that you should be my wife's
lover. I think you are an extremely personable young
man.

Villebosse [*leaping up*]. Sir, I absolutely forbid you to
trifle with the Countess's honor! Take that back, sir!
Take back that word or you'll answer for it!

Count. What word, sir?

Villebosse. The one you just uttered, sir! Your cynicism is a loathsome pose. I will not allow it to soil a lady who is entitled to our respect. The Countess, sir, is above suspicion.

Count. But dammit, Villebosse, what suspicion?

Villebosse. You know perfectly well what I mean! If you take it upon yourself to spread the rumor that your wife is having an affair, you'll have me to reckon with!

Count. Villebosse, you are adorable! I never tire of listening to you. You are the funniest man I ever met.

Villebosse [*disconcerted*]. I am unhappy, that's all. I feel these things. . . .

Count. So I see.

Villebosse. It's no good. I'll never learn to accept the trivial little world you live in. I come from Carcassonne. Our ancestral home has kept its moat and drawbridge since the thirteenth century. We have never lived elsewhere, never put in central heating, and never used a lady's name in vain. The day I fell in love with the Countess, I came to you and offered to fight you to the death. My course was clear. I married the widow or I dropped out of the lists for good. You refused.

Count. I didn't fancy dying at the time. Nor killing you either. I'm very fond of you, Villebosse.

Villebosse. It was you who wanted this complicated and degrading situation.

Count. I wanted to live. That's always complicated and frequently degrading.

Villebosse. I am committed now. The Countess's honor and happiness are my personal concern. I will not stand by and see you make a fool of her, as you are doing—with just anybody. You will toe the line, sir, from now on, or I'll know the reason why!

Count. What do you want me to do?

Villebosse. Break it off immediately with this young person. The Countess is willing to let bygones be bygones. She will overlook your little lapse.

Count. Must I leave Hortensia too?

Villebosse. She tolerates her—weakly, in my opinion. Eliane's indulgence toward you is something I shall never understand. But you must be discreet. Remember to be more attentive to her than to that lady, and to put her first always. Good God, it's odd that I should be the one to point it out—Eliane is your wife, sir!

Count. Villebosse, I like you more and more. Give me your hand, old warrior!

Villebosse. Certainly not!

Count. Why not? I'm sure you're quite fond of me too, really.

Villebosse. It would be most unseemly. Let us keep our distance, sir. But remember, I shall be watching you!

Enter the COUNTESS.

Countess. To think you succeeded in getting us all out of bed at half past ten! Why, this dawn is positively ravishing! Did you sleep well?

Count. Yes, thank you. Eliane, I should like to speak to you a moment.

Countess. Villebosse?

Villebosse [*dashing up*]. Eliane darling?

Countess. Would you like to make yourself useful?

Villebosse [*drunk with devotion*]. Always!

Countess. Go to all the rooms and gather up the late comers. We start rehearsing in ten minutes.

Villebosse. Leave it to me, Eliane! [*He rushes out.*]

Countess. Well? I'm listening.

Count. I shall be brief. But you're a clever woman, Eliane. I know you'll understand.

Countess. Goodness, what a solemn face!

Count. I am in love with Lucile.

Countess [*pleasantly*]. Yes?

Count. We have lived together very intelligently, Eliane, with an identical distaste for scenes. You closed your eyes to my mistresses; I never asked with whom you were taking tea. We have given one or two splendid balls, ours is a house that people like to visit. And considering what one ordinarily makes of marriage, ours has been delightful.

Countess. Thank you, Tiger.

Count. No. It's I who must thank you. I have been impossible, often. We owe that bright success to your marvelous flair for living. In a world where one proudly wears one's dirty secrets on one's sleeve, we have known, you and I, how to greet life with a smile. We have lived as one dances: to music, to set steps and with grace.

Countess [*not looking at him*]. And has all that lost its charm now?

Count. It will always seem to me the only lucid way to live. Only——

Countess. Only?

Count. This graceful, clear-cut outline of my life, from my first successful ball to my probable presidency of the Jockey Club in twenty years from now, and thence to my funeral, with all of Paris in silk hats at the Madeleine, will be, it suddenly strikes me, a charming memory for others, a pretty theme for the obituary columns—and nothing for me. I wondered why I was always so gay. I was bored.

Countess. And it was that little girl, was it, who helped you realize that, up in her attic?

Count. Yes. I love her, Eliane. I had not the faintest idea what it was like. It's quite stupid, without gaiety, or grace, or sparkle, or any of the things I thought I cared about. But there it is.

Countess. Is that so new, Tiger? I've seen you on the brink of suicide two or three times because a girl resisted you.

Count. Yes, I never could bear to be thwarted in desire. There are also little boys who kill themselves because they can't have a bicycle. That's never very interesting. I didn't even feel that haste, this time. My greatest joy is being with her—nothing else matters to me now. But if, for some reason, you asked me to wait, I could wait a very long time, Eliane—and not grow weary.

Countess. I shan't take you at your word. It would be too sad if you lost this brand-new confidence the first time you put it to the test. You know I have never stopped you taking what you wanted.

Count. My poor Eliane, we are talking from different worlds now. That's what frightens me. There's no question of taking, this time.

Countess. I see. Of what, then?

Count [*quietly*]. Of giving.

Countess. You've plenty of time, and money to burn. Give, my dear, give! Who's stopping you? Go on a little trip with her, buy her some clothes. You've talked for ten years of visiting the East. Go and hide your amours in Amsterdam. I'll tell our friends you're in Kashmir.

Count. My poor Eliane, I shall be much farther away than Kashmir.

Countess. That's the second time you've called me that. I cannot tell you how I hate it. I am not your poor Eliane. As a matter of fact, I find the whole thing vastly amusing. Do you want us to part, Tiger? Do you want to marry her?

Count. Why distress your uncle the cardinal with a divorce? That seems to me completely pointless.

Countess. Hasn't she asked you to yet? She will within a week. Those little ladies who give their all to the first comer in a garret have a great obsession with respectability.

Count. That's the only rift I dread between us, Eliane —that anger and resentment will make you say something we'll both regret. I have thought very highly of you, always. There is already an emerald between us. Don't add anything to it.

Countess. So, how do we stand? We shall still give this ball, I presume? And you will leave next day for as long as you love this child, and as long as she loves you, is that it? Very well, I agree. And without too much heartbreak, you see? Enjoy yourself, Tiger. Tell me all about it when you get back.

Enter VILLEBOSSE, HORTENSIA *and* HERO, *glass in hand. The* COUNTESS *darts over to* HORTENSIA *and kisses her.*

Countess. Darling little Hortensia! So soft and sweet and trusting! Oh, what snakes men are! I like your scent so much more now! Hero, my treasure, you do look dismal! Oh, Hero, you've been naughty again! Now, Hero, put down that glass, there's a darling. It's too early in the day for whisky.

Hero. No. [*He wanders away and sits down.*]

Villebosse [*to the* COUNTESS]. He's horribly drunk. He can hardly speak, let alone rehearse. I can't find Damiens and the girl. They aren't in their rooms.

Countess. Tiger will find them. Tiger dear, do go and fetch her.

DAMIENS *appears in his outdoor clothes, a strange blackclad figure among the bright costumes.*

Damiens. I am very sorry, your Ladyship, but I must, regretfully, give up my part and leave the castle.

Countess. Monsieur Damiens, you're raving! The show is in two days!

Damiens. My goddaughter left very early this morning, on foot, for the station. This impulse can only be the result of yesterday's unfortunate misunderstanding. After that painful episode, I do not think I ought to stay here either.

Count [white-faced]. How do you know she's left? She may have gone to the village.

Damiens. I went to fetch her just now, and I found this letter for you on her dressing table. And one for me too.

The COUNT *opens the letter.*

Countess. Come now, Damiens, this is pure imagination! She and I had a very amicable talk last night. The incident was completely closed.

Hero [forgotten in his corner, asks thickly]. What does the letter say?

Count [as if in a dream]. "You were right. It wasn't possible. I am going away. I shan't bother you again."

A pause.

Hero. Is that all?

They all look at the COUNT, *who stands there, pale and unseeing.*

Countess. This is really most extraordinary. Damiens, you know her better than any of us, what do you think?

Damiens. Your Ladyship will excuse me, but my train leaves in a few minutes. I've barely time to get to the station. Her letter to me tells me no more, save her determination never to see me again either. Her feelings must have been hurt—and far more seriously than we think. She's gone, the Lord knows where, all alone with her grief—with no one to go to, no money, nothing.

Countess. Oh dear! If only we'd given her six months' pay!

The Count, *who has been standing as if rooted to the
spot, suddenly turns on his heel and runs out.*

Hortensia. Tiger! Where are you going?

Countess. For his car, I expect. He'll try to find her
on the road. Damiens, catch him up! He'll drop you at
the station.

Damiens. Good-by, your Ladyship! [*He hurries out.*]

Countess [*to Hortensia*]. The girl must have taken the
five o'clock bus for Alençon. She'll have caught her
connection there by now. Tiger hasn't a hope of finding
her.

Hortensia. She may change her mind and write to him.

Countess. I don't think so. We can say it now, that
girl had quality. Her leaving proves it. She loved him,
there's no doubt about that. That's why we needn't
worry. After what happened, she'll never try to see him
again.

Hortensia [*unexpectedly kindly*]. But what will Tiger
do?

Countess [*looking at her, genuinely astonished*]. Why,
Hortensia, what a sweet creature you are! You've quite
a soft streak in you. . . . He'll be sad for a month or
two and then he'll start to play again. Besides, I know
Tiger. He has the strongest sense of social duty. Our first
guests arrive this evening. For the next two days, however
wretched he is, he won't have time to think of anything
but his festivities. Come, my dear, let's have some
breakfast. These upsets give one a furious appetite.

Hortensia. But what about the part?

Countess. I had an inkling this might happen. Leonora,
to whom Tiger gave the part originally—and who'd
learned it all—has agreed to overlook the dirty trick
he played her. She flew in to Le Mans this morning.
I've sent the car to meet her. She'll be here in half and
hour. And I shall telephone Gontand-Biron. I'm sure
his cold is better.

Hortensia. You sent for Leonora! After what you told
me about her and Tiger?

Countess. Hortensia, I love you dearly, but frankly, my
sweet, you simply aren't up to it. I'm sorry, but you
see, the important thing is to help Tiger to forget. Either
I know nothing about him at all, or before the week is

out he'll think of nobody but Leonora. He cannot bear women to resist him. Come and have some coffee. I think we both need it.

They go.

Villebosse [*charging after them*]. Eliane, I haven't had breakfast either!

HERO, *still looking vacantly into space, calls him back thickly.*

Hero. Sir!

Villebosse. Sir?

Hero. One moment, if you please. You are a first-class shot, I believe?

Villebosse. What do you mean by that?

Hero. They even tell me that you have won several important championships—with pistols.

Villebosse. That's quite true.

Hero. Well, sir, I am here to tell you that a certain lady does not love you as truly as you think.

Villebosse. What did you say?

Hero. One never *is* loved as truly as one thinks, that is a general truth. But for you, I have a more specific truth. Since last night, sir, to use a term I find repugnant, you are a cuckold.

Villebosse. You're drunk! Take that back!

Hero. I am drunk. But the drunker I am, the clearer my head. I take nothing back. I was not in my own room last night. I was in another room. Do I make myself clear?

Villebosse [*advancing on him, bristling*]. What did you say? Do you realize what you're daring to insinuate?

Hero. It seems plain enough to me. Don't force me to repeat it. I do so hate dirty words.

Villebosse [*grimly*]. Very good. You are at least frank about it. I've had my suspicions about you for some time. We shall fight this out. Just give me time to get in touch with two of my friends.

Hero [*still seated*]. Make haste. I want it to be tomorrow morning.

Villebosse. At your service, sir. The sooner the better.

He is about to go. HERO *calls him back.*

Hero. Sir!

Villebosse. Sir?

Hero. Just to make it all quite regular, kindly slap my face.

Villebosse. That won't be necessary.

Hero. Yes, it will. No slap, no duel.

Villebosse. But it's all settled! I'll leave you the choice of weapons, if that's what's worrying you.

Hero. I'll claim it only if you hit me. I know the rules. Slap my face, immediately. [*Rising.*] Hit me, damn you— or I'll fling my glass in your face! Well, what are you waiting for? Hit me. Hard. Come on, you dirty cuckold!

Villebosse. You asked for it! [*He hits him across the face.*] This is ridiculous. . . .

Hero [*pale*]. No. It's fine. I choose pistols. [VILLEBOSSE *bows stiffly, a little surprised at* HERO'S *choice, and goes out.* HERO *stands quite still, gazing into space. Then he drops heavily into a chair and slowly drains his glass as he murmurs*] Evangeline. . . . [*Curtain.*]

ROMEO AND JEANNETTE

Translated by

MIRIAM JOHN

CHARACTERS

Frederic
Julia
Lucien
Jeannette
The Mother (*of Frederic*)
The Father (*of Julia, Lucien, and Jeannette*)
Postman

ROMEO AND JEANNETTE

ACT ONE

*A huge, badly furnished room in a large dilapidated house.
It is in a state of the utmost disorder. It opens, at the
back of the stage, onto dark corridors leading to a kitchen
and the bottom of a staircase. The curtains are drawn
over the French windows but are parted to let in* JULIA,
FREDERIC, *his* MOTHER, *and a little light.* FREDERIC *and
his* MOTHER *are rich country people, dressed in Sunday
black.*

JULIA. They always leave everything open. [*Calling.*]
Anybody there? [*There is no reply. She disappears into
the dark passage at the back and can still be heard
calling.*] Is anyone there?

FREDERIC *and his* MOTHER *remain on stage. The* MOTHER
looks around her.

Mother. They don't seem to hear.

As she says this, JULIA *comes back. One has the feeling
she is frightened. She stammers.*

Julia. But they had my letter. I posted it on Monday.
[*She goes briskly to the table and removes some of the
sordid odds and ends that are cluttering it.*] They're
terribly untidy, all three of them.
Mother. So I see. [*She looks around her again suspiciously, an upright, black-clad figure, leaning on her
umbrella.*] May we sit down?
Julia [*hastily*]. But of course. . . . [*She goes to a chair
and tries it.*] No. That one's broken. The stool's all right.
I bought it myself in the market before I went. It's
quite new [*She takes hold of the stool.*] No. That's
broken, too.
Mother [*still standing*]. What do they do with the
chairs?
Julia. I don't know. Stand on them . . . knock them
about. . . .

Mother. Why should they knock them about?

Julia [*with a desperate glance at* FREDERIC, *stammering*]. I don't know. I wonder myself, sometimes.

Frederic [*coming to the rescue*]. Why should you worry, Mother?

Mother. I don't, except that I should like to sit down.

JULIA *and* FREDERIC *look around.* JULIA *is beside herself.* FREDERIC *goes to an armchair snowed under with dirty linen.*

Frederic. Here's a chair! [*He tests it and pushes it toward her.*] A good solid one at that. Sit down, Mother.

Watched anxiously by JULIA, *his* MOTHER *seats herself after having tried the chair. She looks at the clock.*

Mother. It's ten to twelve.

Julia [*blushing if possible even more furiously than before*]. Yes. I don't understand it. [*She has taken up the pile of laundry which* FREDERIC *has thrown on the floor and wanders around the room with it, not knowing how to disguise it, talking as she does so.*] They know very well the train's at eleven.

Frederic. Maybe they went another way to meet us.

Julia. No. At low tide they always go by the beach, across the bay. We should have met them.

Mother. Besides, if your father and brother had come to meet us at the station, your sister should have stayed behind to look after luncheon, surely.

Julia [*still wandering about with her bundle of linen*]. Yes, of course she should. I can't understand it.

Mother. True, there was probably no luncheon to look after. Have you been into the kitchen?

Julia. Yes. There's nothing there.

She has at last succeeded in cramming the linen into a sideboard. She leans against the doors, panting like a hunted criminal. The MOTHER *has noticed nothing.*

Frederic [*amused at* JULIA's *fears, and attempting to find a solution*]. Maybe they intended to take us out to a restaurant.

Julia [*uneasier than ever*]. There isn't a restaurant in the village. Only a sort of buffet bar at the grocer's.

Mother. So we shall have to go back across the bay? [*Pause.*] It is five to twelve.

Julia [*stammering*]. Yes, but . . . now that the tide's coming in, it would be dangerous . . . we'd have to go by the road, and that takes longer.

Mother. Much longer?

Julia [*after a second's hesitation*]. Yes. Nearly twice as long.

The MOTHER *does not reply. There is a terrible silence. She looks slowly around her.* JULIA *begins to tidy up surreptitiously behind her back. Then, as the* MOTHER *looks down and pokes at some rubbish with her umbrella,* JULIA *bursts into tears and, snatching off her hat and throwing it down, she seizes a broom.*

Julia. I think I'd better sweep up!

Mother. Yes indeed. There's need of it.

Frederic [*sorry for* JULIA, *going to his* MOTHER]. I'll help you, Julia. And you can drop your disapproving air, Mother, and go to the grocer's and buy some canned stuff for lunch.

Mother [*eyes turned upward*]. Tins—on a fifteenth of August!

Julia [*taking a step toward her*]. I'm terribly sorry, Mother. I really can't imagine what's going on. Please don't bother. I'll go to the grocer's.

Mother. No, Julia, you're more use where you are. And if you look hard enough you may even find a saucepan and some water. I'll get some noodles.

Frederic. That's right. And some pâté. And you can get some canned lobster and some butter and jam. We don't all have to be on dry bread.

Mother [*from the doorway*]. Shall I get enough for them?

Julia [*in agony*]. I—— I don't know. I don't see where they could be having lunch.

Mother. They must have guessed we were inviting them to a picnic.

Frederic [*pushing her gently out*]. Probably. Make it snappy, Mother. We'll lay the table while you're gone.

When she has gone, JULIA lets go the broom and falls
weeping into a chair.

Julia. I knew this would happen. I knew it! They're
terrible!

Frederic. D'you think they got your letter?

Julia. Of course they did.

Frederic. In fact, they don't want to meet us.

Julia. It isn't that. It's just that they'll all have gone
their own sweet ways this morning, each counting on the
others.

Frederic. Your sister as well? Do the two men usually
help her with the house?

Julia [*with a desolate gesture, tearfully indicating the
disorder around her*]. Look at it.

FREDERIC *bursts out laughing.*

Julia. Oh, don't laugh! Don't laugh! I'm so ashamed.

Frederic. Why ashamed?

Julia. I didn't tell you. I thought I needn't. Why did
your mother want us to come here? As though there were
any need to ask permission to marry me—me! If we
hadn't come, I needn't have said anything.

Frederic. About what, Julia?

Julia. Everything. All the things I'm ashamed of.

Frederic [*smiling*]. Are you really as ashamed of them
as that?

Julia. I always have been, ever since I was little.

Frederic. What's so extraordinary about them?

Julia. You'll see soon enough. [*Suddenly she bursts out
furiously*] They haven't got a meal ready! They haven't
even swept the place! They've all gone their own sweet
ways, and they'll come back any old time, dressed any
old how. And there will be your mother with nothing to
eat.

Frederic. Don't worry about her. She's just getting
some food, anyway.

Julia. It's not as though I didn't warn them. I told
them in my letter; I said, "I'm coming with my fiancé
and my future mother-in-law, so we must have a good
lunch." I even sent them some money.

Frederic. Perhaps they usually have lunch late.

Julia. There's nothing in the kitchen but a drop of sour milk and a hunk of stale bread. Oh, and as for the money—I know what will have happened to that!

Frederic. Poor Julia.

Julia. I wrote them in so many words—I said: "Clean the house up a bit so that I'm not ashamed of it. My mother-in-law loves things to be tidy." And look at it!

Frederic. We'll tidy it up between us. Up you get.

Julia [shouting through her tears]. No! I just want to lie on the floor and cry!

Frederic. Julia!

Julia. I want them to find me here in the mess they've accumulated for over a week, with my fiancé and his mother. Let them be ashamed for once. It's their turn!

Frederic. Get up, Julia.

Julia. Only of course they wouldn't even be ashamed. I know them. They wouldn't care. They don't care about anything. [*She sits up.*] You see, you wanted to meet them, and now you won't love me any more!

Frederic [laughing]. It's already happened. I don't love you any more.

Julia [throwing herself into his arms]. I'm not like them! Even when I was a little girl, I was the one who swept and polished while my sister did nothing but look at herself in the glass. I was the one that made Papa shave and put on clean collars. You'll see, you'll see—he won't even have shaved!

Frederic. You never know. It is the fifteenth of August!

Julia. He couldn't care less about holidays and Sundays and things. And as for what he does the rest of the time—— They none of them care about anything. Eating scrap meals at all hours and living in squalor. So long as Papa can have his card parties at the bar and *she* can run about the woods or sunbathe on the sand all day. Too bad if the house is in chaos!

Frederic. And what about the winter?

Julia. She just lies there, on what she calls her divan, smoking. Or she makes hats and dresses out of bits of old material, the way she did when she was small. You should see them, too. And of course none of them ever has a penny, or when they do, they spend it immediately. She makes most of her frocks out of old curtains. And no sooner are they finished than there's a dirty mark or a tear somewhere, and if her behind shows through or her knees poke out of her stockings—well, so what?

Frederic. Julia, Julia, so you can be bitchy!

Julia. You hate that sort of thing so much—you're going to be so miserable.

Frederic [gently]. But I'm not marrying your sister.

Julia. I know you laugh at me sometimes. You call me a maniac, a busy bee, because I go around picking up litter and rubbing like mad every time I see a spot on something. But it's just that I have the feeling there's always something to tidy up; something that's got to be cleaned up after them.

Frederic. And your brother—what does he have to say?

Julia. He wasn't like them, before. But when his wife left him and he came to live here he soon went the same way. He reads all day long, shut up in his room. I don't like him, either, now. Before, he was just a boy like any other boy, working hard, coming out top at school, wanting to earn his living. Now, it's as though a door had been shut between us. He looks at me the same way as she does, with a sort of sneer on his face, and refuses to have anything to do with anything. After all, it's not our fault if his wife doesn't love him any more.

Frederic. What about your mother, when she was alive?

Julia [shrinking]. Mother isn't dead. I lied to you. She went off with a traveling dentist who used to pull teeth in the street—to music—with a top hat on. [*Pause.*] There, I've told you that, too, now. Now hate me.

Frederic [taking her in his arms]. Idiot! Dear, sweet idiot!

Julia. I shall never, never look you in the face again.

Frederic. That'll be very convenient for the next fifty years—I should say we'd both have about that long to go, with luck.

Julia. Oh, Frederic, do you think you'll go on loving me in spite of them? Don't you think it would be better to get out right away? I'm so frightened.

Frederic [holding her to him]. Why? I'm here.

Julia. I don't know. Just *because* you're there. You're so clear, such miles away from them, so pure. Supposing you began to think I was like them?

Frederic. I know my busy bee.

Julia. Your busy bee's going to die of shame.

Frederic. No. People don't die of shame.

Julia. That's what you say. You say they don't die of love, either. What do they die of?

Frederic. I wonder.

He kisses her. LUCIEN *has appeared in the doorway, having come downstairs from the floor above. His shirt collar is undone and he has a book in his hand. He watches in silence while they kiss. Suddenly* JULIA *sees him and breaks away from* FREDERIC.

Julia. Oh! Were you there?

Lucien. I'm always there when there's kissing going on. It's a plot against me. Ever since I became a cuckold I haven't been able to move a step without running across love. . . . And naturally I have a horror of kissing couples. I seem to find them all over the place. However, do go ahead. Don't let me embarrass you. Actually, it's not true. As a matter of fact, I enjoy it—in a sort of gruesome way. I say to myself: "Well, well! Another two that won't be together long!"

Julia. Is that the way you introduce yourself? I bring my fiancé here, whom you've never met, and that's the way you greet him.

Lucien [*icily*]. Hullo.

Frederic [*holding out his hand*]. Hullo.

Lucien [*recording*]. He's polite, your friend. He holds out his hand and smiles nicely.

Frederic. It's a habit I have. I knew a character like you in the army.

Lucien. A cuckold?

Frederic. No. Just embittered.

Lucien. And I suppose with your nice smiles and your frank handshakes you finally softened him up, this embittered character?

Frederic. No, but I got used to him. We became the best of friends.

Julia. Did you hear me call just now?

Lucien. Yes.

Julia. And of course you didn't budge.

Lucien. Wrong again. I budged when everything went

quiet, hoping that you'd given up and gone. Also,
I budged because I was hungry. Do you suppose there's
going to be any lunch?

Julia. Lunch! Oh, yes, talking of lunch . . . where
are the others?

Lucien [*with a wave of the hand*]. One never knows
where the others are—one hardly knows where one is
oneself in this place. Don't you agree, Monsieur——er
—— You seem the well-educated type, as they call it.
I like you a lot. Frank, loyal, honest, clear, go-ahead, and
all the rest of it. A proper little soldier. You'll make an
excellent cuckold.

Julia. Lucien!

Lucien. A merry little cuckold. They're the best. I'm
the doleful sort.

Julia [*going to him and shaking him*]. Lucien! You
think you're funny, but you're just loathsome. You
think you're being original, but you're vulgar, too vulgar
for words. The commonest, drabbest little guttersnipe
I've ever struck.

Lucien. I'm not a little guttersnipe, I'm a melancholy
cuckold.

Julia [*taking him by the arm*]. Melancholy or not,
you're damn well going to shut up!

Lucien. So we're not allowed to be unhappy, now?
Compulsory happiness, is it? That's great.

Julia. You forget it was me that used to wipe your nose
for you and wash your dirty feet and spoonfeed you
before you could walk. I know you. You're a little beast,
but you're not as wicked as you'd have people think. So
just you listen to me. Just because you've been miserable,
because Denise left you and made you unhappy, that
doesn't mean you're going to stop *me* being happy. I
came here with my fiancé and his mother to tell you I'm
getting married. Frederic's worth more than you and me,
he understands everything. But there's his mother, and
she certainly won't be able to understand you. Not even
if we explain to her that you really have been hurt. She
belongs to a kind that gets hurt more discreetly. So try
to look a bit tidier when she comes back, and comb your
hair, and behave decently. [*Suddenly, pitifully.*] Please,
Lucien! Please don't spoil my happiness!

Lucien [*gently*]. When people ask me nicely, I can't

say no. I'll go and put a suit on. [*From the doorway,
amiably, to* FREDERIC.] You're lucky. She's a brave kid.
Tiresome, but brave. [*Exit.*]

Frederic. Poor chap. He must have suffered a lot.

Julia. He's hateful!

Frederic. No, he's nice.

Julia. Oh, you! Samson! Always stronger than anyone
else. You laugh at everything, excuse everything. But *I'd*
have preferred a brother with decent manners.

Enter Frederic's MOTHER *and* Julia's FATHER, *their arms
loaded with cans of food.*

Father [*with a theatrical gesture*]. Sensation! . . . We
met at the grocer's. I was having a drink at the bar with
Prosper. Then when Prosper says, "Look who's here,"
I take one look at the silk dress and the umbrella and I
have a presentiment. I get up. "Mother-in-law, delighted
to be presented to you!" I say. A manner of speaking,
you understand, since I was presenting myself. The whole
lot of 'em had their eyes popping out of their heads.
[*To* JULIA.] I had to let her pay for the food—I hadn't
a sou on me. Be a good girl and pay her back, Julie.
No, no, I insist, you're my guest! Thank, you, kind sir,
delighted.

Julia. Papa's very talkative.

Mother [*putting down the cans*]. So I've noticed.

Father. What's this? Table not laid? Wine not chilled?
Nothing ready? What's all this?

Julia. I was going to ask you, Papa.

Father. Ask me? Ask *me*? [*Storming.*] Where's Jeannette?

Julia. I was going to ask that, too.

Father. It's astonishing! [*He turns to the* MOTHER,
*whom he waves toward the sofa with a large gesture, and
in quite a different voice says*] Without wishing to be
indiscreet, how many children have you made, dear lady?

Mother. Eleven. Eight living.

Father. Eight living. Not to mention the others. That
still leaves seven more. But no doubt you can keep track
of yours. I've only made three, but I never seem to be
able to lay hands on one of them. [*Shouting thunder-
ously.*] Where is Lucien?

Julia. In his room.

Father. You see. That's the end of it. No warning. No one else about. There's nobody I can rely on any more. You can carry on, that's your strength. But I'm all alone. It's very sad for an old man. Fortunately I have this one—she's the prop of my old age. Although if she goes and marries your son, she'll be yours. That'll make nine for you. Nine props. Well now, are you going to see to everything, Julie, make us a nice lunch?

Julia [*sternly*]. Is there any wine?

Father [*humbly*]. Er——— I'll tell you——— I can cool it for you. . . . I don't know what I could have been thinking of. . . . Besides, my hands were full.

Frederic [*laughing*]. Don't worry. I'll go and get some. Chin up, Julia!

Father [*watching him go out*]. He's a charming young fellow, your son, congratulations! [*He stretches himself out on the divan.*] Well, Julie, are you pleased to see your old father again?

Julia [*who is taking the cans to the kitchen*]. I should have been even more glad to find the table laid and the house cleaned up.

Father [*with a wink at the* MOTHER]. You mustn't believe her when she says things like that. She doesn't mean a word of it. She's delighted. Got a heart of gold. [*He picks something up off the floor and pushes it under the sofa.*] Besides, the place isn't so untidy. Few papers lying about, of course, and as for the dust, well, never mind that; you can't do anything about it, it comes back every day anyway. A bit of old lace. . . . It might strike you as untidy, but it isn't real untidiness. Just confusion. I used to be an artist. I need a certain amount of confusion around me.

Mother [*rising*]. I'm going to lay the table.

Father. That's an idea. I'll help you. It'll make me feel young again. When I was twenty I always used to lay the table, to tease the maid.

Mother. Where are the plates?

Father. I don't know—here, there, and everywhere I suppose.

Mother. How do you mean, you don't know? What do you do when you want to eat?

Father. Look for them. Here—here are three. They're

dirty, though. Oh, never mind, it's only cheese. Just throw away the rind.

The MOTHER *snatches the plates from him and makes for the kitchen, calling to him.*

Mother. Find me some more.
Father. I'll do my best. [*Left alone, he hunts around for a while, then suddenly gets discouraged and throws himself full length on the sofa, pulls a cigar out of his pocket, and bites off the end, grumbling.*] Find me some more . . . find me some more! Hard nut, that. Proper dragon. Pity. Handsome woman, too.

The MOTHER *returns and finds him there. She tries to wither him with a glance, but he meets it stoically and goes on smoking beatifically. She seizes a broom and begins to sweep up around him.*

Father [*after a short silence*]. You know, I'm an optimist. It's a principle of mine that everything always sorts itself out.
Mother [*sourly*]. Yes, when other people take over.
Father. Indeed, yes. But I've always observed that other people were rather willing to take over. It's extraordinary the number of people there must be on this planet that are determined to take action at all costs. If there weren't a few of us philosophers about, keeping ourselves to ourselves, there'd be no elbowroom for the scrimmage.
Mother [*stopping suddenly*]. I've got four farms at home, not counting the town house. My boy has just qualified as a notary—he'll have his own practice one day. Maybe you're wondering why I should let him go to Julia, who hasn't a sou to bless herself with?
Father. Me? I'm not wondering anything. I'm delighted.
Mother. Julia is a good, hard-working girl. Honest, economical . . .
Father. Spit and image of me.
Mother. Her aunt has been my friend for fifty years. She's told me she's leaving her everything when she goes.
Father. Poor Irma. How is she?
Mother. She's fine. I know she won't get anything from you.

Father [*with a start*]. Who, Irma?

Mother. No, your daughter.

Father [*firmly*]. Dear lady, I believe in marriages for love. They always go bad, of course, but all the same, before they fail, they're a better bet than any other sort. A few years, even a few months of good going and there's always that to your advantage. And I think you've got to be happy whatever happens, don't you?

Mother. The most important thing is to be a worker. To be serious.

Father. And don't you think happiness is serious? Don't you think it takes hard work? Damnation, dear lady, I think people are bird-witted not to have only that in their heads, day and night, and be content with the price of a drink, a smile, the slightest thing. We're none of us ever happy enough, for Pete's sake. What are you talking about? One should demand happiness fiercely. [*To* JULIA, *as she comes in with plates, glasses, and a cloth.*] Aren't I right, Julie?

Julia. What is it now?

Father. Why the "now"? I was just saying to your mother-in-law that people are never happy enough. You intend to be happy, I hope?

Julia. Yes, Papa, I do. And it would be nice if you would all help.

Father. Count on me, Julie. I may look like a comic, but my heart's in the right place. That's what your mother-in-law-to-be doesn't realize.

Enter LUCIEN, *dressed in a suit too big for him.*

Mother. Who is this?

Father [*with a bow*]. This is my son, madame.

Mother. Is he a waiter?

Father. What's that? No, he's a lawyer. Oh, yes, well, come to think of it, where *did* you get that suit?

Lucien [*unsmiling*]. It's yours. I'm wearing it in honor of the lady.

Mother [*guardedly*]. That's very nice of you.

Lucien [*bowing respectfully*]. My compliments, madame.

Lucien [*to* JULIA, *who is watching him somewhat anxiously*]. Am I sufficiently elegant in Father's tails?

Mother [*to* JULIA]. He seems very polite, your brother.

Julia [*vaguely*]. Yes, he does seem polite.

Lucien. You see—she said it herself!

Mother. Is this the one that's married? Where's his wife?

Lucien. On her honeymoon.

Julia [*crying out*]. Lucien!

Lucien. No, I was joking. She's at Lourdes, on a pilgrimage. She wants to have a baby.

*The MOTHER looks at him, wondering if he is serious.
JULIA pulls her away hastily.*

Julia. Mother, will you come and help me? I need some advice in the kitchen. Lay the table, you two!

Lucien [*to his FATHER, when they have gone*]. I seem to have made a big impression on her. The outfit, maybe . . .

Father. Oh, she's a personality, but I think she's pretty dumb. All the same, to do her justice, she still has a very pretty bust. I have a weakness for that type.

Lucien. You're slipping. She's a hundred.

Father. You've no imagination. I can just see her, say, in about 1912, with a huge feathery hat. . . . Jeepers creepers! Ah well, forget it, it's too late now.

Julia [*coming in and going up to them*]. Listen, both of you. We've probably only got a minute alone. Let's say no more about there being no lunch and the place being in a state.

Father. But I was the first to be upset about that! You saw for yourself.

Julia. I'll have a word with Jeannette about it when she comes in. If she comes in. You spent the money just the same?

Father [*with a tragic gesture*]. The milk bill had to be paid. Money just gets swallowed up in this house! There were only 120 francs left after that. I wanted to buy myself a made-up tie so as to look respectable today. . . . I had nothing decent to wear. I say I wanted to . . . but as a matter of fact I did and it's already messed up. They're no good, these gadgets. Now look at the one I had before the war. Just one snap and you were all set. Oh well, I've rigged up an old one now with string. Does it show?

Julia. No, but you might have changed your collar.

Father. My collar? It's celluloid. You don't seem to
realize. It's patent. You don't have to change it.

Julia. You could wash it. And you could brush the
dandruff off your jacket, and clean your nails, and not
fasten your first button into your second buttonhole.

Father. Bah! You attach too much importance to details. You must look at the thing as a whole.

Julia. And of course you didn't shave this morning?

Father [*innocent*]. No. How did you know?

Julia [*who has managed to button the jacket properly*].
And don't spend the whole of lunch complaining that you
haven't a bean.

Father. What do you take me for? I've taken some
knocks, but I'm a good loser. On the contrary, I want to
crush her beneath the weight of luxury, this woman. Get
out all the silver, Julie!

Lucien [*in his corner*]. It's been up the spout for years.

Father [*rounding on him, superb*]. I can get it out
whenever I wish! I've got all the tickets.

Lucien. Maybe we could lay the table with those.

Father. In any case, supposing we do have to give up
the idea of luxury for the moment, at least let's be dignified, behave in style. Patriarchal simplicity. We are re-
ceiving her in the family house which misfortune has not
spared but which still stands solidly on its foundations. . . .

Lucien. Talking of that, it's raining in all the rooms,
and the plumber wants an advance before he'll start on
the repairs. Anything you can do about it?

Julia. Always me! Me! You make me sick!

Father. Is it our fault if the roof's caving in? It's the
plumber who should make you sick. Advance indeed!
Little whippersnapper I knew when he was that high.

Lucien. That's right. He knows you.

Father. He doesn't know me yet. I'll call in a rival.

Lucien. There aren't any.

Father. Rubbish. I'll get one from Paris. You can go
so far and no farther with me. [*He lights another cigar
and stretches himself out on the divan, suddenly calming
down.*] Now what about this lunch, is anyone seeing to
it?

Julia. I sent you all I could. Now I've got to think
about my wedding and my trousseau.

Father. Quite right. Do things in style. I don't want it

said that we didn't give you anything. I suppose you earn your keep with your teaching? Do you give any private lessons? I met one of the Academy inspectors at a funeral, incidentally, and he told me you'd done very well in your exams.

Julia. I'll do my best, don't worry. I just want you to realize that now I'm getting married you mustn't rely on me any more.

Father. Obviously. In fact, believe me, if times had been different, I'd have given you a handsome dowry.

Julia [to LUCIEN]. What about you?

Lucien. I'm waiting for an answer from the Ivory Coast.

Julia. And supposing the Ivory Coast doesn't answer? It seems to me that with all your degrees you ought to be able to find a job nearer home than Africa.

Lucien [with a jeer]. What, work here, among the cuckolds, in an office full of cuckolds, who'll spend all day talking about their love lives? Not likely. The wilds for me, and good, black, primitive Negroes with heads thick as boulders and no idea, but absolutely no idea, what love is. Not a white within four hundred miles. I've made that a condition. So if they do answer, it's yes right away and off I shall go with not so much as a good-by. There's a little bag all ready by the coat rack, so I shan't lose a minute. As soon as the letter arrives—hat, kit, vamoose! And don't bother too much about letters. I shan't even open them.

Father [calm]. Children are all ungrateful. [After a pause.] Anyway, I never write letters.

Julia. What I sent you couldn't have been enough, though. What have you been living on this winter?

Lucien. Canned stuff.

Julia. Answer me—what have you been living on?

Father [who has had enough]. I don't know! Jeannette managed somehow.

Julia. Is she working? What does she do?

Father [with a vague gesture]. You know what she's like—one never sees her.

Julia. You must know by experience that money doesn't grow in these parts. Did she get a job in town?

Father. No, no. She's been staying here.

Julia. But I don't understand. Did she advance you much?

Father [*with another wave of the hand*]. Oh! You know what I'm like about money. . . .

Julia. Lucien! You know something about this. Let's have it.

Lucien. It's quite simple. I fully believe, my sweet, that we've been living all this winter on the generosity of Monsieur Azarias.

Julia. You mean the Azarias up at the little château?

Lucien. Yes. The little lamb skips off at nightfall and doesn't come back till dawn. And I have the impression she goes that way, through the woods. All the same, every one of them! I'm delighted.

Julia [*bursting out*]. Oh, I'm so ashamed, so ashamed! And you never said a word! You didn't even write to me so that I could try and do something about it! That's all I need just now. Just before my wedding. Everybody'll know about it.

Lucien [*derisively*]. Wrong tense. Everybody knows.

Julia. Is that all you can find to say? Your sister has a lover, a lover that pays her. She visits him every night, and you just joke about it. You're delighted because everyone knows about it.

Father [*smoking on the divan, with a grand gesture*]. I beg your pardon. I don't know about it.

Just then FREDERIC *comes in with some bottles.* JULIA *goes to him, as though calling for help.*

Julia. Frederic! Frederic!

Frederic. What is it?

Julia. Let's go away—now!

Frederic. Why?

Julia. Go and find your mother in the kitchen—tell her you're sick, that you've got to go home. Tell her anything, but let's get out of here.

Frederic [*to the others*]. Have you been quarreling?

Lucien. Who, us? Not in the least.

Father. Leave her alone. The child's a bundle of nerves.

Julia [*buried against him*]. Frederic, you're so strong. You go through life smiling and thinking that everything's all right, that it's all easy. Oh, Frederic, you're so sure of yourself, but you don't know anything. Ever since you were a little boy there's been your mother to scold you and clean up in a neat and tidy house. How can you know——? But I'll be like her, Frederic, I'll be like her, I swear. I'll make you just as happy as you were when you were little. And you'll always find everything in its right place when you come home—things, feelings, everything.

Frederic [rocking her]. Yes, Julia.

Julia. And when we have a child, it'll have a real mother, like yours, with an apron on, and bread-and-butter cut thin, and a slap when it's naughty, and the same old things going on day in, day out like the ticking of a clock. . . . But I know there's nothing but squalor and nastiness and cold nights in empty houses, and shame.

Frederic [gently]. Yes, Julia.

Father. Charming! . . . Ah, love! Love! . . . I was just the same. Jumpy, nervous, suspicious, irritable. I would never believe I was loved enough. . . . And yet, God knows—— [*Waving his hand and calling to* JULIA.] He adores you, child, he adores you! There's no need to cry, you can see it blindfold.

Julia [pressing herself closer to FREDERIC]. Let's get out, Frederic. I'm frightened.

Frederic [smiling]. Frightened of what? You're with your Samson now, your strong man. You shouldn't be afraid of anything. Come, now, dry your eyes. Be sensible. Smile.

Julia [trying to smile]. I can't. I'm too frightened.

The MOTHER *comes in. She still has her hat on, but has put on an apron over her silk dress and is carrying in her hand a chicken which she has half plucked.*

Mother. Julia! We may yet succeed in making a decent meal. I've found a chicken in the garden. I've just bled it.

There is a stupefied silence from LUCIEN *and his* FATHER. *Then suddenly* LUCIEN *leaps up, yelping.*

Lucien. Leon! She's killed Leon!

Mother [looking at the chicken]. Leon, who's that?

Father. Great jumping snakes! This is going to cause a riot!

Lucien [yelling like a mad thing]. Leon murdered! Leon slain by the in-laws! Stupendous, unique moment!

Mother. But it's only a chicken! I'll send you a couple tomorrow—the biggest I've got.

Lucien. She says it's only a chicken. She says Leon's only a chicken. She has absolutely no conception of what she's done!

Julia. I assure you, Lucien, nobody thinks you're funny.

Lucien. Who said anything about being funny? Nobody thinks it's funny. Look at Papa.

Father [*who seems to have lost his own*]. Keep your heads, now. We must all keep our heads. Couldn't we revive it somehow? Artificial respiration . . . ?

Lucien. Too late. It's bleeding. I see the blood of Leon flowing! Leon has perished at unworthy hands. And we are like a Greek chorus, helpless, ashen, dumb . . .

Mother. Make him be quiet, the lunatic, we can't hear ourselves speak!

Lucien [*standing on the sofa, still in his tails, declaiming*]. Too late, madame, too late! The clouds are gathering round us. Listen. I hear the gate grinding on the hinge; the pine needles cracking beneath a footstep. Fate is about to burst upon this house! It is going to burst, my children, I tell you I have had a warning, it is definitely going to burst!

JEANNETTE *has appeared at the back. She stops as she suddenly sees the chicken in the* MOTHER's *hand. They are all looking at her, but she is staring at the chicken.* LUCIEN *is heard to murmur in the silence.*

Lucien. There we are. It's burst. . . .

JEANNETTE *looks at the* MOTHER *and suddenly makes toward her. The* FATHER *calls out in a strangled voice.*

Father. Be polite now, child!

JEANNETTE *has snatched the chicken away from the other woman and is holding it against her, teeth clenched, terrible. She speaks as if in a dream, in a scarcely audible voice.*

Jeannette. Who is this woman? What is she doing here with an apron over her stomach and blood all over her hands?

Father. I'll explain it all, child; there's been a terrible misunderstanding.

Jeannette. Who is this woman all in black with her low forehead and her big eyes and her respectability? Who brought her here, with her widow's weeds and her earrings and her strangler's hands?

Julia. Jeannette, I forbid you. This is my fiancé's mother.

Jeannette [*still staring at the* MOTHER]. Ah! So she's your fiancé's mother. So you forbid me. Did you forbid her to lay hands on my Leon just now?

Julia [*shouting*]. There was nothing to eat here—whose fault was that?

Jeannette [*shouting, but not looking at her*]. There were canned peas and sardines at the grocer's! I told Papa to get some.

Father [*feigning astonishment*]. Me? You told me to get some? What with?

Jeannette [*not hearing him*]. But no. She had to eat well, didn't she, your mother-in-law, so as not to let the family down? She had to feel nice and smug over coffee, didn't she, and be able to belch politely in her stays. That's hospitality. So she chased him with her knife and you let her do it. [*She turns on the* FATHER *like a Fury.*] You let her do it! What a coward you are! I can just see you, dancing attendance on her: "But of course, madame, by all means!" And to think he used to know you; he used to come and perch on your shoulder and eat out of your hand!

Father. I was lying on the divan here. I didn't hear a thing. I was just smoking. . . .

Jeannette [*pressing the chicken against her*]. I hope you'll all of you die like he did—slaughtered in bed one fine night. I hope you'll be frightened, the way he must have been frightened!

Julia. Jeannette, stop being stupid now and shut up!

Father [*to the* MOTHER]. Forgive her. She's just a child. Underneath, she's a fine kid. You just have to get to know her.

Mother. Get to know her? Thanks very much, I know her already! [*She unties her apron.*] Julia, my child, I do finally believe you were right. We could have done without meeting your family. Come along, Frederic, we're leaving. [*She makes for the kitchen. The* FATHER *runs after her, calling.*]

Father. But what about lunch? Now please, dear lady, compose yourself. . . . We were about to have a meal at last.

Mother [*going out*]. Thank you. We shall dine when we get back. At home, we're free to kill chickens when we like.

The FATHER *watches her go with a gesture of despair.*

Julia [*to* JEANNETTE, *before following the* MOTHER *out*]. I detest you.

Father [*beside himself, to* JEANNETTE]. A chicken! After all, it was just like any other chicken, you stupid little fool! Just because you called it Leon. . . . Admittedly it was a nice creature, but we're all nice . . . that doesn't prevent us from coming to an end one day!

He goes out. There remain ony JEANNETTE, *standing motionless with the chicken pressed close against her;* LUCIEN, *still standing on the sofa; and* FREDERIC, *who has not taken his eyes off* JEANNETTE *since she came in. There is a short silence after all the uproar. Suddenly, without moving,* FREDERIC *addresses her gently.*

Frederic. I'm sorry. [JEANNETTE *looks at him; he smiles slightly.*] But your father is right. We're all mortal. He could have been run over.

Jeannette. That wouldn't be the same. I'm sure he was frightened. He saw the knife and he understood, I'm sure of it. He was so intelligent.

Frederic [*without smiling*]. Maybe he didn't have time to understand exactly what she was going to do.

Jeannette [*in despair*]. Oh, yes. I'm sure he knew he was going to die. As though it was his fault lunch wasn't ready. All he thought of was running about in the grass just quietly looking for little worms and being afraid of the wind blowing the shadows about. Their stomachs, their beastly stomachs, that's all they think of. [*She looks at* FREDERIC *and draws back a little.*] But who are you? I don't know you either.

Frederic. I'm Julia's fiancé.

Jeannette [*regarding him mistrustfully*]. Oh, so you're her son?

Frederic. Yes, but you mustn't be unfair. It's not my fault.

Jeannette [*looking heartbrokenly at the chicken*]. Poor Leon. He did so want to grow into a big, strong cockerel. A real cockerel with a proper red crest, waking everybody up in the morning.

Frederic [*gently*]. Don't you ever eat chicken?

Jeannette [*lowering her head*]. Yes. When I don't know them. I know that's just as unfair, but I've tried to give up eating meat at all, and I can't—I like it too much.

Frederic. So you see, you can't help it either.

Jeannette [*shaking her head*]. Yes I can. When I'm old and understand everything like other people I shall say that, too, I know. That nothing is anyone's fault. It must be fine to become suddenly tolerant about everything; to go about excusing everything; not to kick any more. Don't you find getting old takes a long time?

Frederic [*smiling*]. You just have to have a bit of patience.

Jeannette. I don't like patience. I don't want to be resigned and accept things. She must have told you things about me, my sister.

Frederic [*smiles*]. Yes. Lots.

Jeannette. Well, it's all true. And worse. And it's all my fault. I'm the black sheep of the family—you must have heard; the one that does all the things that aren't done. You're supposed to detest me.

Frederic. I know.

Jeannette. And you don't have to smile at me as if I were a child and needed humoring. I don't like people to snivel and be soft, either. You're right. I eat other birds; why shouldn't I eat this one now that it's dead? Because I loved him? That's stupid. I'll go and give it back to the ogress! [*She goes into the kitchen, calling.*] Here you are, here's your chicken, you two! Pluck it in your old kitchen and cook it if you want to!

She has disappeared. FREDERIC *turns to* LUCIEN, *who has been watching motionless, with his ambiguous smile.*

Frederic [*in a voice that tries to be bright, but does not succeed*]. She's amazing!

Lucien *looks at him for a second without a word, then comes down off the sofa, smiling.*

Lucien. Yes. She'll go on amazing you, too.

Frederic, *surprised at his tone, stands staring at him. Curtain.*

ACT TWO

Scene—*The same, except that the house is now in order. It is evening, after dinner. The room is already shadowy. At the back, in the lighted kitchen, Julia and the Mother can be seen busying themselves with chores. On-stage the Father is sleeping in an armchair, a dead cigar in his hand. Frederic and Jeannette are seated at some distance from each other, looking at each other across the half-cleared table. Farther back, leaning against the windows, a shadow: Lucien looking out into the night.*

The Father suddenly begins to snore noisily, then stops as Lucien begins furiously whistling a military bugle call. Frederic and Jeannette look at the Father, then at each other. They smile at each other for the first time. A clock sounds the half-hour somewhere. Their smiles fade.

Frederic. The train's at half-past ten, isn't it?
Jeannette. Yes.

Pause.

Frederic. How quickly today has gone.
Jeannette. Yes.
Frederic. When shall we see each other again?
Jeannette. At the wedding.

Silence. Lucien moves suddenly and disappears into the darkness. He can be heard whistling the curfew as he wanders off.

Frederic. This could be an evening a long time from now, when we come to spend a few days here with Julia. It'll be just like this. . . . Your father will be asleep in his chair, letting his cigar go out. Julia will be busy in the kitchen. We shall forget to light the lamp, just like this evening, and we shall sit and listen to the night coming on.

Jeannette. You'll never come back here, you know that.

Frederic. Why?

Jeannette. Julia will never want to come back.

Frederic [*after a pause*]. Well, then, it's an evening a long time ago. An old, old evening that doesn't want to come to an end. We must be very old now, worn out, battered, together again after years and years apart; and we're reminding each other of that quiet evening when no one thought of lighting the lamp, when we sat waiting, waiting, not knowing what for.

Jeannette [*pulling herself up and crying out*]. I shan't remember. I hate memories. They're cowardly and useless.

Father [*waking with a start and trying to look as though he has not been asleep*]. What were you saying, child? I didn't quite catch.

Jeannette. Nothing, Papa. I wasn't saying anything. Go back to sleep.

Father [*dropping off again*]. I'm not sleeping. I can hear everything.

Jeannette [*behind him, too softly to wake him up, and gazing somewhere into space*]. All right, then, Papa. If you can hear everything, listen to this. Listen with all your ears. Listen to what your daughter has to say. Your bad daughter. Not the other one. *She* never says shameful things that burn when they're spoken. She always does the right thing, your other daughter, and she's going to get her reward. She's going to be happy. She won't need just the memory of one evening, later on. She'll have the right to every evening, every day, every minute—the right to a whole lifetime. And when she's dead, and there's life everlasting, she'll have the right to remember her own life all over again, for all time, sitting at the right hand of God the Father Almighty!

Frederic [*rising and breaking in*]. Be quiet!

Jeannette [*shouting at first*]. No, I won't be quiet! [*Then she looks troubled and says gently*] Why should I obey you? What are you to me?

At this moment an Old Man *in a dark cloak appears on the threshold with a telegram in his hand.*

Postman [*shouts*]. Children! Children!

Father [*turning in his sleep*]. Post, children, post! Postman's here!

Lucien [*He has loomed up out of the night, and falls upon the postman*]. Is that you, postman? Is it for me?

Postman. No, boy. It's for your sister. Telegram—night rate.

Lucien. When will it be for me, postman?

Postman. When I get it, son.

He disappears into the night. There is the sound of the gate slamming, then, after a second, LUCIEN goes up to JEANNETTE and holds out the telegram.

Lucien. Well! Night rate, my love. Someone has something urgent to say to you. [*Pause. He waits.* JEANNETTE *has taken the telegram but does not open it.*] Aren't you going to open it?

Jeannette. No. I know what's in it.

Lucien [*with a grimace, curious*]. You're lucky! I'd like to know. . . . [*He goes off whistling a military call, after emptying a glass of wine that is standing on the table.*]

Frederic [*suddenly, dully*]. What is in the telegram?

Jeannette. Nothing.

Frederic. Why don't you open it?

Jeannette [*tearing it up without looking at it*]. I already know everything it says.

Frederic. Anyway, you're right. What business is it of mine? I've known you since this morning, and I'm leaving in an hour.

Jeannette. And marrying my sister next month.

Frederic. Yes.

They look at each other.

Jeannette [*suddenly, after a pause*]. It's a telegram from my lover.

Frederic. The man who was following us in the woods this afternoon?

Jeannette. Oh, did you see him? No, not that one, poor lad. He doesn't dare write to me. Maybe he can't even write. This is another one, who thinks he has the right. I visit him every evening.

Frederic. And he's writing because he won't be seeing you this evening.

Jeannette. Not this evening or ever again. I sent him a note by hand this morning to tell him I wouldn't be seeing him any more.

Pause.

Frederic [*with an effort*]. Why are you leaving him?

Jeannette. Because I don't love him. Because I suddenly felt ashamed of belonging to him.

Frederic. And yesterday?

Jeannette. Yesterday I didn't care. I didn't care about anything—about having a lover like him or about going about with bare legs and a torn frock and being plain.

Frederic [*dully*]. You're not plain.

Jeannette. Yes. Julia's more beautiful than I am. Julia's pure, and I'm—— I know what I'm worth. That man that was following us—he's been my lover too, and I didn't love him either. And there were others before that, ever since I was fifteen, and I didn't love any of them.

Frederic. Why do you deliberately smear yourself?

Jeannette. So that you'll hate me. So that you'll go away tonight hating me. So that you'll marry Julia hating me.

Frederic. You knew perfectly well I shan't be able to.

Jeannette [*softly*]. And also so that you'll never be able to forget this moment, when I told you everything bad about myself here in the dark.

Frederic. It's bad to tell someone everything like that, deliberately.

Jeannette. I've only got one evening—not even that, just an hour—hardly that even now. There'll be plenty of time to be quiet after that.

Frederic. Why do you talk like that, when there's nothing we can do?

Jeannette. There's nothing we can do tomorrow, nothing we can do for the rest of our lives. But we can still do something for this one hour if they leave us alone. An hour is a long time when it's all you've got.

Frederic. What can we do?

Jeannette. Tell each other straight out what bad luck we've had. Tell each other about that secret bit of bad luck that we'll have to hush up for ever afterward. Tell each other how stupid it is to deprive oneself of a single day, of a single minute, that might pass us by for ever and ever.

Frederic. But this morning I loved Julia!

Jeannette. Yes. And I expect you still love her. You're going away with her soon, anyway. She'll have you for the rest of her life. That's why I'm daring to say this, because she's better off than me.

Frederic. Julia's good. She mustn't be hurt!

Jeannette. I know. And I know that *my* hurt is too new, it doesn't carry the same weight. I know it's *my* memory that must fade like an old photograph, getting fainter and fainter day after day. I know there's got to come a day when you won't remember any more exactly what my eyes are like—you've hardly looked at them. And then another day, the day Julia's first son is born, or perhaps the day of the christening, when you'll forget them altogether.

Frederic [*with a muffled cry*]. No.

Jeannette. Yes. That's why I dare say all this. I'm talking the way people talk when they're going to die. Not for a good cause, but shamefully, with nobody much to regret them.

Frederic. I shall go away with Julia in a little while, and marry her, I know. But I shall never forget you.

Silence.

Jeannette [*softly, with eyes closed*]. I must say thank you, mustn't I, like poor people have to?

Another silence.

Frederic. This pain, this agony we've both been feeling today, it can't be love—that's impossible. But I shall never be able to get rid of it now.

Jeannette [*teeth clenched*]. I shall. Tomorrow. I swear it.

Frederic. Will you?

Jeannette. I must be able to! I must tear the pain out of me all by myself, like an animal tearing a thorn out of its pad with its teeth. I don't want to go on loving with empty arms. I don't want to go on loving one and being with another.

Frederic. But we don't love each other! We scarcely know each other!

Jeannette [*shaking her head*]. It's true. I can't love you, I hate you too much. What did you come here for? Couldn't you have married her at home, your Julia, without my knowing? Yesterday I could laugh. Yesterday I had a lover I wasn't sure I loved and I didn't care. He said he loved me, and I still liked to hear him say so—yesterday.

Frederic. Why did you write and tell him you were leaving him tonight?

Jeannette. No reason. So that I could be free when I said good-by to you. And if I could have left the others as well, the ones before him, and wiped out the marks of their hands on me, I'd have done it.

Father [*turning in his chair as he sleeps, with a sigh*]. Yes, but of course I'm not doing the paying.

Frederic [*smiling in spite of himself*]. What's he dreaming about?

Jeannette [*also smiling*]. I don't know. The wedding breakfast, maybe. . . . Poor Papa. When Lucien goes as well, we'll be alone, the two of us. Funny sort of setup that'll be.

Frederic [*suddenly, gently*]. I'm sorry.

Jeannette. Why? You've already said you were sorry for no reason once before, this morning, about the chicken. . . . After all, everything's as it should be. The other way around would be terrible. Julia's a real woman. I'm not. You've loved her for months and months, but you've only loved me since this morning, and it's still not certain if you do. I'm the one that's a fool, to have said what I've said. What's happened to us must be going on every day, but other people just give a deep sigh and think, "What a pity it's too late," and go on looking at each other in a special sort of way for years afterward. It adds a little mystery to family life. . . .

LUCIEN *can be heard whistling outside. He suddenly looms out of the darkness behind them.*

Lucien. Well, children? Watching Papa having forty winks? [*Going up to him.*] Doesn't it give you the shud-

ders, rather, this open-mouthed corpse? How surprised
it looks. So that was life, was it? They should have told
me. Too late, my dear friend, much to late. Sleep away.
Have your little foretaste of death. Don't snore, though,
or I'll whistle. I like the dead to be discreet. [*He looks
at the others.*] Not bored with each other, I hope, all
alone here? [*He watches the other two passing to and fro
in the lighted kitchen.*] Look at them, busy little bees.
Scrubbing and scouring away in the kitchen, thinking
they hold the key to Truth like the handle of a saucepan,
not suspecting a thing. They hate us, both of them. They
know that from tomorrow on our squalor will win the day.
It may even make them miss their train, but no matter.
They don't want it said that they left our kitchen
dirty. . . . We all have our own notion of honor, don't
we? What's yours, Jeannie? [*Silence. The others do not
answer. He goes to the table and pours himself a glass
of wine.*] I'm mad about housewives. The image of death.
How absurd it must look from a distance—all these
unfortunate women rubbing away tirelessly at the same
little corner, day in, day out, for years and years, being
thwarted every night by the same dust. . . . There she
is, this housewife, wearing herself out, drying herself up,
getting wrinkled and ugly, until one fine night she
crumples up and pegs out, all in after the last round of
chores. And next day, on that same little corner that's
still there—you bet—plenty of time ahead—there falls
another layer of dust. And this time it stays. [*He stretches,
yawns, and takes another drink.*] True, if they didn't do
that, what would they do, poor dears? Make love? [*He
gets up.*] Not everybody can make love, though—that
wouldn't be right and proper. Would it, dear brother-in-
law-to-be? [*He can be heard laughing mockingly in the
shadows, even when he can no longer be seen. He whistles
another military bugle call as he wanders off into the
garden.*]

Frederic [*suddenly, in a dull voice*]. Love. Does he
really not believe that that's a day-to-day struggle, too?

Jeannette [*smiling a little tiredly*]. Not so hard as today,
though. I could never keep it up.

Frederic [*smiling, also rather tiredly*]. Yes, today's been
tough going. [*Pause.*] And there's still tonight to come.
And having to wake up.

Jeannette. I'm a bad lot, so I shan't budge from my

unmade bed. I shall pull the bedclothes up to my eyes. . . . Papa will come and shout at my door for a bit and then he'll go and warm up the stale coffee himself. Later on, around midday, I shall hear him calling me because he can't find a key to open a can of sardines. And I shall go on lying low until night comes.

Frederic. Then when we've killed the first day, there'll be the others. [*Suddenly, he cries*] I can't do it! [JEANNETTE *looks at him.*] I want to struggle, yes, but not against this part of me that's crying out. I want to struggle, but not against this joy. [*Looking at her, he exclaims*] How far away you are on the other side of this table! How far away you've been all day. . . .

Jeannette. It had to be like that. What would have happened if you had so much as brushed against me?

Frederic. We've been fighting each other all day without touching, without even daring to look at each other. We've been rolling on the ground, stifling each other, without a word or a movement, while other people have been talking. . . . Oh, how far away you are still. And yet you'll never be so close again.

Jeannette. Never again.

Frederic. Never again, even in thought. . . . It must be like that, mustn't it, if we want to be strong? We must never for a moment imagine ourselves in each other's arms. . . .

Jeannette [*motionless, eyes closed*]. Not tomorrow. But tonight I'm in your arms.

There is a pause, then FREDERIC *sighs, also with eyes closed.*

Frederic. I couldn't keep it up. . . . Don't move! It's so good suddenly—it can't be wrong.

They both continue talking with their eyes closed, not moving.

Jeannette. Yes. It's good.

Pause.

Frederic [*in a whisper*]. So it was possible. I feel as though I were drinking water. How thirsty I was.

Jeannette. I was thirsty, too. [*Pause, then dully.*] Maybe we ought to call them now. Wake Papa or go out after Lucien, but we ought to have someone with us.

Frederic [*suddenly*]. Wait! It hurts too much. I didn't know what it was like to be hurt. [*He opens his eyes, takes a step toward her, and asks*] Who is this man?

Jeannette. What man?

Frederic. Your lover.

Jeannette [*recoiling a little into the darkness*]. What lover? I haven't got a lover.

Frederic. You just told me you had. Who is this man you go to see every night?

Jeannette [*loudly*]. Who told you I went to see him every night? Do you listen to what other people say?

Frederic. You told me yourself.

Jeannette. I was lying! It wasn't true. Did you believe it? I haven't got a lover.

Frederic. Then why did you tell me you had? I believe everything you say.

Jeannette. To make you listen to me. Your one thought was to get away; you were trying with all your strength not to love me!

Frederic. And all my strength said no. All my strength went over to the enemy, battalion by battalion. How different it seems tonight, too. Like a host of strange faces that I don't recognize—and no one to offer me a helping hand in the darkness. What did the telegram say?

Jeannette. What telegram?

Frederic. The one you just tore up.

Jeannette. You frighten me. You sound like a judge. Remembering I had a telegram and tore it up. You remember everything.

Frederic. Yes. I used to forget everything. Names of streets, numbers, insults, faces. Julia used to laugh at me. Now I don't forget anything any more. Everything is in its place, with a label, a question mark. Life has become a nerveracking survey of one's accounts. What was in that telegram?—answer me.

Jeannette. How can I answer you? You saw for yourself. I tore it up without opening it.

Frederic. Pick up the pieces and read them.

Jeannette. I don't know where they are any more.

Frederic. I do—they're by your feet.

Jeannette. It's dark. I shouldn't be able to see.

Frederic. I'll put the light on.

Jeannette [*suddenly, in a loud voice*]. Oh, no! Please don't put the light on! Don't make me read it. Don't make me look you in the face. Just believe me. It would be so easy to believe me in the dark.

Frederic. But that's all I ask! To believe you, like a child, like a slave. Everything's crying out inside me that I want to believe you. Can't you hear it? But I can't. You tell lies all the time.

Jeannette. Yes, I tell lies all the time, but you must believe me just the same. They're not real lies. With a little luck they might all have been true. They would all become true, if you wanted it that way. Oh, *please!* It's so much simpler for you. You need only want it.

Frederic. I do want it, I do want it, with all my might, as you do in dreams, but I can't. Who sent you that telegram?

Jeannette. You see, you're questioning me again. So I have to lie to you, to gain time.

Frederic. Why should you want to gain time?

Jeannette. Everything's so fragile still. It's too early to talk yet. Tomorrow we shall know each other. Tomorrow we may be stronger than words. . . . Oh, if you would only wait, if you would only wait a little. I'm so poor as you see me tonight. I've so few possessions yet. I'm just a beggar. Give me a little, just a little bit of quiet.

Frederic [*in a dull voice*]. I can't.

Jeannette. Or ask me some other questions. Ask me why I'm trembling as I talk to you, why I cry when I tell you lies, why I'm getting so mixed up—me, the one that's so sure of everything and laughs all the time!

Frederic. I can't. I want to know who the others are. I want to know all the things that'll hurt me.

Jeannette [*with a sudden desperate gesture, out loud*]. All right, then, you'll have asked for it. Take me or leave me with all my faults. You'll have to take half of them now, though. I can't go on alone. We must share and share alike. It was all true just now—I did have a lover, and he did write to me, to beg me not to leave him, I suppose. And there were others before him that I didn't love. Before I knew I ought to wait, that somewhere on this earth there was someone I didn't know yet, someone I was already about to steal. . . . There, you know everything now. Lying is the only way I know of defending myself. [*Pause.*] You don't say anything. You're standing there close to me; I can hear you breathing in the dark. I can feel that Julia must be like a great patch of light inside you now. You'll never be able to love this fraud as you love her, will you? [*She goes on in a low voice.*] And yet for all my bad ways and my goings-on and my wickedness of heart I'm like a virgin standing here in front of you at this moment—something the others will never know. But there's no bouquet, no white veil, no innocence, no little bridesmaids to carry the train—a bride all in black. . . . [*Her voice lower still.*] And all for you, if you would deign to look at her.

FREDERIC *has stepped toward her suddenly. He takes her in his arms and kisses her. She frees herself with the cry of a hurt animal and runs off. He remains alone and motionless in the dark room. The* MOTHER *comes in and lights the hanging lamp, which casts a gloomy light.*

Mother. You can't see a thing here. What are you doing in the dark? [*She stows some things away in the sideboard.*] There. The kitchen has probably never been so clean. Poor Julia! She was in tears about it, and I can well understand it. She's so unlike them. It was only for her sake I stayed this morning. Thank heavens it's over now. We've done what had to be done and now we'll all three pack up and be off and not come back any sooner than we can help. What's the matter? You're so pale. Are you tired?

Frederic. No, Mother.

Mother. It's this light. [*Looking at the* FATHER.] He's asleep, the old good-for-nothing. Still, he's a bit better than the other two. You saw the other girl, I suppose, leaving everything to Julia and me? The cheek of it! We'll try not to invite her to the wedding. Julia agrees with me. Your uncles would never understand how I could let you marry the sister of a girl like that. Poor Julia! She's suffered enough already on her account. [*She goes back to the kitchen, calling out to* JULIA, *who is just visible.*] We shall have to leave the rest, my dear, if we don't want to miss the train.

She has disappeared with JULIA. FREDERIC *has not stirred.*
A door opens suddenly. JEANNETTE *appears. They talk in*
low voices, like criminals.

Jeannette. What are we going to do?

Frederic. We must tell her.

Jeannette. Now that I'm the rich one, I feel ashamed.
You call her.

Frederic [*calling, but scarcely raising his voice*]. Julia.

Jeannette. Louder. She can't hear. . . . [*Suddenly cry-*
ing out.] Wait! It's wrong, what we're doing.

Frederic. Yes.

Jeannette. Nobody will ever be able to understand, nobody will ever forgive us, will they?

Frederic. No, nobody.

Jeannette. We're like two murderers that daren't look
each other in the face. But we've got to do it. It would be
shabbier still not to say anything.

Frederic. And tomorrow it will be too late. [*He calls*
again, still not loudly enough.] Julia.

Jeannette [*coming up to him and putting her arms*
round him]. Wait! She's going to lose you. She's suddenly
not going to have you in her arms any more. I'm trying
to imagine what it's like to have nothing in your arms
any more.

Frederic. It's like it was just now.

Jeannette [*with a cry*]. I don't remember any more! Oh,
how good it is to be together! When was it—yesterday?—
that we didn't know each other?

Frederic. I don't know. We must call her.

Jeannette. Wait! Oh, if only you'd never known her! If
only you'd known me first. I'm touching you. I'm really
touching you. Forgive me, Julia—it's so good!

Frederic [*looking ahead of him into the distance*]. We
mustn't ask her to forgive us. We mustn't try to explain.
We must tell her quickly, like cutting something with a
knife. We must kill her quickly and get out.

Jeannette. How you love her still!

Frederic. Yes. [*He calls, louder this time.*] Julia!

Julia [*appears, a cloth in her hand, at the kitchen door*].
Are you calling me?

Frederic [*more softly*]. Yes, Julia.

FREDERIC *and* JEANNETTE *have let go of each other and are standing close together looking straight ahead of them.* JULIA *comes into the room and looks at them.*

Julia. What is it?

Frederic [*making a beginning*]. This is it, Julia. It's going to be difficult to say, and you won't be able to understand, I know. I'm not going to marry you, Julia.

Julia [*does not move at first. Then she puts down the cloth on a chair. Looking at* JEANNETTE, *she asks*]. What has she said to you?

Frederic. She hasn't said anything. You don't know. You can't ever know, you can't ever understand. It's not our fault. We've both been fighting against it since this morning.

Julia. Fighting . . . ? Who, you?

Frederic [*with a gesture of the hand*]. Both of us. You must go with Mother, Julia. I'm staying here.

Julia. Staying where?

Frederic. Or if you think it's better for you to stay, we'll go.

Julia. "We" . . . who's "we"? [*They do not reply. She goes on in a lower voice*] When you say "we" . . . you don't mean us any more? Who do you mean you're going with? [*They do not answer.*] You're trying to frighten me, aren't you? And now you're going to laugh at me. Or maybe you want me to laugh first?

Jeannette. I'm going to hurt you, Julia. We've hated each other ever since we were little. But today I want to be humble with you. I want to be your servant.

Julia. Stop trying to be nice to me. You're frightening me.

Jeannette. We've always quarreled over everything— toys, clothes . . . everything. But today I'd willingly give you everything I have. Only I haven't got anything but my old shabby clothes and him—and I can't give you him. I wish I could make myself uglier, so that you didn't feel so hurt. I wish I could spoil my face, cut my hair. But then I don't want to be ugly either, because of him.

Julia. Do you really think he can love you? You're everything he hates most in the world!

Jeannette [*humbly*]. Yes, Julia.

Julia. A slattern, a liar, and bone lazy!

Jeannette. Yes.

Julia. He's so pure, so hard to please, the soul of honor—how can he love you? Is this a joke or something? Have you told him about your lovers?

Jeannette. Yes, I have.

Julia. What about this last one—the one that pays you—does he know about him? I bet he doesn't.

Jeannette [suddenly transfigured]. Thank you, Julia!

Julia. What for?

Jeannette. At last you've been wicked!

Julia. You weren't actually hoping I wouldn't defend myself? She got around you, I suppose? Rubbed herself against you like with the others? Kissed you full on the mouth in a dark corner, or better still, out on the sands?

Frederic [loudly]. We've never been alone. We haven't even talked to each other!

Julia. Oh, it doesn't take her long and she doesn't need much conversation. Ask her how she's done it before with the fisherboys at night, lying on the nets at the bottom of a boat in the stink of fish!

Jeannette. Thank you, Julia, thank you!

Julia. Keep your thanks, you sneak thief!

Jeannette. Now that you're fighting back, I'm not ashamed. Thank you, Julia.

Frederic [trying to pull her away]. Be quite! Leave her alone!

Jeannette. You might have cried or burst into tears, and he might have taken pity on you. But you started defending yourself like a woman about to be robbed.

Julia. Yes. Thief! Thief!

Frederic. Be quiet, both of you!

Julia. Quiet? So I've got to be quiet, too? She's taking you away, and I've got to be quiet!

Jeannette. How clumsy you are. All stiff and dignified. You're only thinking of how much you hate me. You're only thinking of the harm we're doing you. You should be crying. Go on, cry! Melt his heart!

Julia. You'd like me to cry, wouldn't you? but don't be too sure.

Jeannette. Cry! He's only waiting for that to take you back! He loves you still, you can see he does. Look at him at least!

Julia. No.

Jeannette. Now, while I'm shouting and ugly and my hair's all over the place! He hates me like this. He's beginning to miss you already. Cry, quick, Julia, cry!

Julia. No! I've got all the time I need to cry in. That'll do for when I'm alone.

Jeannette. Tear my eyes out, then! Scratch me, hit me —I shan't defend myself. But do something horrible— you've got to, too, so that I'm not the only one! He's only thinking of you now; he's only listening to you. Do something mean and horrible or I shall kill you, I shall spit in your face!

She throws herself on JULIA. FREDERIC *tears her away, hurting her as he does so, and pushes her away from him.*

Frederic. Leave her alone now. I'm telling you to!

Jeannette [*with a cry of triumph*]. He hurt me! Did you see? He hurt me, *me*! *I'm* his wife!

Frederic [*gently*]. Please go now, Julia. You're worth more than she is, I realize that, and she's probably done all the things you said she had, but she's right; she's my wife now.

Julia [*turning suddenly and running to the kitchen, calling*]. Help! Mother! Help!

Jeannette [*with eyes closed, her voice hoarse*]. How you must hate me at this moment!

Frederic [*hard, without looking at her*]. Go up to your room. Get what you want to take with you and wait for me outside.

JEANNETTE *goes out.* LUCIEN *appears suddenly.*

Lucien. You're not going to do it?

Frederic. Yes. Now, this minute.

Lucien. Don't. It always goes wrong.

Frederic. Why?

Lucien. It's too good. And everything that's good is forbidden, didn't you know? [*He pours a glass of red wine.*] Take this glass of wine, for example; it isn't much, but it warms you up a bit on its way down. . . . That's forbidden. You have to take advantage when He's not looking. [*He empties the glass at a gulp.*] There! He didn't notice that one.

Frederic. Who?

Lucien [*pointing upward*]. That One up there. Every time anyone's happy, he gets in a frightful rage. Doesn't like it.

Frederic. You're drunk.

Lucien. Not yet, alas. That doesn't happen till much later. You're not going to do this, are you? You'll never get away with it.

Frederic. We'll see.

Lucien. I can see already. I can see you a week from now, the two of you, in a month, a year. It's all unrolling in front of me like a little movie film. A terrible little movie film. But there's still time. Go and find Julia and your mother in the kitchen and tell them you were dreaming.

Frederic. I wasn't dreaming!

Lucien. Look at me, dear boy. I don't look the sensitive type, do I? Don't do it. Even if only for Julia's sake.

Frederic. I mustn't think of Julia any more!

Lucien. What's love? Nothing. Mockery, lies, wind. I tell you, she'll die now. Don't do it. It's not worth the trouble you cause yourself, let alone the trouble you cause other people. It's not worth a baby crying. Don't do it.

Frederic. I've been over all that. It's too late now.

Lucien. You can't have been over it all; you don't know it all. I know. I know it all! I've completed my education. It cost me somewhat dearly, my dear little ducation, and I'm still paying. I had to do it on the never-never; lifelong installments . . . but now at least I can talk. I'm fully qualified in love. I've got my doctorate in cuckoldry. That makes me an authority. Don't do it, dear boy. The game's up in advance.

Frederic. But why?

Lucien. For no reason at all. Because she's a woman. Because we're alone in the world. Because one night in a month or a year or ten years from now, when you think you're holding your little mate in your arms, you'll suddenly realize you're like everybody else; that it's only a woman you've got in your arms, there's nothing there.

Frederic. That's enough. You shut up, too.

Lucien. Marry Julia. Have children. Become a man. A man with a profession, with money, with a girl friend later on—nobody'll mind that—a real man. Don't try to be clever. It's so easy to be happy! There's a formula; men have spent centuries perfecting it. Cheat, old man. Cheat at everything. Above all, cheat yourself. It's the only way of getting That One up there to leave you alone. He's got a weakness for tricksters, or else He's shortsighted. Or maybe He's asleep. [*He indicates the* FATHER.] Like him, with his mouth open. And if you don't make too much noise, He won't interfere. . . . But He's got a nose, a terribly keen sense of smell, and the whiff—just the merest whiff—of love, and He's on to it. And He doesn't like it. He doesn't like it at all. So He wakes up and starts taking an interest in you. He pounces on you like a sergeant major. About turn! No good trying to be smart with me, my fine friend. Don't care for refractory types. Brought plenty like you to heel. You'll be a cuckold. What's that? What? Not satisfied? You can die of it, then, that'll teach you! Death! Death! Death! Death! You've read that little page at the back of your service certificate, where they promise you it served up in all sorts of different ways when you're a new recruit? That's love.

Jeannette [*appearing with a coat, hat and small bundle*]. I'm ready.

Frederic. Let's go.

He takes her hand and they go out and disappear into the darkness. LUCIEN has not moved. He helps himself to the rest of the wine, lifts his glass ceilingward.

Lucien. Here's to them. Do you mind?

Father [*awakened by the silence, and trying to look as though he has not been asleep*]. Well, now, where are we, children? I hope this is going to be over soon.

Lucien [*smiling*]. Quite soon. It's just beginning.

Curtain.

ACT THREE

SCENE—*A deserted summer house in the woods. The room is quite empty. At the back the bottom of a staircase is just visible. There is an overturned sofa lying on*

*the floor. Hanging at the broken window is a dark curtain,
bellying out in the wind. The room is in darkness. A storm
can be heard outside.* JEANNETTE *comes in with* FREDERIC.
They are drenched with rain.

JEANNETTE. Let's come in here for a bit. At least we'll be
out of the rain. [*They come in and shut the door. Everything suddenly seems quiet.*] It used to be used as a summer house in the woods, but it's been neglected for a
long time now. I shelter here now and again when I get
caught in the rain. [*Silence. They stand in the middle of
the dark room. She murmurs.*] It would be better to wait
here.

Pause. A gale blows the curtains out again.

Frederic. What a storm!
Jeannette. Yes. The glass has all gone out of the windows. [*Short silence.*] There's a hurricane lamp in the
corner there, if you've got any matches. [*He passes her a
box of matches.*] The owner's very kind. He knows I come
here sometimes and he leaves this for me.
Frederic. You know him?
Jeannette. Slightly. [*She pins back the flapping curtain
with a plank.*] If we light up, we'd better draw the curtain. The light can be seen a long way off in the woods.
[*He looks around him. She goes to the sofa and pulls it
back into position.*] There's only an old rickety sofa, but it
does stand up.

FREDERIC *has caught sight of the staircase.*

Frederic. What's up there?
Jeannette [*seeming to hesitate slightly*]. It's a sort of
hayloft. There's just an old mattress on the floor and some
ancient moth-eaten curtains that I put up on the wall and
an old trunk for a table. It's my home. I sleep there sometimes in the summer. I'll show it to you presently. [*Pause.
They are standing face to face, not daring to move. She
whispers*] So here we are.
Frederic. So here we are.

*Pause. They are embarrassed, and do not move. There is
the sound of the storm outside.*

Jeannette. Still, it is better to stay here than at the station.

Frederic. Are you shivering?

Jeannette. Yes.

Frederic. You're wet through. Are you cold?

Jeannette. No, I'm not cold. It's only my coat that's soaked. Take off your jacket and let it dry. I'll go upstairs and find you something. [*She runs lightly upstairs and can be heard walking about in the room above.* FREDERIC *takes off his jacket. She comes down again with a blanket which she throws over his shoulders.*] There! You look wonderful like that—like an old redskin chief. [*He goes to take her in his arms, but she disengages herself almost imperceptibly, murmuring*] I'm frightened.

Frederic [*gently*]. I'm frightened, too.

There is a short pause. She smiles.

Jeannette. I'm frightening you with my hair all wet like this. I'm so ugly.

Frederic. No, you're not.

Jeannette. They say I look like a crazy thing when my hair's wet.

Frederic. Who are "they"?

Jeannette. The others. [*Correcting herself.*] People.

Frederic. You look like a wood nymph.

Jeannette. I'd like to have been a real wood nymph, sitting all by myself up in the branches, with my hair all tangled, shouting insults at people. There were never any real ones, though, were there?

Frederic. I don't know.

Jeannette [*raising her eyes, suddenly serious*]. Anyway, you probably like girls with their hair all tidy; the sort that brush it for ages and ages every morning in the bedroom. [*She passes her fingers through her hair, then runs suddenly to her little bundle and rummages feverishly in it. She gets up, vexed.*] No, I don't seem to have brought a comb with me. I'll buy a brush tomorrow. [*She is standing facing him; suddenly she cries*] And I'll tidy my hair, properly, and make it smooth—the way I hate it and you like it. As smooth as Julia's! [*They stand looking at each other for a while, disconcerted, then she lowers her eyes, humble again.*] I'm sorry. But I should so much like to be

beautiful. I do so want you to like me. [*Pause. She cries*]
Wait a minute! I haven't got a comb, but I did bring
something else—in this box. [*She takes up a cardboard
box, badly tied up with string, which she was carrying
when she came in, and climbs upstairs. He remains alone
on the stage, somewhat disconcerted. She can be heard
calling from above.*] But you mustn't look! If you move
an inch I shall come down again and you won't see a
thing. I shall be rather a long time—it's dark up here.

Frederic. Do you want the lamp?

Jeannette. No, thanks. I don't need it. Don't move.
Are you bored waiting?

Frederic. No.

Jeannette. Anyway, this will make up for it, I hope.
[*There is a short pause, during which there is no sound
from her, then suddenly she appears on the staircase in the
eerie light of the hurricane lamp. She has hurriedly put
on an unusual, flimsy white dress, but is still wearing her
clumsy boy's shoes. She stands there for a while without
a word.*] There. Now, I'm dying of shame. I'll go and
take it off!

Frederic [*dully*]. No. [*She stops.*] Did you bring that
with you in your bundle?

Jeannette. No, not in that. In that big cardboard box
that I kept banging against the trees on the way. It's the
only precious thing I have in the world.

Frederic. But it's a wedding dress. . . .

Jeannette. No. It's white, but it's a ball dress, a real
ball dress, like the ones in the catalogues. . . . [*She looks
slightly troubled.*] It's not new, though. . . . I bought it
from a secondhand shop that was selling it for the material
alone. I just managed to scrape up the money selling some
of the wild duck eggs I go nesting for in the reeds. They're
very rare around here, you know. People have them hatched
by their own hens, and get a much more valuable breed
that way. [*She has the feeling he probably does not believe
her and adds*] I'd been selling eggs for a whole season,
so I did have the money. Because of course the dealer
wouldn't let me have a dress like this for nothing. It looks
almost new, too, now that I've washed it. [*Her voice trails
off. He says nothing, but stands looking at her. She turns
back up the stairs, murmuring*] I'll go and take it off.

Frederic [*tonelessly*]. No. Keep it on. [*She comes down again and walks silently toward him, never taking her eyes off him. When she is close, he takes her in his arms.*] I don't care if it is new—or even if you got it as a present from someone.

Jeannette. Why don't you ever believe me? I'm sure you believe anything Julia tells you.

Frederic. Yes, I do.

Jeannette. But not me.

Frederic. No.

Jeannette [*disengaging herself*]. Well, go and find her, then. I want to be believed, too! [*She comes back to his arms.*] No. Don't move. I'll tell you everything. Sit down. [*She makes him sit down and then sits at his feet.*] I didn't do it just with the wild-duck eggs, of course. I'd have needed much more than that. But it is true they paid for some of it. I didn't want you to know the rest because I didn't think you'd like it. Papa had had some silver in pawn for ages and ages. He was always asking for renewals, but the time was running out. I stole the pawn ticket from a whole pile of them he keeps in a drawer and took the silver out, with the duck-egg money actually, and sold it to buy this dress. He'd never have had enough money to take the things out himself, and he'd just have lost the silver. Besides, there was a bit of money over, and I bought him a box of cigars with it. Only a small box, because this was expensive. [*Pause.*] I don't mind you knowing that, now that you know how I got the money. I bought it new in a big Paris shop. I chose it from the catalogue and they sent it through the post. So now you know. [*Another pause.*] Does that make you unhappy?

Frederic. No.

Jeannette. Do you believe me now?

Frederic. Yes.

Jeannette [*sighs and lays her head on his knee*]. How simple it is to tell the truth. Somehow you just don't think of it.

Frederic. Do think of it, please, so that I don't get too hurt.

Jeannette. Are you hurt, truly? But you said just now you didn't care if the dress was new, or if someone had given it me.

Frederic [*with his eyes closed*]. It wasn't true.

Jeannette. Oh, good! I'm glad. Because if you only loved

me that way, if you only desired me and didn't mind about anything else, I should be terribly unhappy. You must believe in me, make lots of demands on me.

Frederic. I want with all my might to believe in you; I shall go on asking you for the truth, every morning, like daily bread, to keep me going for the day.

Jeannette. That's right. Every morning when we wake up I shall tell you the truth. How good it'll be to give you all the truth I have in me, like a little piece of luggage to carry. It'll make me feel so light. And then at night I shall give you another little lot, before I go to sleep. But of course at night it will be a bit complicated.

Frederic. Why?

Jeannette [*sighing*]. Because days are so long! Because I love you so much. Because I'm so afraid of hurting you.

Frederic. How else would you hurt me except by lying to me?

Jeannette. Oh! There are other ways. People are frightened of lies, but they're really only like little clouds; they pass without leaving any trace. And you mustn't think I can remember all mine, either. If I were to remember them all, if they were all to be stuck all over me like flies, then maybe it would be frightening. But when the cloud has passed, I feel all relaxed again; rather as if we'd been able to change the subject and I'd kept my mouth shut— all calm and innocent! Do you see?

Frederic [*sighing*]. I'll try.

Jeannette. A step to the right—that's fine; a step to the left—that's bad. It's like being little again and not knowing quite which hand is which. [*Pause. Suddenly she asks*] I'm not really the sort of woman you were thinking of as a wife, am I?

Frederic. Not altogether.

Jeannette. But here I am, with my head on your knee.

Frederic. Yes. Here you are.

Jeannette. I suppose that's what they call fate?

Frederic. I suppose it is.

Jeannette [*sighing happily*]. What a good thing fate is.

Frederic [*after a pause, in a hard voice*]. Yes. What a good thing. There's Julia, crying in her empty room back there, with everything around her shattered and insecure, but fate is good. And whatever it is inside me that's broken and will go on hurting for always—that's good, too. Everything's good. A terrible luxury, an appalling sweetness.

Jeannette. And me being the way I am?

Frederic. That's good, too. I suppose it was really the simplest thing in the world that we should be so unsuitable for each other, so full of contradictions, both of us. And that I should have to love Julia first, and meet you through her, and that you should be so different.

Silence.

Jeannette [*murmurs*]. Even when we were small, we couldn't have been much alike.

Frederic. No.

Jeannette. Did you used to come out top at school?

Frederic. Yes.

Jeannette. I can just see you, looking so tidy and clean with your school satchel over your shoulder. I was always dirty and tousled and covered with ink spots, with my hair falling into my eyes. I was always cutting school, to go and fight with the roughs.

Frederic [*smiling*]. I can just see that, too!

Jeannette. There used to be a whole gang of us. We called ourselves the Kings of Trumps. They even said we killed a boy one night by throwing clogs at him. We were terrible. We had ink tattoo marks and real saber cuts all over us. And we had a charm, too—a bit of red paper that we chewed to make us strong. We called it Mininistatfia. And all the while, there you were—I can just see you—with your clean white collar!

Frederic [*smiling*]. I expect I pretended not to see any of you. I must have hated you all. We had a good crowd, too. We called ourselves the Dauntless. We had a system of military ranks, and we'd made up our minds to rid the world of roughs.

Jeannette. What a hope. Don't worry, they'll always be around.

Frederic. They used to steal fruit from our parents and show their backsides and pull our sisters' hair.

Jeannette. Yes, lovely plaits! Just made for pulling!

Frederic. We all agreed to put a stop to it once and for all and there was to be a big fight on the Fourteenth of July. We had a week's truce to get ourselves ready.

Little bastards! They put knife blades on the ends of their
sticks.

Jeannette. We had a big fight, too. One of the others
got his arm broken. Ours was on Saint John's Day. We'd
been dancing around bonfires like savages before it started.
I'd made myself an American knuckle-duster with some
nails. I buried it in the seat of the deputy mayor because
they'd brought in their parents to help them, the cowards,
when they saw we were winning!

Frederic. Our crowd only had sticks and stones. We
fought in the open with fair weapons. But we aimed better
than they did. You should have heard the yelling when we
got one of them in the dark!

Jeannette [*softly*]. You threw a stone at me once. I've
got a hole the size of a nut in my knee. Give me your
hand. Look, it's there.

Pause. His hand is lying on her knee.

Frederic [*gravely*]. I'm sorry.

Jeannette. That's all right—so long as you don't hurt
me any more. [*Silence again. She sighs happily.*] It's nice
to feel your hand there. Like being a horse that knows it'll
never stumble. How quiet everything is all around us suddenly. Has the rain stopped?

Frederic. I don't know.

Jeannette [*after a pause*]. It's as if something were being
gently torn inside me. I have the feeling I shall never hurt
you. Is that what they call tenderness, do you think?

Frederic. I don't know.

Jeannette. I didn't before, either. I'd only read about it
in books. I thought it only happened after a very long
time.

Frederic. I thought so, too.

Jeannette. It can't be true, can it? It's happened so
quickly. I can desire you and be happy in your arms, but
I can't love you like that, surely? How can I possibly? I
don't even know you.

Frederic. I don't know you, either, but tonight you're
going to be my wife. Wife and younger brother all in one,
till death do us part—you, this little stranger with the
shut face. How simple it is.

Jeannette. Holding hands is simple, and sitting like

this with my head on your shoulder. But what about our real feelings . . . ?

Frederic. All we need to do is make ourselves think the opposite. I used to say to myself: She'll be very serious, and dressed in black like the girls where I come from. She'll have a shiny face with light eyes and hair brushed back—a little soldier bravely carrying her pack beside me. But no. It had to be your eyes, that I daren't look into; your straggly hair, your urchin face, and your lies. Everything I don't like I had to love.

Jeannette. Supposing I stop telling lies and brush back my hair, too?

Frederic. I used to tell myself: I'll have two children. The older one will be called Alain—he'll be a terror— and then there'll be the little one, Marie, and she'll be gentle as a bird. And every evening when I come home I shall go over their spelling with them, out of a book. But there aren't going to be any of those quiet evenings. It's as simple as that. No spelling by lamplight, no attentive little faces . . . only bare hotel rooms, lies, scenes, hurt.

Jeannette. You sound so contented when you say that.

Frederic. I am contented. Not the way I was hoping for —but differently. With the sort of contentment you feel when you've arrived somewhere, even if it should be the pit of despair; when you can say: Oh, good, this is it. I'm there.

Jeannette. And you think we're there?

Frederic. Yes. This time, we're there. It's taken a long time and we came a strange way around. But I can feel you all warm against me, and these few minutes before we take each other are almost like a betrothal. I'm there all right.

Jeannette. Am I really there, too?

Frederic [*smiling*]. You should know.

Jeannette. And it's too late to go back? You've finished with all the things you wanted before? That means you feel responsible. If I'm hurt, you'll have to feel guilty about me, and if I'm unhappy, no matter what for, you'll share it?

Frederic. Yes, no matter what for.

Jeannette. I can understand their being so solemn about it.

Frederic. Who?

Jeannette. Real fiancés. [*She gets up.*] But what I don't understand is that they cheat afterward. They whisper things to each other in kitchens. If I'd once given a solemn oath like that, all dressed in white in a church with a bouquet, if I'd said to a boy, "From now on I'm your wife, we share things—good and bad we both have to share," I'd be like a soldier with his captain; I'd rather cut my arm off! [*She turns away, saying in a loud voice*] Why are you always thinking of Julia? Why are you always talking about Julia?

Frederic. Julia? Why, what have I said?

Jeannette. Can't you hear yourself? Every time you stop talking, you're calling "Julia." Every time your eyes look my way, they're looking at her, and I turn away in spite of myself. You know I shall never be like her. You know I'm just the opposite of her. Look at me. It's me, here, nobody else. Me, with the good and bad in me all tied up together in a knot. You have to take me as I am, it's no good trying to undo it.

Frederic. Be quiet!

Jeannette. What are you doing away from her, away from your mother and the lawyer and your own village, away from everything safe and good in your life? What are you doing here with this bedraggled woman that shouts and tells lies and makes you feel ashamed and will go on making you suffer? You want her, don't you? so take her quickly. She's yours for tonight. She'll co-operate. And in the morning, when you've had what you want, get back to Julia, quickly. She's the one you really care for.

Frederic [*taking her by the wrist*]. We've been hurt quite enough. Now will you be quiet!

Jeannette [*struggling free*]. That's right, hurt me! Twist my arm like you did just now to protect her! It's Julia you care for—always have and always will, my lad. If she'd had the courage to fight just now at the house, and forget about her clean apron and her nicely bound books and all the rest of it, she'd have been in the right camp now, I bet, along with the Dauntless against the Kings of Trumps.

Frederic. You're crazy!

Jeannette. And you'd have stood in front of her, wouldn't you, if I'd started throwing stones at her? So that she wouldn't be hurt and her dear sweet blood shouldn't flow? You would have, wouldn't you, like this evening, when I wanted to hit her?

Frederic [*hard, looking her full in the face*]. Certainly!

Jeannette [*shouting like a child*]. Well, I'd have let loose all my roughs on you. They'd have tied you to a tree and I'd have scalped her, your Julia! I'd have scalped her with all her pretty, well-groomed hair, before your very eyes! Oh, why aren't we kids any more? Why can't we have a good fight? [*She throws herself into his arms and cries out in anguish.*] Oh, if you could only take your knife out of your pocket and cut my heart in two, you'd see how good and red it is inside.

Frederic [*won over, pressing her against him*]. How fast it's beating. . . .

Jeannette. Can you hear it? Oh, if I tell any more lies, if I can't undo all the strings I'm caught up in like a poor little fly, and if I hurt you and say wicked things, just think of my heart all helpless there in its prison. Because it's only my cunning or my wickedness or my pride that talks; I'm just a woman with all that she's done behind her and all that she's capable of in front of her, but my heart's like an animal that can only jump about to make itself understood. And it's jumping up at you now, can you feel it? So whenever I push you away or laugh at you, even if I seem to want to hurt you, just listen to that. Don't take any notice of me. [*She presses herself against him.*] Hold me tight now—I shan't have your strength for long to boost mine up. [*She goes to the window, draws the curtain, and opens the door wide. The wind bursts into the room and makes the lamp flicker.*]

Frederic. What are you doing?

Jeannette. I'm opening everything so that the light can be seen right into the woods.

Frederic. Why?

Jeannette. So that no one can say I've given less than real fiancées do. And since we're going to be together for better or worse, we can start right now, can't we? It's like the swimming race across the bay on the Fourteenth of July. There's always one left out. But anyone who isn't fit can easily not enter. [*She is standing at the open French window, facing the wind, in a state of exaltation.*]

Frederic. Shut that door. The lamp'll go out.

Jeannette. We'll light it again. We'll light it and wait until a man that's wandering about in the woods now like an old black sad owl sees it shining through the branches and comes knocking at the window. [FREDERIC *has taken a step toward her but stops as she goes on.*] He knows he's lost me. He's looking for me, I feel sure. But he's just an animal. He's ugly and ashamed—maybe he won't dare come in. All right, so he doesn't come in—good! But I shall have done all I can to bring him here. It's like something I read somewhere at school—when the innocent and the guilty both had to take hold of the red-hot iron. After that it was just a question of courage and luck . . . it was well worth another trial.

Frederic. Do you want me to meet this man?

Jeannette. It's like an operation, Frederic. If I don't lose too much blood, if I'm not too mutilated, there may be just a chance I'll go on living. [*She adds, gravely*] Only afterward I want you to love me like Julia.

FREDERIC *suddenly goes to the window, shuts it, and turns toward her.*

Frederic. If that man comes in here—if I look him in the face—I may not be able to love you any more.

Jeannette. I know. With the red-hot iron there was always the risk you'd die of burns. But you had to take hold of it just the same.

Frederic. Isn't what we've done enough? Isn't it enough that she's been hurt?

Jeannette. No. Each of us has to pay his share.

Frederic. I love you, and we're alone at last after that interminable day. Don't let's wait any longer! The night's coming on so quickly. I've accepted it all—the wrong and the hurt we've caused, and your being so different—provided we're there now. [*He draws the curtain.*] Please, please don't ask any more. Don't look for any more ways of being hurt. Look, I'm not asking any more of you. Men fight and die for dreams, too, but there comes a time when they feel tired; when they want to call a halt, feel their wives near them, and snatch a bit of happiness at long last.

He has taken a step toward her. She draws back.

Jeannette. No, Frederic. When we were in the woods, I thought we should never be here quickly enough, I wanted you so much; but now if you touch me I think I shall call out.

Frederic. I don't recognize you any more. Who are you, so tense and pale all of a sudden, so on the defensive?

Jeannette. I'm their sister.

Frederic. Whose sister?

Jeannette. Of the women in your life—all that trail of women hanging on to each other's black skirts, stretching way back over the generations and mounting guard over your heart. Aunts, cousins, grandmothers, and Julia, too. I'm not afraid of them any longer. I'm like them. It isn't difficult. It's love that does it.

The door opens suddenly. LUCIEN *appears on the threshold, his clothes streaming.*

Lucien. Excuse me. I'm disturbing you, I'm afraid. We shall have done quite a bit of walking in the rain tonight, all of us. Funny sort of weather for romance. [*He closes the door again.*] Azarias sent me. He daren't come in, he's shy. But he's not a bad chap, and I should think he loved you. He says I'm to tell you you can keep the dress. [JEANNETTE *has not moved.* FREDERIC *turns to her without a word.* LUCIEN *opens a box he has been carrying in his hand.*] And I'm to give you the veil you left behind. [*He calmly places the huge tulle veil on a chair.*]

Jeannette [*softly in the silence*]. Yes, it was a wedding dress.

Frederic. And he gave it to you?

Jeannette. Yes. Yesterday.

Frederic [*after a silence*]. Why did you bring it with you?

Jeannette [*like a child*]. It was the only nice thing I had.

They stand facing each other, silent and motionless.

Lucien [*smiling*]. Is that beyond your comprehension? Be fair, now. She was going away with you for ever and always—the great love. You must admit it was the best possible time to give a bit of thought to her appearance. It's a mere man's idea to wonder who bought her dress. . . . Besides, I must point out that she left the veil behind—a very delicate sentiment. And of course a no less delicate sentiment prompted us to bring it back to her.

Jeannette [softly]. I hate you, Lucien.

Lucien. Yes. It's a lousy part I'm playing in all this—not very clever, I must confess. [*He looks at the two of them standing there dumb and out of countenance. Then he says mockingly*] Poor lambs! It's pitiful. Wanting the truth, the whole truth, and nothing but the truth, and then when it's there in front of them they just shut up and want to cry. You need to be hard-boiled like me to welcome the lady Truth.

Frederic [suddenly]. Why did you lie to me?

Jeannette. You saw it was new, so I realized I'd never be able to tell you.

Frederic. Tell me what? That he'd given it you yesterday?

Jeannette. Yes.

Frederic. But you brought it with you just the same.

Jeannette. Yes.

Frederic. I was only offering you escape and poverty, you knew that. You followed me at once, with nothing. Like me you broke off with everything, left everything behind, and the crime we're guilty of was only excusable because we both abandoned everything. I wish I could tear it off you and rip it to pieces and dirty it all over.

He goes toward her but she draws back with a cry, holding the dress against her.

Jeannette. No!

The cry brings FREDERIC *to a standstill.*

Lucien [softly]. It isn't nice to spoil things! Besides, she loves her dress, bless her. Not as much as you, of course, but very much. If you ask her to choose, she'll choose, and go and take it off. But we've been weeping over the catalogues for months now and we've dreamed of this dress for so long, with nothing but our shabby old sweaters to wear. Think of it, we might even have married Azarias, just for that.

Frederic [loudly]. It's not true!

Lucien. Oh, but it is. What do you think women are made of, anyway? Steel, platinum, diamond? But of course that's something the law wouldn't teach you. They're nothing but sighs, dreams, whims; there's good and there's bad all mixed up together, and according to the chemical equation they either combine or cause an explosion. Women have a knack of taking on the aspect of something eternal, so that you want to die suddenly, they're so beautiful; and then one fine morning they become terrifying, monstrous. They've slipped through your fingers. Azarias is rich, and he loves her. She's leaving him tonight for you, with no regrets. And don't think for a minute she used to go to him for the sake of his cash—she's not a whore, my sister. She went to him because it amused her, and she's going off with you because it amuses her more, but she's taking her dress with her. That's all.

Frederic. Shut up!

Lucien. You'll be well away by the time you have to admit it yourself. It does me good, so leave me alone.

Frederic [*suddenly*]. You were lying! You were lying again! You've been lying to me all the time. When am I going to be able to believe you now?

Lucien. Oh—tomorrow—in five minutes' time—or even right now. You've only got to go away with her—just leave it to her. From tomorrow on, you'll believe her. It's a solution, and no sillier than feeling hurt.

Frederic. I couldn't do it.

Lucien. I thought I couldn't either. But it's the solution, I assure you, however wise you are, or however silly.

Frederic. I wish I could understand!

Lucien. Understand what? What goes on in their flimsy little carcasses at such times? Nobody's ever understood that, not even themselves. What would be the good of it, anyway? It can't be so pretty. Give it up. You just have to get used to them. You might as well try to understand disease, stupidity, poverty, war, death. We're children at the game.

FREDERIC *has dropped onto the sofa, head in hands.* LUCIEN *seats himself beside him.*

Lucien. Oh, we put up a good show with our manly exploits, explaining to all and sundry that we're scientists, poets, heroes, that we'd rather die than not live in freedom, that we are capable of abstract thought. Fat lot that has to do with anything. [*Silence for a while between them.*

He goes on.] Better hang on to your mother, or a Julia if you can find one, or to the women in books. . . . [*He points to a picture, a huge engraving hanging in a large black frame and yellowed from exposure through the broken window.*] Take the wife of Poetus, for instance. This old summer house has been very useful to our family. When my wife left me, I used to come and hide myself away here many a time. And one day, when I'd been staring blindly at the wall, I discovered this engraving, hanging lopsided in the middle of a panel. The glass is dirty, so you can't see it very well. It's the wife of Poetus, a Roman condemned to death by Nero. She has just snatched the sword from the centurion's hand and, as Poetus hesitates, she stabs herself first, then hands the sword to her husband with a smile, saying, "*Non dolet.*"

FREDERIC *has glanced up at the picture, but lets his head fall into his hands again. Silence.* JEANNETTE *is the last to turn to the picture.*

Jeannette. What does it mean—*Non dolet?*
Lucien. It means "It doesn't hurt." First Empire style, you know. She's no beauty, of course, maybe a little rotund for aesthetes such as ourselves, but all the same . . . [*He sighs, half wistfully, half mockingly.*] Lucky Poetus!

Pause.

Jeannette [*softly*]. Frederic, I just want to tell you something. I opened the door myself just now so that this man should come in and tell you more or less the same as Lucien has just told you. I'm a liar, it's true, and I'm not worth much, and it's true I brought the dress with me, too. [*Pause. She continues with an effort.*] You heard what he said. Julia, your mother, and now the ladies of Rome as well, they're all against me! All the women that have been strong and pure. . . . Well, I can be that, too, more than they can. What has Julia given you, after all? Her little bit of goodness, or her fear of being compromised? And what about your mother? I suppose she used to rock you in her arms at night when you couldn't sleep? Do you think I wouldn't have done the same? Do you think I wouldn't have looked after

you when you were sick and held you in my arms? I
would have been ten mothers to you for a thousand
nights! I'd have been like a mother hen that never pecks
at a single grain for herself. I'd have been like a she
wolf, standing in front of her young and fighting for
them to the death. But *she's* had ten other children;
she's done all the same things ten times over because it
moved her guts to see a little piece of herself living and
moving after it was born, the way it moves the guts of
all animals!

Lucien. True, even the worst of women become
mothers. Maybe it'll move you one day, the same as it
did her, and then we'll all have to revere you.

Jeannette [*turning on him, ablaze*]. No! I don't want
to feel the way all mothers do about just any of their
children! I don't want to be twelve times exalted in spite
of myself, twelve times true to the death, twelve times
unique! This isn't just some vague instinct I've given
way to, something that makes it absolutely necessary for
me to have a child to suckle. I love *him*! It's for him
I want to sacrifice myself and die. This isn't the sort of
love that'll come surging up again like sap every time
my waistline gets thick. It's the first and last time, I
know it, till the skin of my stomach clings to my spine.
The last time I shall be ready to give my blood, here and
now, and my milk, if it would come!

Lucien [*getting up, spitefully*]. Your blood, your milk!
You work fast. You've only known him a day.

Jeannette. That's all you can think of to say, all of you.
Is it my fault it's only a day?

Lucien. Your blood. . . . Ah, they're good talkers if
you listen with your eyes shut. Fortunately you only have
to look at them, with their fluttering eyelids and their
little nervous grin. You've given him your mouth and
the taste of your skin on his tongue. That's all there is
to it. You're just a girl he's picked for the night.

Jeannette. No! I'm his wife!

Lucien. His wife? You? Don't make me die laughing.
Look at him. Firm, frank, reliable—a real honest-to-God
little French soldier, fairly bursting with the right sentiments. You, his wife? You want him; he wants you.
Good luck to you. Get on with it, quick. But don't
start building a cathedral on it.

Jeannette. Supposing I were to become everything he

loves in one night? Supposing that all of a sudden I stopped being lazy and untidy and a liar and became brave and honorable?

Lucien [*bursts out laughing*]. All the same! Every one of them! They're quite capable of drowning Mama and Papa one fine night in order to make off with the dear boy; they're ready to steal for him, sell themselves at the street corner, descend to whatever depths may be necessary. But if he, the angel child, prefers modesty, sentiment, virtue, he has only to say so. It's so easy! They can turn that on, too. It's all one to them. And sincerely, what's more. Refusing to give themselves, lowering their eyes, blushing if one uses the wrong word, looking down from their pedestal. They can do anything, for as long as it lasts.

Jeannette. Yes, I can do anything, I can do anything!

Lucien. Only what they can't actually manage is to make it last.

Jeannette. That's a lie!

Lucien. What they can't do is to see that it's all still true next day. They're honest from day to day. It's a way the pretty little things have. And the unfortunate thing is that *we* need just that tomorrow. We couldn't care less about this love they offer us just for today. It doesn't mean a thing if tomorrow isn't safe. That's why we put all we've got into trying to be happy with them until in the end they leave us when they get tired and we have to take the blame.

Jeannette. He'll be happy! He'll believe me. You couldn't believe Denise, but I'll give him so much that he'll believe me!

Lucien. What'll you give him? You've nothing to give. You've none of you anything to give, except your body for a minute, and your everlasting changes of mood.

Jeannette. It isn't true!

Lucien. And he hasn't anything to give you, either. You're lovers. You've played your cards. You can dance the dance to the end, now. Throw yourself in the river in despair, kill yourselves for each other, nurse each other through leprosy, sell yourselves. It's all a sham, a mirage, nothing but show! You've nothing to give. . . . You've chosen love, you've chosen to take, always, to think of nothing but yourselves.

Jeannette. It's not true!

Lucien. Oh, yes. You've chosen love, and you're here to hate each other, to be revenged on each other, you'll never know what for. No need to beat your breast about it, it's always been the same, ever since there were men and women, pairing off like flies in the small hours.

Jeannette. No!

Lucien. Yes. And maybe you'll go off now into the wide world, the two of you, hand in hand, but you'll be watching each other like two enemies in the desert. And people will say, "What a sweet couple! How they must love each other." Yes. Sweet couple of murderers! Capable of anything, dear ladies! Claws out and fangs bared. One of 'em's got to have the other's blood and the sooner the better. That's love for you!

Jeannette [*who has thrown herself on the sofa beside* FREDERIC]. Oh, you're too horrible—you're too horrible!

Lucien [*coming up to her and speaking more softly*]. What do you believe, then? That it's Philemon and Baucis for the asking? A pushover? Tenderness, devotion, confidence, the lot, day in, day out? You have to pay for that, my sweet, day after day, with sweat and boredom and petty scraping and fear all rolled into one. You pay for it with kids that get sick and you don't know whether they're going to live or die; with nights and nights of lying next to each other and listening to each other breathing, and all the time the wrinkles are getting deeper and deeper. . . .

Jeannette. I know I shall have wrinkles! I know I shall get old. And people will say, "There are those two old people." And when he dies, I shall die next day.

Lucien [*dropping down wearily beside them, muttering*]. Die . . . die. . . . What is there in dying? You've got to begin by living. That's not so funny, and it lasts longer.

Jeannette. You're saying all this to stop us living.

Lucien [*suddenly strangely tired*]. No. To stop you dying, silly kid. You get everything mixed up.

There is a short silence. All three of them are sitting sedately side by side, looking straight ahead of them.

Jeannette [*softly, humbly*]. You hate love. But the women you've known aren't everything—you haven't known them all. There must be some who've loved with all their might, forever. Isn't there just one? If there is, I can, too.

Lucien. I've never had her number.

Jeannette. That one you were talking about over there in the picture, was she in love?

Lucien. The wife of Poetus, you mean?

Jeannette. I don't know. Yes. What was it she said when she took the knife first, to give her husband courage?

Lucien. Non dolet.

Jeannette. Non dolet. Didn't that mean she loved him?

Lucien. Yes, I suppose so.

Jeannette [*getting up*]. Well, if it's no more difficult than that . . .

Lucien. Where are you going?

Jeannette. To take off this dress. [*She disappears upstairs.*]

Lucien [*when he and* FREDERIC *are alone*]. I've told you all I know, anyway. I've warned you about my own little experiences. Now maybe you'd better judge for yourself all the same.

There is the sound of glass breaking upstairs.

Lucien. What's she doing now, the little lunatic? Smashing the windows?

After a minute or so, JEANNETTE *reappears, very pale in her white dress. She holds out her arm to* FREDERIC. *Blood is running freely from a jagged cut.*

Jeannette. Look. It doesn't hurt. I've forgotten how they say it in Latin.

The two men have got up. There is a second's stupefied silence, then FREDERIC *falls on her and wraps her arm in his handkerchief, kissing her and stammering.*

Frederic. Jeannette, my love . . . forgive me. I'll believe you. I'll always believe you!

They have their arms around each other. LUCIEN *raises his arms heavenward.*

Lucien. Right, fine! If they're going to start lopping their arms off now, what can one say?

At this moment, the door opens, the wind hurtles through the room again, the light almost goes out; and the old Postman *is revealed, standing outside the door in the rain, hesitating on the threshold.*

Postman [*softly*]. Children, children!
Lucien [*going to him*]. Is it for me, postman?
Postman. No, boy. It's your father sent me, to tell you to go straight to the town to fetch the doctor. They're mighty worried at the house. Your sister's drunk something. They think she's poisoned herself.

FREDERIC *has disengaged himself from* JEANNETTE'S *embrace.* LUCIEN *turns to him.*

Lucien. Go on back. I'm taking Azarias's car to fetch the doctor. [FREDERIC *does not move immediately. He goes to him and takes him by the arm.*] Come on, quickly. This time it's the real thing.

He goes out, dragging FREDERIC *with him. The* Postman *follows, leaving the door wide open. There is a long silence.* JEANNETTE *remains alone, motionless, looking very small in her white dress with the wind buffeting her and her arms clasped around her. Suddenly she turns her head toward the open door.*

Jeannette [*murmuring*]. You can come in now.

A man appears like a shadow in the doorway, his coat streaming with rain. As the shadow advances into the room, the curtain falls.

ACT FOUR

SCENE—*Same as in Act One. Late afternoon a week later.* FREDERIC *is stretched out on the sofa, his head buried in his arms. The* FATHER *is pacing up and down the room,*

watching him with an air of hostility. Enter LUCIEN. *The*
FATHER *goes toward him.*

FATHER. Is the trap there?

Lucien. Yes.

Father. Good. [*He takes him aside.*] I can't pretend I'm
sorry to see the back of them. A week, I tell you. This
boy's been here a whole week and not once has he opened
his mouth. I'm old-fashioned. Politeness first, I say. My
girl friend could have been at death's door, but as a man
of the world first and foremost I'd at least have kept up
the conversation. Not he.

Lucien. You can keep up both sides of a conversation.

Father. Julia nearly died. Right. But she's been out of
danger since yesterday. . . . I said to myself, Now he'll
make an effort. But still not a word.

Lucien [*softly*]. Maybe he isn't out of danger.

Father. I'm delighted he's getting out of here. I make no
secret of it. I'd rather talk to myself and have done with it.
At least one knows where one is. [*There is a sound of
music in the distance. He shouts suddenly*] Stop that
music!

Lucien. Not a hope.

Father. I may look calm, but my nerves are all to pieces.

He settles himself calmly in his chair and lights a cigar.
LUCIEN *goes up to* FREDERIC.

Lucien. Not very delicate, I must admit, giving us the
full orchestral works. What you probably don't know is
that in the ordinary way one wouldn't be able to hear it
—the house is too far away. She must have arranged to
have it somewhere this end of the grounds, to make certain
wc'd hear. It should be a very smart wedding. There are
five Citroens in front of the gate. Monsieur Azarias has
connections.

Father [*from his corner*]. And not even a card from
them. [*Pause. Then, in a detached voice.*] Where do you
think they ordered the food?

Lucien. At Biron's.

Father [*contemptuously*]. Pooh! Conventional stuff.
Fish balls, lamb cutlets, chicken. I can feel myself swallowing it.

Lucien. Then what are you complaining of?

Father. The snub.

Lucien. You'll swallow that, too.

Father. Never. I'm a good chap, but I've got the memory of an elephant. I never forget and I never forgive. I don't say a word, and people think I'm easygoing, but fifty years afterward the worm turns. [*Pause.*] Cheese, ice bombe, mocha cake, champagne. That fellow can only think of one menu. If they'd condescended to consult me, I'd have said, go to Thomas. Thomas is the only one in this part of the country that knows how to serve food. *Oeufs mimosa,* lobster Thermidor, stuffed shoulder . . . magnificent!

Lucien. It didn't make much difference to you, though, did it?

Father [*rattled*]. True. [*Pause.*] Do you think I'd have been able to wear it if they'd invited me?

Lucien. Wear what?

Father. My dinner jacket.

Lucien. Certainly.

Father. It'd have been a great honor for them. After all—this Azarias fellow—I knew his father.

Lucien. And now he knows your daughter. That makes you quits.

Father. You ridicule everything. But with me, it's all engraved here. [*He points to his forehead. The music becomes louder. He leaps to his feet, shouting.*] Make them stop that row!

Lucien. You make them stop it.

Father. That's just what they'd like. They can keep it up for a week, I'll play deaf as a post. The musicians'll be the first to tire. What do you suppose an orchestra like that costs a day? There must be at least six of them. Say about two thousand francs a day each, you see what this little bit of nonsense adds up to? [*He goes out into the garden.*]

Lucien [*coming back to* FREDERIC]. She just wanted us to hear her wedding. Julia's got to hear it in bed, Mama's got to hear it in the kitchen, the whole village has got to hear it. The bells this morning weren't enough. She's scattered fiddlers all over the shrubbery. She must hate them all up there, but I can just see her in the thick of it. She'll make 'em all dance until morning. drive 'em to a standstill, and all for our benefit.

Frederic. Julia's going to get up. In an hour from now, we shall be gone.

Lucien. We'll try and let her know. That may shut it up. I imagine these waves of harmony are aimed more particularly at you.

Frederic. Possibly.

Lucien. She wants to be quite sure you're suffering at the same time. She adores you, that kid. You saw how nicely she cut her arm. What was it? "I've forgotten how they say it in Latin." Splendid entrance, that.

Frederic. But then why? Why immediately after . . . ?

Lucien. You really are incorrigible, old man. You want to know everything! You must get out of this terrible habit. Nobody will ever know why. She doesn't know herself. [FREDERIC *has thrown himself down with his face in the cushions.*] It hurts, doesn't it, at first? You have the feeling you just can't stand the pain another second. You ought really to yell out, or break something. But what? You can't break *them.* How about the furniture? Grotesque. It's when you realize there's nothing to break that you begin to grow up. [*Pause. He comes and sits beside* FREDERIC.] You can live quite comfortably with a pain, you know; you'll see when you get to know it. You find out the subtleties and hidden crevices of it. You become a specialist in it. You know what to feed it on every day, and what may not be good for it. You get to know the sort of whisper that stirs it and the sort of music that lulls it to sleep. And later, much later, when you stop being lonely at last and can talk about it to other people, you begin to show it off to the public, like a guide at a museum. You become the peak-capped employee of your own pain. You die just the same, but more gradually. [FREDERIC *gets up to escape him, and goes to look out the window.*] Don't be in such a hurry to be unhappy. You've got all your life before you. What's so splendid about being a cuckold is that it gives you plenty of time. I'm not talking of the uncouth type that murder their wives at the first suspicion and then blow out their own brains. . . . I refer to the artist cuckold, the good craftsman that likes a job well done according to the rules, a job that does justice to him.

The music grows louder.

Father [*appearing at the French windows*]. That's splendid! They've brought in some brass, now. We're not going to get a wink of sleep tonight.

Lucien [*sharply*]. We shouldn't have got that anyway. [*The* FATHER *goes away again.* LUCIEN *goes up to* FREDERIC, *suddenly harsh.*] A wink of sleep . . . funny expression, isn't it? You can just imagine a huge, dark, open eye that fills the room and watches you. And you can't get a wink out of it. You summon up all your strength and hang on like grim death to that enormous eyelid, but there it is, always open, watching you, thoughtless, vacant, imbecile, a real human eye. Do *you* sleep?

Frederic [*shrugging*]. Yes.

Lucien [*shouting*]. You'll never sleep again!

Frederic [*turning abruptly*]. What are you getting at? What are you trying to do to me?

Lucien [*softly*]. Watch you. Watch you being hurt. It does me good.

Frederic. Watch away. Is it pretty—the sight of someone being hurt?

Lucien. No. It's frightful, it's obscene. But when it's your own reflection in a mirror, it's worse. I used to look at myself in the glass the whole night long, you know, watching my death's-head grin and my idiot eyes. I used to watch my chin tremble and wait like a huntsman stalking his prey for hours and hours, just to see if that smackable cuckold's face would burst into tears. Now, at last, it's somebody else—that makes a nice change.

Frederic. Quick, then. Take a good look. I shan't be looking at myself in the glass. I'm a man, and tomorrow, whatever happens, I'm going to live.

Lucien [*jeering*]. Bravo, little man!

Frederic. I shall have work to do. I shall marry Julia. I've got a whole house to decorate and a garden to clear and wood to cut for the winter.

Lucien [*one confidence deserving another*]. I took up gym. Yes, I thought, this has only happened because you're thin and don't stand up straight. It's all because you've no muscles on your chest and arms to make a man of you. No muscles, no women. Everything quite suddenly became simple, and I set out to conquer the mighty muscle. I bought a book—ninety francs. The secret was cheap. And every morning by my open window, clad in my little singlet, more cuckold than ever, I would go through my Swedish drill. [*He goes through some motions.*] One, two, three, four. One, two—— [*He stops suddenly, already exhausted.*] But believe me, it's all a lie—muscles take a long time to grow. What's more, if you look a little closer at the face of the instructor on the cover, you'll notice that in spite of his athletic body he was probably a cuckold, too. One piece of advice. Start right away with plenty of red wine. You get results much quicker that way. [*He helps himself, drinks, and offers wine to* FREDERIC.] Shall I pour you some?

 Frederic. No, thanks.

 Lucien. As you wish. But to have real class as a cuckold means you have only one privilege—to suffer twice as much. And what's the point of being a cuckold with class, anyway? Is there such a thing as having cancer in style or wearing your leprosy with an air? You might as well writhe in your colic, spit out your phlegm, or cough up your lungs and yell when it hurts. Have a good moan, get on people's nerves. You might as well be a puny, cringing little cuckold, unseemly in the eyes of God— just to show Him. Know what I did the first day? I fell off my chair suddenly during dinner and lay still on the floor to make them think I was dead. For no reason. Just so that they'd be scared; so that something should happen. They dabbed my temples with vinegar, they tried to unclench my teeth with spoons, and I could hear them fussing and bustling about, and there I was all the time, breathing away quietly. I wasn't dead, but I was a cuckold. I'd have liked to go one better, too. Whip off my pants, piss all over the wall, black my face, and walk the streets with a huge false nose so that people would say, "What's he doing, that young man there with the big false nose?" "Nothing. He's just a cuckold. That's a cuckold's nose!"

 Frederic. Oh, shut up!

 Lucien. Am I embarrassing you? The gentleman wants to suffer in peace, perhaps, in the grand manner? Maybe he wants to play cuckolds all by himself? Nasty, common cuckolds aren't quite his style? Maybe he's a special sort of cuckold. All the same, we are brothers, monsieur, we've drunk out of the same cup. And since there's nobody to kiss us, we shall have to kiss each other.

He goes to embrace FREDERIC *playfully, but* FREDERIC
pushes him away.

Frederic. Let me go! You're drunk. You stink of
alcohol.

Lucien. Maybe I do stink of alcohol, but drunk at five
o'clock? Never. My dear chap, it's like that business of
the muscles, it takes time. Everything takes time. No, I
shan't be drunk until tonight, and then I shall be quite
speechless; that's when I become respectable. [*Declaiming.*] The Count used to shut himself up alone every
evening in his library, and the Countess would hear him
staggering upstairs in the middle of the night. . . . I only
stagger when I'm sober. I get drunk so as to be able to
go up to the Countess every night without staggering.
[*Short pause.*] Only there's always a slight disappointment
awaiting me up there—no Countess.

Frederic [*after a while*]. I'm not going to go back to my
suffering like a dog to its vomit. Let it bleed itself away
and have done with it. This juvenile world you've
dragged me into, the two of you, doesn't belong to me.
Neither my father nor my mother nor any of the people
in my village have ever had time to pay much attention
to their own troubles, though their children died of unknown diseases and their wives left them just the same.
They simply had other things to do besides brooding
over their own woes.

Lucien. Oh, a farmer's life for me!

Mother [*coming in*]. Julia's up now. The journey will
tire her a little, but she prefers to go tonight. Like me, she
has only one desire—to get out of this place as soon as
possible.

Lucien. But it's so pretty at this time of the year.

Mother [*to* FREDERIC, *paying no attention to* LUCIEN].
Are you ready?

Frederic. Yes, Mother.

Mother. I'll call you to help Julia downstairs. I'm just
going to get her a cup of coffee. [*She goes into the
kitchen.*]

Father [*who has come back and is watching her go*].
Ever since she cleared out the cupboards, she's been cutting me dead. I don't know what she could have found
there.

Lucien [*in a low voice, to* FREDERIC, *as though continuing a conversation*]. And if you're strong enough to get over the days (and you may manage that—you seem pretty tough) there'll always be the nights. Nights when the sleeping cuckold relives his agony. Even if I got her back, even if she stayed faithful to me after that and I managed to forget about it during the day, I'd still be a cuckold to the end of my nights. [*Pause.*] And yet it's the only chance of being no more than half a cuckold. That's why I've never given up waiting.

Frederic. How long is it now?

Lucien. Two years. She'd gone out to buy some stockings, if you please! I must say, I'm beginning to get a bit worried. . . .

Frederic. You'll forget her.

Lucien. No, brother. Another illusion to discard. You find someone else, maybe. But you don't forget. [*He gets up.*] Besides, cuckolds always tend to make themselves out more pathetic than they are. I'm not waiting for her any more exactly. Just a letter. A letter from the Ivory Coast with a beautiful green stamp on it. I'm told they're blacker and stupider there. I shall get on fine with the niggers.

Father [*getting up and going over to them*]. I'm listening to you two talking away there. I don't understand you, my dear boys. There you are, torturing each other, frightening each other. Life and love have always seemed so much simpler to me. And don't go thinking I haven't been in love. When I was twenty, I had three mistresses. A girl in the records department, a dizzy blonde who learned the whole thing from me from A to Z; then there was the little waitress at the restaurant where I had my meals; and a young girl from one of the best families in the town. A virgin, my dear boy, before she knew me. Used to take me to her room at night, a couple of steps from where her parents were sleeping. J.P. . . . Forgive me if I only tell you her initials. She got married later on to one of the district high-ups.

Lucien. I knew her. She was hunchbacked.

Father [*riled*]. Not really. A slight malformation that didn't affect her charm in the least.

Lucien. She was plain, too!

Father [*concurring*]. Her nose was rather prominent.

But a fine pair of eyes! [*He goes up to* LUCIEN.] Anyway, dear boy, we're both men, aren't we, damn it all? I was a bit of a lad, too, you know. What's a hump or a nose once you're in bed? . . . [*He makes a vulgar gesture.*] One mustn't be romantic, after all. Love is just an enjoyable moment. Once the pleasure is past—— [*This time the gesture is lofty.*] Careful! Utmost gallantry and politeness, of course. I've always respected women. But that's the end of it. I wouldn't have given up billiards with the boys on that account. I arranged my life so as never to suffer! And it was a principle of mine to be the first to clear out. Never more than three months. Once that was up, I was relentless. I've seen some of them howling like animals, running out naked into the street after me. But I was always deaf to prayers, threats, everything. Once, a big brunette—a dressmaker from Cahors—a Juno, dear boy, with breasts like that—leaped into the kitchen as I was on my way out, seized a bottle of bleach, and said if I took another step she'd drink it. I walked straight out.

Lucien. And did she?

Father. I'm convinced of it. I met her three weeks later, and she'd got considerably thinner. But things always work out, hang it all! She married a gendarme. Now she has a grown-up son—a hairdresser. What do you think life's all about, anyway? The main thing is never to be taken in.

Lucien. And if you get hurt?

Father [*sincerely amazed*]. But you don't get hurt! That's where I don't understand you!

Mother [*coming in with a cup in her hand*]. There. I'll just take her her coffee, and we'll be off.

Father. We shall miss you, dear lady.

Mother. The mare's in good trim. Charles says we shall be back for dinner. It only took him three hours to get here. He's brought a blanket, but I'm afraid Julia may catch a chill in the night air. I'll take one with me from here and send it back to you.

Father [*in lordly manner*]. Dear lady, the house is yours.

Mother. The wedding will take place on the date we arranged, but Julia thinks as I do that after what has happened it would be better not to ask anyone.

Father. But the family . . .

Mother. Julia prefers that neither of you should be there.

Father [*who dare not understand*]. Neither of us . . . ?

Mother. Her brother or you.

Father [*out of countenance*]. But, after all, her father . . .

Mother. Frederic's uncle will give her away. She wants to have only one family from now on.

Father [*abdicating, proud*]. I was just having a jacket made. . . .

The MOTHER *does not reply. Suddenly* LUCIEN *shouts.*

Lucien. If I marry a Negress out there, Papa, I'll invite you! It'll be magnificent. Everyone will be quite naked, quite black, and they'll all stink. And there you'll be, all alone in your dress suit, sweating away in the procession with my blonde inamorata on your arm. We, too, shall be thoroughly respectable; we, too, shall be snug in the bosom of the family, Papa, all among the blacks.

Father [*with a Shakespearean gesture, as an exit line*]. I no longer have any children!

Lucien. Where are you going?

Father. To Prosper's. Lend me five hundred francs.

Lucien. Take a thousand, dear King Lear. Go and get drunk, it's well worth it.

The MOTHER *watches them go out, shrugs her shoulders, and goes upstairs again to Julia.* FREDERIC *is left alone. Suddenly* JEANNETTE *appears in the doorway, dressed in white. She stands there for a while without moving, looking at* FREDERIC. *He sees her and gets up.*

Jeannette [*softly*]. Yes, I got married in white, to infuriate the villagers. And of course I had to find some use for the dress. [*A momentary silence. He does not respond.*] Are you still going to have your wedding next month?

Frederic. Yes.

Jeannette. Mine's all over now. [*Pause.*] It's good when things are over and done with, when there are no more decisions to make, no turning back. That's why I came to say good-by.

Frederic. Go away!

Jeannette [*gently*]. Yes, I will. But don't say it so un-
kindly. I've already gone away, once and for all. I'm talking
to you now from the other end of the earth. This is just
one of those special moments granted by Fate sometimes
when people can't turn back. We're like two trains that
have gathered speed and go faster and faster in opposite
directions as they pass. And we're giving each other a last
little smile through a window. [*Pause. As though recording a finding.*] Not even a smile.

Frederic. No.

Jeannette. How solemn you are. Don't you know how
to play at life?

Frederic. No.

Jeannette. I'm unhappy, too, but I play. I'm merry as
a cricket up there at the house, making them all drink and
dance. My husband's guests have never stopped paying me
compliments. He's the only one who always knows everything in advance, and he's frightened.

Frederic. Frightened of what?

Jeannette. He's like a man who's won a raffle and isn't
quite sure of his prize.

Frederic. Will you make him unhappy, too?

Jeannette. He's unhappy already.

Frederic. Does that amuse you?

Jeannette. I don't care one way or the other. I don't
know him.

Frederic. And this morning you said in front of all those
people that you were his wife.

Jeannette. That's what they thought they heard, but I
said nothing of the sort. This morning, in front of the
curé and the man with the sash, I said, not that I was
taking this man for better or worse, forever, but that I was
giving you up till the end of my life and after. Yes, it's
strange. The priest called out in church: "Mademoiselle
Jeannette Maurin, do you consent never to take Monsieur
Frederic Larivière to be your lawful wedded husband?"
And nobody moved a muscle; nobody seemed to think it
unusual to put it that way or call out your name like that
at someone else's wedding. It was the same at the town
hall. Nobody was at all alarmed that there should have to
be all that dressing up, that great fat man with the multicolored sash, all that prize-giving paraphernalia, and a husband rigged out like a sacrificial bull, just to tell me that

I was never to love and honor you, never to follow you throughout the world.

Frederic. What the others heard was true. You've tied yourself for always to another man.

Jeannette. No. I've cut myself off from you for always. It's a solemn sacrament. The Church should have provided for it along with the others: the sacrament of renunciation. [*Silence. They stand looking at each other. She murmurs*] How far away you are!

Frederic. Yes. All this week I've been trying to pull myself up out of the pain, inch by inch, but I kept falling back into the pit. Now I'm at the top. With sweat running off me and my nails torn and bleeding. And I'm going to try not to fall back again.

Jeannette. It's a long climb.

Frederic. Yes. There isn't far to go, but it's a long climb.

Jeannette. I came to ask you to forgive me for hurting you, too.

Frederic [*with a gesture*]. Never mind.

Jeannette. Did you go back to the summer house in the night?

Frederic. Yes. As soon as the doctor said Julia would be all right.

Jeannette. Did you wait for me?

Frederic. Until morning.

Jeannette [*after a pause*]. Perhaps I ought to have left you a note.

Frederic. Perhaps. [*Pause.*] When I went off with your brother, there was a man standing outside. Was that the one?

Jeannette. Yes.

Frederic. And did he come in when we'd gone?

Jeannette. I called him in.

Frederic. Why?

Jeannette. To tell him that if he wanted me, I'd marry him.

Frederic. And it was settled then and there?

Jeannette. Yes. We even cheated a bit over the banns. In a small place like this, you can manage things like that. I hoped you'd still be here on my wedding day.

Frederic. Everything's turned out very well. We're only just going. [*Short silence.*] So all that remains is for me to wish you happiness.

Jeannette [*softly*]. You're not serious.

Frederic. I wish I weren't. It must be good to be able to laugh.

Jeannette. They do say so.

Frederic [*suddenly, loudly*]. But I shall laugh later on. Tomorrow, in a year, in ten years maybe, I swear to you I shall laugh. When the children begin to talk, they're bound to say something funny; or the puppy we'll have bought them to play with will run away from a shadow in the garden; or perhaps for no reason—just because we suddenly get a hot day with the sun shining on the sea— then I'll laugh.

Jeannette. Yes.

Frederic. I've still got this pain, and everything's uncertain still. But there'll be a morning, a bright new morning without any memories, when I shall get up with the sun and everything will fall into place again. It'll be like waking from a bad dream, and I shall find the place all freshly painted, and my little black table by the study window, and the hours going slowly by and the shadow of the church growing longer and longer across the square, and Julia's smile, like quiet water at night. One day I shall be strong again and all the people and things around me will stop being a perpetual question mark and become an answer, a certainty.

Jeannette. Yes, my darling.

Frederic. Oh, I've asked far too many questions this last week! Let things speak for themselves from now on! Let the warm stones say, "Look, it's summer, we're warm." And the evening, creeping up over the bench in front of the house: "I'm evening, full of the noise of birds, you must rest now." And then afterward the stillness of night: "Don't think any more, I am peace." I don't want to ask any more questions ever again!

Jeannette [*softly, after a pause*]. You love so many things in this life. They'll answer you sometime or other. Just be patient for a while. But I hate evening, and peace, and summer. I shan't wait for anything.

Frederic [*suddenly, without moving*]. Why didn't I find you when I went back there in the night? [JEANNETTE *makes a small, weary gesture, but does not answer.*] I'd put my handkerchief around your hurt arm! I'd taken you in my arms. I'd said, "I'll always believe you." You told me you loved me.

Jeannette [*in her small voice*]. You shouldn't have left me alone.

Frederic. I thought Julia was going to die.

Jeannette. Yes. It was very sensible and very good of you to go to her at once, but it was just precisely the moment when sensible things and good things aren't quite fair any more.

Frederic. She'd taken poison because of us.

Jeannette. Yes. A bit earlier maybe, or a bit later, I might have thought "Poor Julia!" too. And I would have waited patiently all night, happy to know that you'd be reassured by morning. But we were unlucky. That was just the moment not to leave me.

Frederic. Why?

Jeannette [*with a sad little smile*]. You always ask why. Do you think I know? All I know is that just at that moment I was like a bird in the topmost branches of a tree, ready either to fly away or to build my nest there.

Frederic. But you did love me?

Jeannette. Yes, I loved you. I still love you.

Frederic. And yet that man had only to come into the summer house . . .

Jeannette. No, poor thing. You flatter him. . . . I called him in. It was already over by then.

Frederic. What was already over?

Jeannette. I can tell you exactly when it finished. You hadn't even left the room yet. It finished when you took your arms from around me.

Frederic. What finished?

Jeannette [*with eyes closed*]. You're starting all over again, the way you did the first day. You're going all over it again, like a judge.

Frederic [*taking her by the wrist*]. What was it that finished? I want to know.

Jeannette [*softly*]. You won't make it easier for me to tell you by hurting me. [*He lets her go.*] I'm doing my best to explain, but it's difficult for me, too. If you like, it was the certainty that I felt, deep inside me, that I was stronger than your mother, stronger than Julia and all those Roman women; that I deserved you more than anyone else. That was what came to an end after you'd gone. I'd just put my arm through that window; I could see my own blood running for you, and I was proud. You could have told me to jump out the window, to enter into the fiery furnace, and I'd have done it. I could have been poor for always with you; I could have been faithful to you forever. The only thing I couldn't bear was not to feel you touch me any more.

Frederic. Why didn't you call after me? Why did you let me go?

Jeannette. It was already too late. The very moment you took your hands away from me, I stopped being stronger. It was like falling down into an enormous chasm. There was no more I could do. You hadn't even quite let go of me, you hadn't even taken a step toward the door before I became the weaker one, the less certain, the one less right for you. Even if I'd wanted to, I couldn't have called you back.

Frederic. Did you think I would come back?

Jeannette. Yes. But to have waited for you would have been dishonest. I hadn't anything to give you any more. I couldn't be your mistress and lie to you afterward, like the others, could I? Dead or alive, Julia would at once have been stronger in your thoughts than me. Once we'd made love, and that wouldn't have taken long, we'd have been a pretty sight, the two of us, wouldn't we?

Frederic. You could have run away, without calling him in.

Jeannette. Alone?

Frederic. Yes.

Jeannette. I can't be alone. And anyway I knew that Julia wouldn't die and that you'd finish up by marrying her. I wanted to get married right away, to be the first.

Frederic. But why?

Jeannette. To hurt you.

Frederic [*after a pause*]. You have. Are you satisfied?

Jeannette. No. Whenever you suffer, I suffer, too. Every time I hurt you, I hurt myself the same way. And if you were to die of it, I'd die, too, at the same time.

Silence.

Frederic. Oh, if only I'd never met you! The world made sense before, for good or bad. Everything around me had its right place, and a name. It was all simple. Now, as I listen to you, I can't think as you do at all, and yet childish and false as your suffering is, I can't bear it.

Jeannette. Yes, the other one's pain always hurts.

Frederic. I want with everything I've got to believe you and understand you, but you must come a little way to meet me. Our chance of happiness together couldn't just have depended on that split second when I took my arms away. It's childish!

Jeannette [*smiling*]. We're so different, my darling. We really did have only the tiniest chance, and only once.

Frederic. Oh, why do you look so sad when you smile? I don't ask you to be sensible like me—I only ask you not to shut yourself up in that dark little world where nobody can get at you. I feel so clumsy with my great, coarse man's hands; it's as though your secret were running away like water through my fingers. But maybe I could learn just the same, even if I don't really understand. There are games and languages that stupid people learn that way, without ever having understood the rules. I'll learn.

Jeannette [*smiling*]. You won't.

Frederic. I'm strong, and patient, and humble. You're not the only human being I'm no good to, all the same. Let's forget all the things that go to make up my strength and justify my existence—they don't count any more.

Jeannette [*after a pause*]. Do you think I would ever consent now to drag you along at my apron strings, with your face looking anxious or composed, according to my moods, and with all my ugly misdeeds caterwauling around me? I'm no longer the little soldier that cut her arm for you the other night. Do you think I'd ever consent to deceive you eventually, as I did the others, without any reason, and to have you forgive me till the next time because I looked unhappy? I'd rather die. [*Another silence while they stand looking at each other. She goes on, more gravely.*] That was what I came to tell you. That evening when I agreed to marry this man, I gave myself to him again. I've become weak and cowardly all over again, and lazy and untidy and a liar. I'm everything you hate again, and I can't even be your wife! [*She stops, and then continues in her small voice.*] But if you like, there is something I can do tonight, so as to make it last forever in spite of everything, and that's die with you.

Pause.

Frederic [*in a hard voice, without looking at her*]. No. That's too cowardly. We've got to go on living.

Jeannette [*softly*]. With all the ugliness and failure, until we're old and hideous and finally die in our beds, sweating and struggling like animals. The sea is so clean. It washes everything with its great big waves.

Frederic. No. [*Pause again.*] The sea isn't clean. It has thousands of bodies buried in it. Death isn't clean either. It doesn't solve anything. It filches part of you away, but it botches the job and leaves behind a great caricature of a body that decomposes and pollutes the air—an enormous, disgusting thing that has to be hidden quickly. Only children and people who've never watched over a dead body can still think of death as something to adorn with flowers, something to call on at the first sign of age or the first pang of suffering. People have to get old. They have to grow out of the world of childhood and accept the fact that things are not so pretty as when they were young.

Jeannette. I don't want to grow up. I don't want to learn to accept. Everything's so ugly.

Frederic. Maybe it is. But all this horror, this fuss about nothing, this absurd, grotesque adventure that life is—it belongs to us. We've got to live through it. Death's absurd as well.

The orchestra starts up again.

Jeannette [*softly*]. Very well, then, I shall go back and dance. They must be waiting for me. [*She cries out suddenly.*] Forgive me for coming!

She runs into the garden and disappears. JULIA *appears, followed by the* MOTHER. FREDERIC *has not moved.*

Julia. Are you ready, Frederic?

Frederic [*seeing her, replies after an almost imperceptible pause*]. Yes.

Julia. Do you think we can go?

Frederic. Come along. [*He goes to help her downstairs.*] Aren't you afraid of catching cold in the trap?

Mother. I've got a second rug for her.

Frederic. We won't go by Les Baux. We'll cut across

the Marsh. They mended the road last winter. We'll be home before nightfall that way.

Mother. I must say, your father and brother might have been here to say good-by to you, my dear. Do you know where they are? They're at that bar.

Julia. So much the better. I'd rather not see them again.

They are walking across the stage as they talk. FREDERIC *stops in the doorway and takes a last look at the room, standing aside to let* JULIA *pass.*

Frederic [*mechanically*]. Go ahead. Sure you haven't left anything behind?

Julia [*stopping, suddenly*]. How about you?

Frederic [*simply, with an absent look*]. I didn't bring anything.

They go out. LUCIEN *bounds out of the kitchen like a demon, calling after them like one demented and making ridiculous farewell gestures from the sofa in front of the window, on which he is standing, throwing flowers after them.*

Lucien. Long live the bride! Health, wealth, and happiness! Long live the bride!

Father [*dashing in like a whirlwind*]. Did you see her?

Lucien. Who?

Father. Jeannette.

Lucien. Where?

Father. Down on the beach. [*He pulls him round to show him.* LUCIEN *looks, but says nothing.*] What does she think she's doing?

Lucien [*softly*]. Going for a swim.

Father. Fully dressed?

Lucien. That's right, fully dressed.

Father. But the tide's coming in.

Lucien. The tide's coming in.

Father. Doesn't she realize that if she goes that way she'll be caught in a current?

Lucien. She knows the bay better than you do.

Father [*yelling*]. Hey, there, Jeannette! Coo-ee-ee! Jeannette! Oh, my God!

Lucien [*softly*]. She's running. She can't hear you against the wind. And even if she could, she'd take no notice. She's done for, Papa, the little sister's done for.

Father. What are you talking about? You mean you think she . . .

Lucien. Sure of it.

Father [*running wildly about the room*]. God Almighty! We must do something! We've got to do something! Come on, fetch some ropes. We'll go up to the house and get help.

Lucien [*stopping him*]. No.

Father. What d'you mean, "no"?

Lucien. I tell you, there's nothing to be done. Leave her alone. First of all, it's too late and, secondly, you'll be doing her a favor.

Father [*pulling himself away*]. You——you——that's monstrous! I'm going to cut down through the woods.

Lucien. You do that. It'll give you some exercise and it won't look so nasty as it does from here.

Father [*goes out and comes back immediately, shouting*]. Hurrah! Hurrah! It's Frederic! He's seen her from the road and jumped out of the trap! Run for it! There's a man for you! He's got to the beach by the little bridge. He's cutting across by the lagoon; he's up to his knees in water. He'll never make it.

Lucien [*coming up to him and speaking softly*]. He will.

Father. He's doing it! He's made it! Bravo there! Come on, now, come on! Oh, well done, my boy! What a sportsman! Come on! Come on!

Lucien [*shouting suddenly*]. Shut up! What do you think you're watching—a football match?

Father. What do you mean, a football match?

Lucien. You're disgusting when you yell like that. I said shut up!

Father [*taken aback*]. But I'm your father.

Lucien [*who has taken him by the lapels as if to start a fight and is shaking him*]. I know that! Only you're so stupid and unsightly that there are times when I just can't bear it any more that you're my father. And this is one of them. So shut up! Do you hear me? Shut up, or I'll knock you cold!

Father [*who can see* FREDERIC *down on the beach,*

pulling himself away]. He's caught up with her! He's caught up with her! Let me go! If they run to the signal station, they'll be all right. There's a bend just there with a stretch of sand still uncovered. Jeannette knows about it, she must know! It's their last chance. . . . But they'll have to run for it, good grief! They'll have to put on a spurt. Why the hell aren't they running?

Lucien. You can see what they're doing. They're talking.

Father. But it's insane! But . . . they must both be mad! Why doesn't someone go after them and tell them? I'm too old! Holy Moses! This is no time for talking! [*He begins to shout grotesquely, cupping his hands into a megaphone.*] Stop talking there, both of you! Stop talking!

Lucien [*in a low voice*]. Stop that or I'll strangle you! Let them talk. Let them talk while they can. They've got plenty to say to each other. [*Pause, while the two of them watch, breathing hard and clinging to one another.*] Now —do you see what they're doing, you old optimist? Do you? They're kissing. Kissing. With the sea galloping up behind them. You just don't understand it, do you, you scruffy old Don Juan, you old cuckold, you old rag bag! [*He shakes him mercilessly.*]

Father [*at the top of his lungs, trying to tear himself free*]. The tide! The tide! Oh, Jesus! [*Yelling helplessly, ridiculously.*] Mind the tide!

Lucien. A fat lot they care about your tide or your bawling or Julia or that woman watching from the road or any of us! They're in each other's arms and they've only got about a minute to go.

Father. They shan't say I didn't do anything about it. I'm going after them by the Customhouse path!

Lucien. That's right. Don't get your feet wet. [LUCIEN *is left looking far out to sea, perfectly still. Suddenly he says in a dull voice*] Love. Unhappy love. Are you happy now? With your hearts and your bodies and your romance. Haven't we still got jobs to do, books to read, houses to build? Isn't it still good to feel the sun on one's skin, to drink wine freshly poured, to have water running in the streams, shade at noon, fires in winter, snow and rain even, and the wind and the trees and the clouds and the animals, such innocent creatures, and children: that is, before they get too ugly? Isn't that right, Love? Every-thing's good isn't it? [*He turns abruptly away from the window, as though he does not want to see any more. He goes to the table, pours himself a glass of wine, and speaks softly, looking at the ceiling.*] Well, there it is. Are you satisfied? That's the way it had to be. But I told them you didn't like the idea. [*Pause. He pours another glass.*] Forgive me, Sir, but you make me thirsty!

He empties his glass at one gulp. The Postman *appears in the doorway, dressed in a dark cloak.*

Postman. Children! Children!
Lucien [*makes toward him precipitately*]. Is it for me this time, at last?

He has snatched the letter from the old man's hands and opened it nervously. He scans through it and crams it in his pocket. Then, without a word, he goes to fetch his bag and hat from the stand.

Postman. Well?
Lucien [*turns to him and speaks gently*]. There are no more children, now. Good-by, postman.

He gives him a friendly little shove and dives out into the darkness without looking back. Curtain.

DRAMABOOKS

MERMAID DRAMA BOOKS

Christopher Marlowe (Tamburlaine the Great, Parts I & II, Doctor Faustus, The Jew of Malta, Edward the Second) (0701–0)

William Congreve (Complete Plays) (0702–9)

Webster and Tourneur (The White Devil, The Duchess of Malfi, The Atheist's Tragedy, The Revenger's Tragedy) (0703–7)

John Ford (The Lover's Melancholy, 'Tis Pity She's a Whore, The Broken Heart, Love's Sacrifice, Perkin Warbeck) (0704–5)

Richard Brinsley Sheridan (The Rivals, St. Patrick's Day, The Duenna, A Trip to Scarborough, The Schoo! for Scandal, The Critic) (0705–3)

Camille and Other Plays (Scribe: A Peculiar Position, The Glass of Water; Sardou: A Scrap of Paper; Dumas: Camille; Augier: Olympe's Marriage) (0706–1)

John Dryden (The Conquest of Granada, Parts I & II, Marriage à la Mode, Aureng-Zebe) (0707–X)

Ben Jonson Vol. 1 (Volpone, Epicoene, The Alchemist) (0708–8)

Oliver Goldsmith (The Good Natur'd Man, She Stoops to Conquer, An Essay on the Theatre, A Register of Scotch Marriages) (0709–6)

Jean Anouilh Vol. 1 (Antigone, Eurydice, The Rehearsal, Romeo and Jeannette, The Ermine) (0710–X)

Let's Get a Divorce! and Other Plays (Labiche: A Trip Abroad, and Célimare; Sardou: Let's Get a Divorce!; Courteline: These Cornfields; Feydeau: Keep an Eye on Amélie; Prévert: A United Family; Achard: Essays on Feydeau) (0711–8)

Jean Giraudoux Vol. 1 (Ondine, The Enchanted, The Madwoman of Chaillot, The Apollo of Bellac) (0712–6)

Jean Anouilh Vol. 2 (Restless Heart, Time Remembered, Ardèle, Mademoiselle Colombe, The Lark) (0713–4)

Henrik Ibsen: The Last Plays (Little Eyolf, John Gabriel Borkman, When We Dead Awaken) (0714–2)

Ivan Turgenev (A Month in the Country, A Provincial Lady, A Poor Gentleman) (0715–0)

George Farquhar (The Constant Couple, The Twin-Rivals, The Recruiting Officer, The Beaux Stratagem) (0716–9)

Jean Racine (Andromache, Britannicus, Berenice, Phaedra, Athaliah) (0717–7)

The Storm and Other Russian Plays (The Storm, The Government Inspector, The Power of Darkness, Uncle Vanya, The Lower Depths) (0718–5)

Michel de Ghelderode: Seven Plays Vol. 1 (The Ostend Interviews, Chronicles of Hell, Barabbas, The Women at the Tomb, Pantagleize, The Blind Men, Three Players and a Play, Lord Halewyn) (0719–3)

Lope de Vega: Five Plays (Peribáñez, Fuenteovejuna, The Dog in the Manger, The Knight from Olmedo, Justice Without Revenge) (0720–7)

Calderón: Four Plays (Secret Vengeance for Secret Insult, Devotion to the Cross, The Mayor of Zalamea, The Phantom Lady) (0721–5)

Jean Cocteau: Five Plays (Orphée, Antigone, Intimate Relations, The Holy Terrors, The Eagle with Two Heads) (0722–3)

Ben Jonson Vol. 2 (Every Man in His Humour, Sejanus, Bartholomew Fair) (0723–1)

Port-Royal and Other Plays (Claudel: Tobias and Sara; Mauriac: Asmodée; Copeau: The Poor Little Man; Montherlant: Port-Royal) (0724–X)

Edwardian Plays (Maugham: Loaves and Fishes; Hankin: The Return of the Prodigal; Shaw: Getting Married; Pinero: Mid-Channel; Granville-Barker: The Madras House) (0725–8)

Alfred de Musset: Seven Plays (0726–6)

Georg Büchner: Complete Plays and Prose (0727–4)

Paul Green: Five Plays (Johnny Johnson, In Abraham's Bosom, Hymn to the Rising Sun, The House of Connelly, White Dresses) (0728–2)

François Billetdoux: Two Plays (Tchin-Tchin, Chez Torpe) (0729–0)

Michel de Ghelderode: Seven Plays Vol. 2 (Red Magic, Hop, Signor!, The Death of Doctor Faust, Christopher Columbus, A Night of Pity, Piet Bouteille, Miss Jairus) (0730–4)

Jean Giraudoux Vol. 2 (Siegfried, Amphitryon 38, Electra) (0731–2)

Kelly's Eye and Other Plays by Henry Livings (Kelly's Eye, Big Soft Nellie, There's No Room for You Here for a Start) (0732–0)

Gabriel Marcel: Three Plays (Man of God, Ariadne, Votive Candle) (0733–9)

New American Plays Vol. 1, ed. by Robert W. Corrigan (0734–7)

Elmer Rice: Three Plays (Adding Machine, Street Scene, Dream Girl) (0735–5)

The Day the Whores Came Out to Play Tennis . . . by Arthur Kopit (0736–3)

Platonov by Anton Chekhov (0737–1)

Ugo Betti: Three Plays (The Inquiry, Goat Island, The Gambler) (0738–X)

Jean Anouilh Vol. 3 (Thieves' Carnival, Medea, Cécile, Traveler Without Luggage, Orchestra, Episode in the Life of an Author, Catch As Catch Can) (0739–8)
Max Frisch: Three Plays (Don Juan, The Great Rage of Philip Hotz, When the War Was Over) (0740–1)
New American Plays Vol. 2 ed. by William M. Hoffman (0741–X)
Plays from Black Africa ed. by Fredric M. Litto (0742–8)
Anton Chekhov: Four Plays (The Seagull, Uncle Vanya, The Cherry Orchard, The Three Sisters) (0743–6)
The Silver Foxes Are Dead and Other Plays by Jakov Lind (The Silver Foxes Are Dead, Anna Laub, Hunger, Fear) (0744–4)

THE NEW MERMAIDS
Bussy D'Ambois by George Chapman (1101–8)
The Broken Heart by John Ford (1102–6)
The Duchess of Malfi by John Webster (1103–4)
Doctor Faustus by Christopher Marlowe (1104–2)
The Alchemist by Ben Jonson (1105–0)
The Jew of Malta by Christopher Marlowe (1106–9)
The Revenger's Tragedy by Cyril Tourneur (1107–7)
A Game at Chess by Thomas Middleton (1108–5)
Every Man in His Humour by Ben Jonson (1109–3)
The White Devil by John Webster (1110–7)
Edward the Second by Christopher Marlowe (1111–5)
The Malcontent by John Marston (1112–3)
'Tis Pity She's a Whore by John Ford (1113–1)
Sejanus His Fall by Ben Jonson (1114–X)

SPOTLIGHT DRAMABOOKS
The Last Days of Lincoln by Mark Van Doren (1201–4)
Oh Dad, Poor Dad . . . by Arthur Kopit (1202–2)
The Chinese Wall by Max Frisch (1203–0)
Billy Budd by Louis O. Coxe and Robert Chapman (1204–9)
The Devils by John Whiting (1205–7)
The Firebugs by Max Frisch (1206–5)
Andorra by Max Frisch (1207–3)
Balm in Gilead and Other Plays by Lanford Wilson (1208–1)
Matty and the Moron and Madonna by Herbert Lieberman (1209–X)
The Brig by Kenneth H. Brown (1210–3)
The Cavern by Jean Anouilh (1211–1)
Saved by Edward Bond (1212–X)
Eh? by Henry Livings (1213–8)
The Rimers of Eldritch and Other Plays by Lanford Wilson (1214–6)
In the Matter of J. Robert Oppenheimer by Heinar Kipphardt (1215–4)
Ergo by Jakov Lind (1216–2)
Biography: A Game by Max Frisch (1217–0)

For a complete list of books of criticism and history of the drama, please write to Hill and Wang, 72 Fifth Avenue, New York, New York 10011.